ACADEMIC DISCIPLINES

Vanderbilt Issues in Higher Education is a timely series that focuses on the three core functions of higher education: teaching, research, and service. Interdisciplinary in nature, it concentrates not only on how these core functions are carried out in colleges and universities but also on the contributions they make to larger issues of social and economic development, as well as the various organizational, political, psychological, and social forces that influence their fulfillment and evolution.

ACADEMIC DISCIPLINES

Holland's Theory and the Study of College Students and Faculty

JOHN C. SMART
KENNETH A. FELDMAN
CORINNA A. ETHINGTON

VANDERBILT UNIVERSITY PRESS

Nashville

First Edition 2000

04 03 02 01 00   5 4 3 2 1

Library of Congress Cataloging-in-Publication Data

Smart, John C.
Academic disciplines : Holland's theory and the study of
college students and faculty / John C. Smart, Kenneth A. Feldman,
Corinna A. Ethington.—1st ed.
p. cm. — (Vanderbilt issues in higher education)
Includes bibliographical references and indexes.
ISBN 0–8265–1305–0
1. Education, Higher—Social aspects. 2. Universities and
colleges—Sociological aspects. 3. College teachers. 4. College
students. 5. Holland, John L. I. Feldman, Kenneth A., 1937- II.
Ethington, Corinna A., 1944- III. Title. IV. Series.
LA184 .S42 2000
378.1'2—dc21   00–008765

Published by Vanderbilt University Press
Printed in the United States of America

We dedicate this book
to the memory of
Dr. Charles F. "Chuck" Elton

CONTENTS

PREFACE

Two fundamental convictions permeate our entire book. First, we believe that advances in knowledge about the professional lives of college faculty and the educational lives of college students depend on a full understanding of the important influences of academic disciplines. Academic disciplines are the professional—and sometimes personal—homes of both faculty and students in the academic community. Knowledge of why people select disparate disciplinary settings and how they interact with others in these settings is essential to understanding the fundamental issues of interest to higher education researchers and policy makers—issues such as persistence, satisfaction, and success. Thus, greater knowledge of similarities and differences across disparate disciplinary settings is needed in order to understand better how those settings influence both faculty and students. Second, we have a genuine commitment to theory in efforts to determine the direction and magnitude of actual change (or stability) in the interests, attitudes, and abilities of students resulting from their involvement with faculty and peers in disparate disciplinary settings. We believe that theory-based inquiries hold the greatest promise for the long-term development of systematic knowledge of college students and faculty. Our commitment to theory is in accord with Hobbs and Francis's (1973) conviction that "it is by explanation, by theory, if you will, that we gain understanding." In sum, "theory is what scholarship is all about" (p. 57).

These two fundamental convictions informed our selection of an appropriate theory to guide our exploration of the direction and magnitude of actual change (or stability) in college students resulting from their involvement with faculty and peers in disparate disciplinary settings. We sought a theory that had four essential features. First, the theory would have to have a classification scheme for academic disciplines that was theoretically based and empirically defensible. This attribute of an appropriate theory is necessary since it would be virtually impossible to study separately each academic discipline and since there is abundant empirical evidence that some clusters or groups of disciplines share more in common with one another than they do with disciplines in other disciplinary clusters or groups (Braxton & Hargens, 1996). Second, the theory would have to provide a basis for the consideration of both individuals and their environments since much evidence exists suggesting that the direction and magnitude of change in undergraduate students is a function of the characteristics of individual students and the collective attributes of college and university environments (Baird, 1988; Pace, 1990; Pascarella & Terenzini, 1991). Third, the theory would have to provide a basis for the selection of theory-based measures used to examine patterns of change or stability in students and offer theory-based hypotheses concerning the direction and magnitude of such change based on the attributes of students and their respective environments. This provision is desirable as it would guide our selection from among myriad measures of college student outcomes and allow us to examine theoretical assumptions or hypotheses. Finally, the theory, and research on the validity of its hypotheses, would have to provide guidance for the use of appropriate research procedures to reveal the presence of actual change (or stability) in the interests, attitudes, and abilities of students. This feature is desirable because many of the research methodologies used by contemporary scholars actually mask such change in students, as noted in chapter 1.

Seeking these desired features led us to select Holland's (1966, 1973, 1985, 1997) theory of careers as the theoretical framework for our book because this theory has a theoretically based and empirically defensible classification of academic disciplines, considers both individuals and their respective environments, provides guidance for the selection of theory-based measures and offers hypotheses concerning the direction and magnitude of assumed change in students, and suggests appropriate research procedures to be used in efforts to discern the presence of change in students. Thus, we used Holland's theory as the guiding framework to further our understanding of how academic disciplines influence the professional lives of college faculty and the educational lives of college students. The findings that emerged strongly support the three primary assumptions of the theory: college students search for and select academic environments compatible with their personality types (self-selection assumption); academic environments—distinctive clusters of academic disciplines—reinforce and reward students for their display of different competencies (socialization assumption); and students flourish in academic environments congruent with their personality types (congruence assumption).

Audiences

Because our book is about college faculty and students, we hope our findings will be of interest to any one concerned with these two primary sets

of contributors to the fundamental purposes of colleges and universities—
teaching and learning. Faculty members and those directly responsible for
academic programs on campuses should be especially interested in our
findings about the distinctive norms and values of different clusters of academic disciplines (i.e., academic environments) and their respective degree programs. These findings suggest wide variation in the instructional
practices of faculty members in different academic environments and in
their expectations about the relative importance of alternative student
competencies. In addition, faculty members and graduate students who
seek to understand the differential patterns of change and stability in students' learning as a result of their college experiences should benefit from
a more thorough understanding of the applicability of Holland's theory to
the study of the educational lives of college students—in specific, how
those differential patterns of learning are associated with the distinctive
norms and values of their respective academic majors. Institutional, state,
and federal policy makers responsible for improving the effectiveness or
performance of colleges and universities may be especially interested in
the organizational, managerial, and educational implications of Holland's
theory and our findings based on the use of this theory.

   We have made a conscientious effort throughout the book to take our
data seriously. By this we mean that we have attempted to stay within the
bounds of our data and to provide the reader with full information that re-
lates to our many findings. The book is not, and is not intended to be, an
easy read. In some respects it is an old-fashioned theory-based research
monograph, one which seeks to provide detailed information on analytical procedures and empirical findings. Because of the sometimes technical
nature of many chapters as well as the book's potential interest to a diverse
audience, we offer the following overview of the book's contents to assist
readers with different interests and different levels of technical expertise.

Overview of the Contents

The introductory chapter (chapter 1) explicates our fundamental thesis
that thorough knowledge of academic disciplines is a prerequisite to understanding variations in the professional attitudes and behaviors of college faculty and differences in the patterns of student change and stability
that result from the college experience. We specifically contrast the general perspectives of scholars who study college faculty with the general
perspectives of those who study college students. Chapter 2 presents an
overview of Holland's theory and its three basic assumptions. We discuss

the implications of each assumption for the study of college faculty and students to illustrate the potential of Holland's theory to provide a theoretical framework for studying the professional lives of college faculty and the patterns of stability and change in college students. Chapter 3 provides a full description of our faculty and student samples, the variables used to assess the validity of the three basic assumptions of Holland's theory, and the analytical procedures used to assess empirical support for each assumption. These three chapters provide the conceptual and analytical background for the next five chapters, which present our empirical findings relative to the basic assumptions of Holland's theory.

Chapter 4 reviews extant research findings on variability of faculty members' professional attitudes and behaviors in disparate clusters of academic disciplines and presents the findings from our original analyses pertaining to the assumption in Holland's theory that faculty in the different disciplinary clusters reinforce and reward different student interests and abilities. The next four chapters, focusing on college students, present our findings pertaining to the three basic assumptions of Holland's theory. Chapter 5 presents our findings regarding the self-selection assumption that students search for and select academic environments compatible with their personality types. Chapter 6 focuses on students whose majors were in four different academic environments in order to assess the socialization assumption that their patterns of change and stability in different interests and abilities vary across the academic environments since these environments reinforce and reward different student competencies. Chapter 7 presents our findings concerning the congruence assumption that students flourish in academic environments congruent with their personality types. Chapter 8 presents the findings from our analysis assessing the relative strengths of the socialization and congruence assumptions in Holland's theory. This chapter also summarizes the findings given in chapters 4 through 8 framed in terms of Holland's theory and the importance of academic environments. The concluding chapter (chapter 9) builds upon the findings of the five preceding chapters to discuss the educational and organizational implications of Holland's theory in colleges and universities. Specific examples are presented to illustrate how Holland's theory might be used to understand and promote student learning and to improve the organizational structure and administrative processes of colleges and universities. The chapter ends with some suggestions for future research using Holland's theory.

A few words about the internal organization of the chapters are in order. We have attempted to make each chapter rather self-contained, which is most evident in chapters 1, 2, 3, and 9 but is also apparent in the other chapters. Chapters 4 through 7 contain a mixture of information. Each begins with a review of extant research findings on the specific assumption in Holland's theory that is the focus of that chapter. This review is followed by a brief description of the analytical procedures used to produce our findings on the specific assumption of Holland's theory. Each of these chapters ends with a summary of our findings pertaining to that specific assumption. Readers not interested in the detailed information on the procedures used and the specific findings for each assumption are advised to read only the beginning and concluding sections of chapters 4 through 7. Chapter 8 begins and ends with a summary of our research findings—the first in terms of the three major assumptions of Holland's theory and the second in terms of the importance of academic environments.

Acknowledgments

This book benefited from many contributions by several valued colleagues who read and provided their comments on initial chapter drafts. We wish to express our special thanks to James C. Hearn and Peter M. Magolda, whose suggestions were very helpful in making improvements in chapters 1 through 8, and our appreciation to George D. Kuh, Patrick T. Terenzini, and William G. Tierney, who provided comments that improved chapters 1 through 3. We are also indebted to John M. Braxton, editor of the Vanderbilt Issues in Higher Education Series, and Charles Backus, former director of the Vanderbilt University Press, for the opportunity to write this book and for their stewardship throughout its preparation. We are most appreciative of the hard work of Bill Adams, managing editor of Vanderbilt University Press, in overseeing the book's production, and the able efforts of Sherrye Young in putting together the index. Finally, we are especially grateful to John L. Holland for his thoughtful comments and invaluable support throughout the writing of this book.

We have dedicated this book to the memory of Dr. Charles F. "Chuck" Elton, who passed away on March 21, 1999, in Lexington, Kentucky. His death is a loss to all of us who were honored to have known him. Chuck was perhaps best known for his high and unwavering standards of scholarship, his candor, and his humor. His impact on the lives of many higher education scholars was profound. Chuck's legacy to the field of higher education goes well beyond his impact on the lives of individuals and is most evident in his founding of *Research in Higher Education* and his stewardship of the journal as editor from 1973 to 1990, when he retired from his position as professor of higher education at the University of Kentucky. The journal grew in quality and stature each and every year as a result of his exemplary leadership. The journal now stands as a tribute to him, and higher education scholars are indebted to Chuck for the knowledge they have gained through articles published in the journal and by the opportunity the journal affords them to share their knowledge with others. As a man who loved and respected scholarship as much as anyone else we have known, there could be no more fitting tribute to him than the journal, which he founded and left for us. Our lives were enriched by having known Chuck, and we are pleased to have the opportunity to dedicate this book to his memory. We only hope that our efforts would have satisfied the lofty intellectual standards that his life exemplified.

This book is the product of a collaborative effort in the very best sense. Each of us initially brought to the project certain distinct talents and viewpoints. We quickly realized that our professional strengths and individual personalities were not only complementary but also could be mutually reinforced to the benefit of the book, so long as we integrated the strands of our thinking. A collaboration that works is an exhilarating experience. Thus, we found the three years of work required to prepare this book to have been professionally and personally most rewarding.

ACADEMIC DISCIPLINES

1

Academic Disciplines and Academic Lives

THIS IS a book about college students and faculty. We focus on students and faculty because they are the two primary constituencies involved in the fundamental purposes of colleges and universities—teaching and learning. We analyze how systematic knowledge of distinctive clusters of academic disciplines is essential to understanding the diverse patterns of thought and behavior of college students and faculty. Why do some faculty, for example, use more formal and structured teaching-learning strategies that are clearly subject matter oriented, while other faculty place strong reliance on informal and unstructured teaching-learning strategies that are more student centered? Why do some students become more independent thinkers and acquire stronger analytical, mathematical, and scientific competencies over the course of their undergraduate careers, while others become more group oriented and acquire stronger interpersonal and leadership competencies? We believe answers to these important questions emanate from a basic understanding of the influences of academic disciplines and the manner by which they shape the distinctive patterns of thought and behavior of both college students and faculty.

This book is also decidedly theory based because theory is essential to the development of systematic knowledge about most any human endeavor. In particular, this book is grounded in the theory of careers developed by John L. Holland (1966, 1973, 1985, 1997). We selected Holland's theory as the theoretical framework for our study because of its

1

proven usefulness in explaining and understanding variability in different patterns of faculty thought and behavior as well as differences in students' choices of, stability in, satisfaction with, and achievement in disparate academic environments. Holland's theory is basically a theory of person-environment fit, based on the assumptions that there are six personality types and six analogous academic environments and that educational persistence, satisfaction, and achievement of students are functions of the congruence or fit between students and their academic environments. Thus, if one wants to know more about what colleges and universities might do to facilitate the retention, satisfaction, and learning of their students, then one must understand the inherent diversity of academic disciplines and the distinctive academic environments that their respective faculties create.

Our fundamental thesis throughout this book is that thorough knowledge of academic disciplines is a prerequisite to understanding variations in the professional attitudes and behaviors of college faculty and differences in the patterns of student change and stability that result from the college experience. Furthermore, we believe that the centrality of academic disciplines to the professional lives of faculty and to the educational lives of students has important implications for how institutions of higher learning are organized and operated. To persuade readers of this guiding perspective's merits, we will rely both on a presentation of *extant research findings* (about the variability of academic disciplines in various components of the professional lives of faculty and alternative patterns of educational change and stability of college students) and on an analysis of *our own research findings.*

Prior to an extended discussion of Holland's theory of careers and our empirical findings related to that theory in subsequent chapters, we provide in this chapter a rationale for viewing academic disciplines as central to the study of college faculty and students by overviewing two separate but related streams of research. We look first at research findings concerning variability in the professional attitudes and behaviors of college faculty who are members of different academic disciplines; we then turn to the extensive research literature on alternative patterns of change and stability in the attitudes, interests, and abilities of students who major in different academic disciplines. Our purpose is not to provide an exhaustive review of the two research streams; that has been done by others (Birnbaum, 1983; Braxton & Hargens, 1996; Feldman & Newcomb, 1969; Pascarella & Terenzini, 1991). Rather, our aim is to discern the focal interests of scholars, to overview the salient findings that have emerged, and to offer our critique of the merits of the two research streams in terms of their conceptual richness and methodological rigor in investigating the contributions of academic disciplines.

Academic Tribes: The Professoriate
The Evolution of the American Academic Profession

The historical development of the American academic profession prior to this century was heavily influenced by three European models, each of which placed a differing emphasis on academic disciplines and their respective subject matters (Light, 1974a, 1974b). First was the English, or Oxford, model, which emphasized mental discipline for the ruling elite with the implicit goal of providing a common social, moral, and intellectual experience for the offspring of that elite. The central role of the professor in this model was that of an intellectual and moral teacher. Academic disciplines and their subject matters per se were not so important but rather served as occasions to instill moral and intellectual values. This was followed by the Scottish model, which emphasized practical subjects and valued applied knowledge and the education of anyone who was qualified to learn. This model differed from the English one in at least two respects: it was much more egalitarian in terms of serving broader segments of the population; and it viewed the central role of the professor as that of teacher of subject matter content, especially useful knowledge. Thus, the importance of academic disciplines in the American academic profession surfaced initially with the adoption of the Scottish model in many of this country's institutions. The third model to influence the development of the American academic profession came from Germany and had a strong emphasis on scientific training and research to expand knowledge. In this model the central role of the professor was that of scholar who forged new frontiers of knowledge through research and who also taught secondarily. This dominant focus on scientific research, publications, and graduate education fully recognized the centrality of academic disciplines in the professional lives of faculty.

These three models, each of which had a great influence on the evolution of the American academic profession, contribute to our understanding of similarities and differences in the professional interests and activities of faculty associated with different types of institutions and different academic disciplines. The rich institutional diversity that has traditionally characterized American higher education is in large part a function of these models' influences. For example, the English, or

Oxford, model is apparent in elite liberal arts colleges; the Scottish model is evident in land-grant universities and in community colleges; and the Germanic model continues to thrive in large research universities.

Multiple Influences on Academic Careers

The growing dominance of the Germanic model—with its unique emphasis on scientific research, publications, and graduate education—contributed to a particular focus of attention by scholars who study only the small percentage of faculty actively engaged in scientific research and located primarily in large research universities. Indeed, only twenty-five years ago Light (1974a) concluded that "we know little about the careers, hopes, sources of satisfactions, and fears" (p. 262) of the large majority of men and women who constitute the American academic profession. The intervening years since Light's (1974a, 1974b) observations have witnessed a burgeoning amount of research on the professoriate, and much of this research has focused on general members of the academic profession instead of on the "publishing elite" that had characterized most previous studies (see, for example, Blackburn & Lawrence, 1995; Bowen & Schuster, 1986; Fairweather, 1996; Finkelstein, 1984). As a result of these inquiries we now have a much richer tapestry showing the multidimensionality of faculty careers.

As a case in point, Light, Mardsen, and Corl (1973) provided a three-strand model for the analysis of academic careers focusing on their distinctive, yet interrelated, disciplinary, institutional, and external dimensions. This contribution was important in that it distinguished among the alternative backgrounds, interests, and activities of faculty associated with these three strands. The authors described the different background factors affecting the selection of an academic career and the distinctive research perspectives (as well as the representative teaching opportunities) experienced during graduate school by faculty in disparate academic disciplines. Engaging in research and the training of future researchers represent the primary *disciplinary activities*, and Light, Mardsen, and Corl noted vast differences in the publication styles and rates of faculty in different disciplines. Teaching undergraduates and assisting with administrative responsibilities represent the primary *institutional activities* of faculty located in dissimilar colleges and universities. Here the authors found a clear pattern of faculty in less selective institutions spending greater time on undergraduate teaching activities. The primary *external activities* of faculty were work-related contributions outside the institution but within the discipline. Light, Mardsen, and Corl noted that much less is known about the external careers of faculty, which they characterized as "a residual rag-bag both in concept and in research" (p.68). Clearly, however, consulting with outside agencies is an important component of external careers.

The interplay among the multiple dimensions of faculty careers identified by Light, Mardsen, and Corl (1973) has also been a focal interest of Clark (1987b), who has provided an extensive analysis of the interworkings of disciplinary, institutional, and societal influences on faculty careers. Appreciation of these multiple influences has led to specific research on each source of influence. For example, Perkin (1987), Mommsen (1987), and Metzger (1987) have shown how governmental and societal forces have influenced the development of the academic professions. Perkin described how structural changes and governmental actions have contributed to the vulnerability of the academic profession in the United Kingdom; Mommsen showed how a reduction in competition among institutions and a decline in the mobility within the German academic profession was related to societal and governmental reforms; and Metzger described how historical and societal forces within the United States have contributed to the large, diffuse, and open attributes of the American academic profession. Similarly, the contributions of Halpern (1987) and Ruscio (1987) illustrate research on how faculty careers in the United States are shaped by various institutional forces. For instance, Halpern's work analyzed the influence of the "professional-school difference" on the changing character of academic work, thought, and action through an examination of the inherent duality confronted by faculty in professional schools. These faculty members pay allegiance to the central norms of universities through their research production, while at the same time they are pulled and pushed toward the practices and norms of the profession. Ruscio provided an elaboration of the multiple and competing differences in the work activities, authority structures, and belief patterns of faculty affiliated with different institutional sectors of the American system of higher education.

Centrality of Academic Disciplines in Academic Careers

The very scholars who have contributed so greatly to our appreciation of the complexity of faculty careers at the same time appear to be in agreement about the centrality of academic disciplines in shaping those careers.

For instance, Light, Mardsen, and Corl (1973) noted that of the three strands in their model, "faculty careers are dominated by disciplinary activities" (p. 2). Clark (1987b) also attested to the centrality of academic disciplines in his conclusion that the professional attachment of faculty "forms first around the discipline" (p. 382) and that "the disciplinary imperative may well be *the* driving force in modern higher education" (p. 383, emphasis in original).

Metzger (1987) identified four processes that stimulated the growing importance of academic disciplines in the lives of American academic professionals in the late nineteenth and early twentieth centuries. The first was "parturition," the tendency of new subject matter to be born out of the more inclusive, established subject matter areas. This influence on growing academic specialization was enhanced by the widespread adoption of prescribed curricula in most colleges by the 1860s. The second process was "program affiliation," most evident with the emergence of professional schools and their distinctive academic curricula. Clark (1987a) has noted, for example, that the modern academic "professions, as we know them today, took shape in the 1880s and 1890s . . . [when undergraduate education] increasingly became a preliminary to professional study" (p. 29). The third process identified by Metzger, whereby subject matter areas that previously had poor reputations were converted into credible ones, took place at the turn of the century. Metzger called this process of academic legitimization "dignification." The final process, "dispersion," was the tendency of subject matter areas to spread their substantive boundaries steadily. Clark has characterized dispersion as the process by which "an academic subject spreads itself imperialistically far beyond its initial boundaries" (p. 30).

The centrality of academic disciplines may also be seen in their influence on the very attributes that define a profession. For example, Parsons and Platt (1973) suggested that a profession has the following characteristics:

1. It has exclusive powers to recruit and train new members as it sees fit;
2. It has exclusive powers to judge who is qualified;
3. It is responsible for regulating the quality of professional work;
4. It has high social prestige; and
5. It is grounded in an esoteric and complex body of knowledge.

Academic disciplines obviously play a key role in each of these areas, so much so that Light (1974a) concluded that each of the five prerequisite characteristics of professions identified by Parsons and Platt "center on each discipline" (p. 12). Clark (1987a) concurred in his assertion that "academic disciplines have become authoritative communities of expertise" (p. 63).

Thus, as knowledge of the multiple influences on faculty careers has expanded considerably in recent years, the academic discipline has come to be recognized as the single greatest influence shaping the professional attitudes and behaviors of college faculty. The growing conceptual consensus about the large magnitude of disciplinary influences on faculty careers, along with subsequent research findings about disciplinary variability that have emerged, is the primary reason for our in-depth focus on disciplinary variability in the professional attitudes and behaviors of college faculty and on alternative patterns of student change and stability resulting from the college experience. We wish to acknowledge, however, that such variability of disciplines not only is based on their unique perspectives but also is influenced by the institutional and societal contexts in which they exist.

Research on Disciplinary Diversity of College Faculty

The sheer growth in the amount of research on faculty in the past several decades, together with its focus on a more broadly representative sample of faculty nationwide, was assisted by the availability of large-scale national surveys of faculty sponsored by such distinguished organizations as the American Council on Education and the Carnegie Foundation for the Advancement of Teaching. Such surveys enabled researchers to examine variability in the professional interests, attitudes, and activities of more representative samples of faculty on a nationwide basis. More recently an international perspective has been added as a result of the survey of faculty in thirteen countries sponsored by the Carnegie Foundation for the Advancement of Teaching (Boyer, Altbach, & Whitelaw, 1994).

Concomitant with the availability of these massive data sets was the emergence of several seminal writings questioning the conception of a single or uniform academic profession that had characterized much of the prior research. While acknowledging many potential sources of fragmentation in the academic profession, most all of these writings placed great emphasis on the roles of academic disciplines. For example, the centrality of academic disciplines perhaps has been most aptly stated by Clark (1987a), who has suggested that "there is no more stunning fact about the academic profession anywhere in the world than the simple one that academics are possessed by disciplines, fields of study, even as they are located in institutions" (p. 25). Clark's perspective has much in common with Light's (1974b) contention that "there is no single academic profession. Rather, there are academic professions, because the knowledge base for each profession is its discipline" (p. 259). Light (1974a), reaffirming his own contention that a single academic profession is a misnomer, has suggested that "theoretically, at least, we have the academic professions, one for each discipline" (p. 12).

Clearly, however, each and every academic discipline is not unique, as Light (1974a) has suggested. The initial absence of established conceptual frameworks by which to classify academic disciplines with similar orientations historically has been a major contributing factor to the marginal advancement of systematic knowledge about disciplinary diversity in the professional attitudes, interests, and behaviors of college faculty. The development of an acceptable conceptual framework to guide such inquiries is admittedly an exceedingly difficult task. Several attempts were undertaken prior to the 1970s, but they focused on alternative governance models, and many of them have remained as mainline concepts used to understand variability in the professional attitudes, interests, and behaviors of college faculty. Among the various efforts were the "community of scholars" model proposed by Goodman (1962) and Millett (1962), the "bureaucratic" model developed initially by Weber (1947) and modified by Stroup (1966), and the "political" model of academic life advanced by Foster (1968) and Baldridge (1971). The differing assumptions inherent in these alternative governance models reflected the lack of agreement among scholars at the time on an adequate conceptual framework to guide analyses of the professional lives of college faculty. The lack of agreement reflected in the governance models has commonly been found in research on academic departments which, as Clark (1987a) noted, have become "the basic unit of organization because it is where the imperatives of the discipline and the institution converge" (p. 64). Conceptual disarray was thus a dominant condition facing researchers of college faculty prior to the early 1970s.

In examining numerous studies of college faculty prior to 1970, Lodahl and Gordon (1972, 1973) and Light (1974a) concluded that the absence of appropriate theory or conceptual frameworks had been a major impediment to the development of systematic knowledge about the professional lives of members of the academic professions. For example, Light (1974a) identified "disorganization" and "the lack of good theory on which to base research" as the two primary deficiencies of the extant scholarly literature. Disorganization was manifested in the unco-ordinated nature of the research to the extent that "the absence of refer-ences to the work of others . . . bespeaks of egocentrism which has hurt this field" (p. 2). Light asserted that the lack of good theory to guide in-quiries contributed to a condition in which "most studies reflect either the interests of those financing them or the questions of the day" (p. 3). He suggested that the lack of theory not only inhibited comparative re-search over time but also abetted the neglect of fundamental questions underlying the research issues that had been addressed.

The development of theories and conceptual frameworks to guide inquiries of college faculty began in earnest in the 1960s and continues today. These efforts, and the empirical research based on them, have been reviewed by Braxton and Hargens (1996). Scholars have developed theoretical distinctions among academic disciplines on the basis of dozens of dimensions. Representative of these dimensions are efforts to distinguish among disciplines in terms of their respective levels of codi-fication (Zuckerman & Merton, 1971), paradigm development (Lodahl & Gordon, 1972), normative and functional integration (Hagstrom, 1964, 1965), knowledge domains and social features of knowledge communities (Becher, 1989), and consensus (Hargens & Kelly-Wilson, 1994). Readers interested in these and other theoretical formulations of disciplinary differences can consult Braxton and Hargens for an extensive treatment of their premises and the subsequent research based on them.

A salient contribution to higher education scholars' investigations of differences among disciplines is the work of Anthony Biglan (1973a, 1973b), who developed and tested an empirically derived classification schema that has evolved over the years into a major conceptual frame-work for the study of the professional attitudes, interests, and behaviors of college faculty. Biglan's three-dimensional classification schema of academic subject matter areas was developed through the use of non-metric multidimensional scaling procedures. These procedures were ap-plied initially to the responses of faculty at a large state-supported university and at a private, denominational liberal arts college to ques-tions concerning their perceptions of the relative similarity of thirty-three different subject matter areas. Three dimensions were found to be common for both groups of faculty.

The first dimension, reflecting the existence of a paradigm in a spe-cific discipline, was labeled "hard" versus "soft." Paradigmatic develop-ment, a concept advanced initially by Kuhn (1962), represents the extent to which a discipline has a commonly agreed upon set of problems for study and approved methods to be used in their explorations. Traditionally, the "hard" or more "scientific" areas of study, such as the physical sciences and mathematics, possess more clearly delineated paradigms. Such "hard" disciplines are at one end of a continuum on Biglan's first dimension, and "soft" disciplines such as the humanities and education, characterized by less consensus, are at the opposite end of the first dimension.

The second dimension, reflecting an academic discipline's concern with the practical application of its subject matter, was labeled "pure" versus "applied." At one end of this dimension are such fields as accounting, education, engineering, and finance, which tend to be concerned with the practical application of knowledge. At the opposite end are disciplines that traditionally express less concern with practical application (for example, history, mathematics, philosophy, physical sciences).

The third dimension, reflecting an academic discipline's involvement with living or organic objects of study, was labeled "life systems" versus "nonlife systems." Disciplines such as education and the biological sciences traditionally place greater emphasis on the study of living systems and are located at one end of this dimension; computer science, engineering, languages, and the physical sciences—disciplines characterized primarily by their relative lack of emphasis on organic objects of study—are located toward the opposite end of this dimension.

The contribution of Biglan's (1973a, 1973b) three-dimensional schema to the study of college faculty is perhaps best substantiated by its frequent citation in the scholarly literature. A search of citations to Biglan's two seminal articles in the annual volumes of the *Social Science Citation Index* from 1973 through August, 1996, revealed a total of 177 citations in over three dozen journals. The specific importance of his contributions to higher education researchers' investigations of college faculty is evident in the fact that nearly two-thirds (114 of 177) of all citations to his two articles appear in four general higher education research journals (*Higher Education, Journal of Higher Education, Research in Higher Education*, and *The Review of Higher Education*). While an exhaustive review of research findings based on Biglan's schema has been provided recently elsewhere (Braxton & Hargens, 1996), we note here that the schema has been instrumental in developing more systematic knowledge of disciplinary variation in the goals of academic disciplines (Smart & Elton, 1975), in teaching goals of faculty members (Smart & Elton, 1982), in administrative roles of department chairs (Smart & Elton,

1976), and in departmental reward structures (Smart & McLaughlin, 1978).

Without question, Biglan's three-dimensional schema has been a major contributor to providing a common basis by which scholars classify and investigate differences among faculty in decidedly distinct clusters of academic disciplines. This contribution alone has done much to reduce the disorganized, uncoordinated, and fragmented nature of the previous literature noted by Light (1974a). The question, however, as to whether Biglan's schema also has filled the theoretical void that Light noted remains open to debate. Bayer (1987) properly commented that the common reference to the "Biglan model" is a misnomer since it is an *"atheoretical,* empirically derived division of general academic areas of concentration" (p. 213, emphasis added). He further asserted that "the model" is not a typology, since there is an emphasis on differences rather than on similarities among academic disciplines. Bayer suggested that "the Biglan schema would be more appropriately described as a *classification* system . . . [because] it connotes an emphasis on differences . . . and it does not carry any theoretical implications" (p. 214, emphasis in original). Thus, it seems clear that Biglan's contribution fails to satisfy the minimal conditions of either a model or a typology.

Nonetheless, the Biglan classification system remains prominent in research on disciplinary differences in the professional attitudes, interests, and activities of college faculty as evidenced by its frequent citation in the scholarly literature (noted earlier). Thus, the body of knowledge that has evolved from use of Biglan's classification system "has yielded a stronger theoretical underpinning to the 'model' as well as providing broad empirical validation for its utility" (Bayer, 1987, p. 221). The evolving "theoretical" knowledge that has accrued from use of the empirically based "model" could conceivably be construed as "grounded theory" (Glaser, 1978; Glaser & Strauss, 1967; Smith, Harre, & Van Langenhove, 1995; and Strauss & Corbin, 1990).

Walsh (1973) has suggested that a common element in most definitions of theory is seeing theory as "a device which enables us to recognize the relationships among facts" (p. 5); theory development grows from our need to make sense out of life. He developed five formal criteria of a sound theory:

> *comprehensiveness:* sound theories should make predictions concerning a diverse array of behavior;

clarity and explicitness: the assumptions and concepts of sound theories should be clearly, precisely, and explicitly stated;

inclusion of known findings: sound theories incorporate extant empirical findings within a logical consistent framework;

parsimony: sound theories are communicable and understandable, and do not overexplain phenomena; and

empirical research generated: sound theories have a developmental effect upon relevant areas of research. (p. 5)

The Biglan model, which is both communicable and understandable, appears to have had a strong developmental effect on subsequent research. Yet accepting the common characteristics of formal theories and the criteria for such theories developed by Walsh (1973) and knowing the atheoretical, empirically based procedures used in its initial formulation (Bayer, 1987), we conclude that the Biglan model lacks most of the essential characteristics of a formal theory. For example, it makes no predictions about faculty attitudes, interests, or behaviors; its basic assumptions and concepts are not clearly or explicitly stated; and it does not by itself incorporate known findings. Thus, we wonder whether the model has the long-term potential to resolve the disorganized and fragmented character of research on the professional lives of academic professionals and to fulfill the need for a good theory on which to base subsequent research noted by Light (1974a) and others over two decades ago.

Using the same common characteristics of formal theories and the criteria for evaluating the merits of such theories developed by Walsh (1973), we believe the theory of careers proposed by John L. Holland (1966, 1973, 1985, 1997) is a much stronger theoretical foundation to assist research on college faculty to progress beyond its present stage of uncoordinated, fragmented, and conflicting findings to a more systematic level of scientific inquiry. We will describe this theory and discuss the rationale for our conclusions about it in the following chapter, and we will present research evidence in support of our position in subsequent chapters. Before doing so we turn to a discussion of the centrality of academic disciplines in the educational lives of college students.

Academic Disciples: College Students

One reason academic disciplines/departments are a potentially strong influence on patterns of change and stability of college students is the increasingly large size of institutions of higher learning. The phenomenal growth rate of American colleges and universities over the past four decades has been documented by Trow (1988), Finn and Manno (1996), and many others. One consequence of this growth is the difficulty students have in finding a "home" within increasingly large and diverse institutions. The growing importance of academic departments in this milieu is aptly reflected in the following vignette of San Francisco State College, which we assume to present a picture as accurate today as it was over thirty-five years ago: "San Francisco State is no longer, if it ever was, a homogeneous college, and its different departments and divisions are moving toward different models at quite uneven rates. . . . It is the departments and divisions that carry the main burden of State's efforts to upgrade its . . . student body, both in the classroom and in the departmental activities outside class. . . . It is understandable, if hardly ideal, that the Dean should advise incoming students that "The College is too big to provide a focus for your education. Your department will have to be your home" (Riesman & Jencks, 1962, pp. 187–188).

The potential influence of academic departments on patterns of change and stability of college students is assumed to be manifested in large part through student interactions with departmental faculty, for, as Feldman and Newcomb (1969) noted, academic departments "are the basic units in which faculty members organize their administrative, teaching, and research efforts" (p. 152). Parsons and Platt (1973) and Vreeland and Bidwell (1966) noted that departmental faculty are a potentially important influence on students because they possess powerful normative and utilitarian sanctions for the differential socialization of students; these sanctions are manifested through the expressed goals of faculty for undergraduate education and through the ability of faculty to reward students differently for performance by the assignment of grades and the encouragement of interaction. Kelly and Hart (1971) and Lipset and Ladd (1971) interpreted the strong influence of academic departments on student change and stability, when found, as being a consequence of an underlying selective recruitment process of distinctive personality types into academic disciplines that have prevailing orthodoxies, biases, and definitions of "the right way" to think and act. It is reasonable, then, to expect differential change and stability of students across dissimilar departments given the demonstrated wide variations in the professional attitudes, interests, and behaviors of faculty associated with different academic disciplines (see Braxton & Hargens, 1996, for a review of the extensive literature on faculty).

As part of their comprehensive reviews of the massive research literature on what happens to students in college, Feldman and Newcomb
(1969) and Pascarella and Terenzini (1991) synthesized the subliterature
concerning the general importance of academic departments' contributions to differential patterns of change and stability in college students
and the specific features of academic departments relevant to these differential patterns. Below we briefly compare the respective conclusions
of Feldman and Newcomb with those of Pascarella and Terenzini in
terms of the general frequency and magnitude of differences in the patterns of change and stability of college students majoring in dissimilar
academic departments.

Differential Patterns of Change and Stability: Magnitude of Academic Department Differences

Prior to the mid 1960s. Feldman and Newcomb (1969) devoted an entire chapter to research on the differential impacts of academic fields.
They were able to document that students in different academic majors
typically differ from each other on certain characteristics. Based on findings from studies using the Allport-Vernon-Lindzey Study of Values instrument, for example, they concluded that students in the natural
sciences and engineering scored highest on *theoretical* values, students in
business and industrial management ranked highest in *political* values, students in general education and the social sciences tended to score higher
on *social* values, and business students consistently ranked highest in *economic* values. They also found substantial differences in the literature for
students majoring in different fields on political-economic attitudes, religious conservatism, career orientations, intellectual ability, intellectual
dispositions, authoritarianism, psychological well-being, and a number of
personality characteristics. They noted, however, that the findings across
academic majors were not sufficiently consistent to provide a comprehensive typology that consistently reflected differences among the fields,
and they concluded that "individuals enrolled in different curricula do, as
a group, show certain distinctive characteristics, . . . even though each
field does not have one unique type of student" (p. 170). Pursuing the
question of whether these differences show anything more than self-
selection by students into various academic majors, Feldman and
Newcomb concluded from the analysis of data available to them that the
"evidence is clear . . . that differential experiences in the several major

fields do have impacts beyond those attributable to initial selection into those fields" (p. 193). In essence, they found both initial selection and subsequent accentuation effects on numerous outcome measures for college students as a result of their chosen field of study.

As noted earlier, the development of theories and conceptual frameworks to guide investigations of disciplinary differences among faculty affiliated with disparate fields of study did not begin in earnest until the 1960s. The significance of this in terms of explorations of differential patterns of student change and stability is that the studies on which the Feldman and Newcomb (1969) synthesis was based were unlikely to have used any systematic theory or conceptual framework to classify fields of study for comparative purposes. Thus these analysts were left to explore differences among approximately two dozen individual academic majors and lacked any theoretical basis for expecting or interpreting the differences that emerged as a result of their inquiry. This lack of sound theory on the part of researchers who conducted the studies on which their synthesis was based may well have contributed to the inability of Feldman and Newcomb to discern systematic, consistent differences across dissimilar academic majors. Nonetheless, it is clear from their efforts that there were frequent and substantial differences in the attitudes, values, and abilities of students in disparate academic majors at the time they began college *and* at the conclusion of their undergraduate experiences. Moreover, analyses of a number of studies showed that the differences sometimes appeared to be larger at the conclusion of college than on entrance—an instance of what Feldman and Newcomb (1969) referred to as "accentuation" of initial group differences.

Between the mid 1960s and 1990. The differences between the conclusions of Feldman and Newcomb (1969) just described and those of Pascarella and Terenzini (1991), in terms of the contribution of students' major fields of study on their change and stability during college, are dramatic. Unlike the former, the latter concluded that, with the exception of a few "selective impacts," they "found little consistent evidence that one's major has more than a trivial net impact on one's general level of intellectual or cognitive outcomes" (p. 614). They further noted that "the impact of major field of study on noncognitive outcomes is substantially less apparent or consistent" (p. 614) than in cognitive domains. The few selective impacts in the cognitive domain were based primarily on subject-matter tests with students scoring higher in areas of knowledge most congruent with their academic majors.

The rather dramatic differences in the conclusions derived from these two large-scale syntheses of the research literature are especially surprising given the growing interrelatedness and consistency of results in studies of the professional attitudes, interests, and behaviors of faculty members following the emergence of (at least) empirically derived classifications systems of academic disciplines such as the Biglan schema. Because many of the studies available for consideration by Pascarella and Terenzini (1991) were arguably superior in terms of the representativeness of samples, research design, and sophistication of statistical analysis, it might be thought that the conclusions of Pascarella and Terenzini are more sound than those of Feldman and Newcomb (1969). We are reluctant to come to this conclusion, for there may be other reasons for the discrepant conclusions of the two sets of analysts.

Three possibilities come to mind in efforts to reconcile the discrepant conclusions. First, it is possible that the influence of academic departments actually declined after the mid 1960s. We know of no cause to support this possibility, however, and consider it unlikely. Second, the two research syntheses were based on somewhat different epistemological orientations or analytic stances. These differences may have led the respective pairs of authors to focus on (or to give differential attention to) different sources of influence on patterns of change and stability in students. Third, it is possible that the authors of the original studies of college students on which the Pascarella and Terenzini synthesis was based, unlike their counterparts who studied faculty, failed to incorporate into their studies the classification systems of academic disciplines that had emerged in the intervening years and, instead, devoted their attention to other potential influences on student change and stability. These last two possibilities are elaborated in the next two sections.

Studying the Impact of Colleges on Students:
The Two Social Psychologies

The difference in the analytic stance of Feldman and Newcomb (1969) and that of Pascarella and Terenzini (1991) is roughly captured by Gamson's (1991) distinction between a "process" approach and an "effects" approach to the study of what happens to students in college. Both syntheses are concerned with both the *effects* that colleges have on students and the *processes* that produce these effects. However, the "ratio" of emphasis between the two concerns differs, as signaled in the pattern of chapter titles in each of the books. The chapter titles in Feldman and

Newcomb (1969) mainly refer to the social structures and social arrangements of colleges that presumably influence students (for example, "The Diverse American College," "The Diversity of Major Fields," "Impacts of Residence Groupings"). By contrast, the chapter titles in Pascarella and Terenzini (1991) in general refer to attributes of individuals ("Cognitive Skills and Intellectual Growth"; "Psychological Changes: Identity, Self-Concept, and Self Esteem"; "Attitudes and Values," for instance) potentially influenced by colleges.

One way to make clear the difference in analytic stance (and thus the organization) of these two books is to contrast two extreme approaches—one psychological and one sociological—to specifying the origin of changes in persons (even though neither book takes either of the extreme approaches). In an extreme developmental approach, the origin of change is sought *only* in internal or ontogenetic forces that initiate development, whereas in an extreme environmental approach the origin of change is sought *only* in the external or what have been called "sociogenic" forces (Dannefer, 1984a, 1984b; Featherman & Lerner, 1985) of the prevailing social system and culture. As an example, suppose it is found that a group of young people who *do not* go to college typically change over a four-year or five-year period on some outcome measure in exactly the same way as do a group of young people who *do* go to college. Ontogenetic theorists would explain this finding by assuming or postulating internal laws of development that affect individuals in the two different categories in similar ways, whereas sociogenic theorists would explain the same finding in terms of the impact of societal-wide social and cultural forces on a certain age group (or perhaps on the population as a whole).

As it happens, neither Pascarella and Terenzini (1991) nor Feldman and Newcomb (1969) opted for either an ontogenetic or sociogenic approach taken to its extreme; nor did either pair of authors use *only* a psychological approach or *only* a sociological approach, extreme or otherwise. However, a developmental perspective is an important aspect of Pascarella and Terenzini's view of the interplay between student and college and does underlie a good portion of their analysis of college student change and stability. They are anything but doctrinaire or one-sided in their analysis. They warn of the possibility that what is sometimes referred to as development in college students may in large measure be the results of individuals' responses to the anticipated norms of new social settings or roles, and they suggest that "we need to be wary of the tendency to equate the learning of social or cultural norms with development" (p. 364). Any psychological approach they do take in their book is heavily tempered by consideration of the nature of interpersonal settings of colleges, the structural and organizational features of colleges' social environments, and the institutional characteristics of colleges. Feldman and Newcomb essentially took the reverse tack in synthesizing the research on college impacts by heavily tempering their more sociological approach with psychological considerations. A brief formulation of the difference would be this: Feldman and Newcomb leaned toward *sociological* social psychology, whereas Pascarella and Terenzini leaned toward *psychological* social psychology (cf. Stryker, 1977).

The more psychological of the two social psychologies in higher education—particularly when the developmental perspective predominates—is well known and need not be described in detail here. In this approach student outcome variables are chosen that are direct "growth" or "maturity" variables or are more or less directly interpretable in such terms (even if, in some cases, an interpretation within a developmental framework is made somewhat arbitrarily, as shown in Feldman, 1972). Although there may be some analysis of the contents and forms of the social structural arrangements and pressures of both the school and the larger society, more systematic concern is typically paid to the psychological dynamics of change rather than to the possible social impetus for such change. Moreover, even when environmental and social structural parameters are systematically analyzed, they tend to be considered only insofar as they are seen as immediately impinging on personality development, cognitive development, attitudinal development, or the like.

Compared to psychological social psychologists, social psychologists who are sociologically oriented in their study of higher education tend to focus considerably more on the structure and dynamics of the social pressures impinging on students than on the internal psychological dynamics initiating change or buttressing stability. They are interested in systematically measuring and describing a relatively full range of social structural features of the college environment and subenvironments even though implications for student change and stability may not as yet have been completely or systematically explored in higher education theory and research. Although they may study some of the same outcome variables as do developmentally oriented theorists, the interpretations they make of change or stability of these attributes of students are not necessarily made within a developmental framework. Moreover, they may choose student outcome variables that have little or nothing to do with maturity or growth or that, in some instances, are even incompatible with the developmental approach (see Feldman, 1972).

Sociological social psychologists analyze the structural impacts of colleges' environments and subenvironments on student newcomers' socialization into their organizations. The term *socialization* is not used as a synonym for *development*; rather, it refers to the social pressures on new members to adhere to prevailing ways of thinking, feeling, and behaving found in the group. This social organizational approach focuses on how college environments and subenvironments (such as academic disciplines, to take one case in point) vary, from which variation pertinent differential impacts are conceived and predicted. Thus, "impacts" are not necessarily conceived in terms of the "development" or "growth" of the individual.

One way of locating an analysis of college students and their colleges in the landscape of the two social psychologies of higher education is to see how the college environment and subenvironments are brought into play in the analysis (see Feldman, 1991, 1994). At the outset of their book, for instance, Pascarella and Terenzini (1991) inform the reader that one of their difficult decisions in attempting their synthesis was deciding on an organizing principle for presenting findings; they report that "after a fairly lengthy consideration . . . [they] decided to organize the evidence in terms of different types of outcomes" (p. 5). This decision, which is a perfectly reasonable one, does tilt their approach toward psychological social psychology, we believe. Rather than initially focusing on and describing the features of the college environment in their own right and then asking how such features might or might not affect students regardless of whether or not there are studies about each possible impact, the analysis of the environment essentially has been made dependent upon the student outcomes under investigation and the empirical work that happens to have been done on these outcomes. The tilt of the book by Feldman and Newcomb (1969) is in the opposite direction from that of Pascarella and Terenzini. After initially establishing trends in the change and stability of college students following their matriculation, Feldman and Newcomb focused on the college environment and subenvironments, speculating on how they might affect students and then looking at the ways in which, in fact, they do have impacts on students.

The two books, of course, are anything but polar opposites; there is a good deal of overlap. Feldman and Newcomb (1969) considered psychological development as well as the psychological dynamics of change and stability, just as Pascarella and Terenzini (1991) considered socialization and other social forces that create impacts on individuals. Still, the differences in interpretive frameworks remain—subtle as they may be at times and not so subtle at others. And these differences in analytic stance may have contributed in part to the differences in the authors' conclusions about the relative importance of academic departments' contributions to differential patterns of student change and stability during college as well as to suggestions about the possible reasons for any differential effects on students—but only up to a point, we would assume. After all, both sets of authors depended on a set of research studies and empirical findings for their conclusions, which allowed only so much leeway in their interpretations. Thus, it might be informative to consider in a broad way the studies that provided the "raw data" for Pascarella and Terenzini's analysis of college impact—particularly the general epistemological orientation and analytic models underlying many of these studies. We do so in the next section.

Studying the Impact of Colleges on Students: Recent and Current Models and Typologies

We note first that the two most prevalent and respected typologies of academic disciplines developed by Biglan (1973a, 1973b) and Holland (1966, 1973, 1985, 1997), which have proved useful in studying college *faculty*, have received scant attention by higher education scholars in their efforts to determine the primary factors associated with various manifestations of *student* change and stability. For example, Biglan's schema has been used almost exclusively in studies of the professional attitudes, interests, and behaviors of faculty members. Only a handful of the citations to his schema that appear in the mainline higher education journals focus on college students. Similarly, excluding the citations of one of the present authors, there have been no more than twenty-five citations to Holland's theory and classification system in these journals. A second consideration is the possibility that higher education scholars have chosen to direct their attention to sources of influence other than academic departments in their efforts to understand stability and change in college students. Support for this possibility comes from inspection of the key factors in models used to guide most recent studies of college effects on students. Included among these models are those of Tinto (1975, 1987, 1993); Bean (1985); Pascarella (1985); Cabrera, Nora, and Castaneda (1993); Astin (1984, 1985); Pace (1980, 1984); and Weidman (1989). Following are brief overviews of these conceptual models that have guided much of the recent research on college students.

Tinto's (1975, 1987, 1993) model was developed initially to help explain and understand student drop-out behavior but has subsequently been used to guide research on a wide range of college outcomes. His model focuses on two central concerns: the extent of students' integration into the academic and social systems of their institutions; and the degree of students' commitment to their institutions and their educational aspirations. While faculty-student interactions are hypothesized to be central to students' academic and social integration, the proposed model is silent in terms of the roles played by academic departments in fostering these interactions and integrations. Tinto's elaboration of the model and scales developed to measure the key constructs of academic and social integration (Pascarella & Terenzini, 1980) are similarly silent about academic departments. Instead, the writings focus on the general issue of the frequency and nature of faculty-student interactions with no attention to variability across disparate academic departments.

Tinto's theory has been a major contribution to the study of college students. Its importance may be seen in the frequency of citations to it in actual studies and to its influence on alternative "models" that have been subsequently proposed. Most of these subsequent models have accepted the core constructs in Tinto's initial model and represent efforts to extend the initial model to more heterogeneous groups of college students (e.g., nontraditional students) and to multi-institutional settings. Like Tinto's original model, they too, with the single exception of Weidman (1989), are silent about the roles of academic departments' contributions to differential patterns of change and stability in college students.

The distinctive contribution of Bean's (1985) model was the introduction of factors external to campus settings that may influence the behaviors and intentions of students while they are in college. These "environmental variables"—finances, opportunity to transfer, and outside friends—have been found to be especially important contributors to the drop-out behaviors of nontraditional-aged students and under-represented students (Bean & Metzger, 1985; Metzger & Bean, 1987; Nora, 1987). The model proposed by Cabrera, Nora, and Castaneda (1993) similarly emphasized the potentially important roles of "significant others" within and outside educational institutions in students' drop-out behavior. Particularly key to their model is the role played by students' parents. This role is manifested in the authors' constructs concerning parental educational aspirations for and encouragement of their offspring and those concerning parental knowledge of postsecondary costs and financial aid.

Pascarella's (1985) model of learning and cognitive development represented a major extension of Tinto's (1975) initial model through the incorporation of institutional characteristics. While Tinto's initial model implied testing within individual institutions, the inclusion of structural characteristics of institutions in Pascarella's model facilitated the inclusion of multiple institutions within studies of college effects on students. The model and subsequent adaptations to it have been used to guide dozens, and perhaps hundreds, of inquiries in the past decade.

Astin's (1984, 1985) conceptualization of involvement, in hypothesizing simply that students learn by becoming involved, is grounded in five basic propositions: (1) involvement requires the investment of both psychological and physical energy; (2) involvement has both qualitative and quantitative dimensions; (3) involvement is a continuous construct, and different students will invest varying amounts of energy in their collegiate experience; (4) the amount of student learning or development is directly proportional to the quality and quantity of effort invested; and (5) the educational effectiveness of any institutional policy or practice is related to its ability to induce student involvement. His conceptualization suggests the importance of both students and their institutions in promoting student learning and development. On the one hand, students have a central role based on the quality of their effort or involvement with the resources provided by the institution (which determines the extent and nature of their learning). On the other hand, institutions play a critical role in students' learning or development to the extent that they afford students a great number and variety of opportunities for encounters with other ideas and people. While the propositions in Astin's conceptualization of involvement have attracted a great deal of attention from higher education researchers and administrators, Pascarella and Terenzini (1991), among others, concluded that "they probably do not meet generally accepted definitions of theory" (p. 51) such as those elaborated by Walsh (1973), Kerlinger (1986), and others.

Pace's (1979, 1980, 1984) work on the quality of student effort has much in common conceptually with Astin's (1984, 1985) theory of involvement in its assumption that student learning and development are dependent not only on what institutions do or do not do, but also on the extent and quality of effort that students invest in their collegiate experiences. Pace, however, is much more explicit than is Astin about the specific dimensions of the college experience that contribute to different aspects of student learning and development, and he has developed fourteen "quality of effort" scales to assess student involvement and to estimate students' use of institutional facilities and opportunities. These scales, which are the bases for the College Student Experiences Questionnaire and the Community College Student Experiences Questionnaire and which have been used by hundreds of four- and two-year institutions, have strong psychometric properties (Ethington & Polizzi, 1996).

Weidman's (1989) conceptual model of undergraduate socialization is alone among the models reviewed here in explicitly incorporating academic departments as a key element in efforts to understand how the college experience contributes to change and stability in students. Weidman considers the academic department to be "a particularly important locus of both faculty and peer influences on students . . . [and a potentially] powerful source of normative influence on student majors" (p. 306). While his conceptual framework "calls attention to the various normative pressures exerted by different types of majors" (p. 315), it is general in its orientation and does not suggest specific variables to be incorporated and operationalized. To date, no published studies have directly and explicitly "tested" the hypothesized relationships suggested by this conceptual framework.

In sum, the weak influence of academic departments on students' change and stability noted by Pascarella and Terenzini (1991) could well reflect a declining interest among scholars in examining this potential source of influence. The declining interest is evident from the virtual omission of academic departments as a source of influence on students in all models just described, with the exception of Weidman's (1989). Rather than focusing on the more proximal departmental context, these models direct the attentions of scholars to the more distal institutional environment. Regardless of the terminology used—integration (Tinto), involvement (Astin), or quality of effort (Pace)—primary focus has been students' fit with their *institutional* environments or the use of *institutional* facilities, programs, and services. Moreover, there has been a virtual neglect of studying how patterns of change (and stability) vary across departmental settings within institutions of higher education.

Methodologically, the models that have guided most of the recent research on the effects of college on students are longitudinal in nature and have encouraged the use of regression-based, causal-modeling procedures. Such methodological procedures do not focus specifically on whether or not students change, but rather focus primarily on the relative importance of the models' constructs to students' scores on selected outcome variables one or more years after entering college. That is, the concern is whether or not students differ on one or another outcome

variable after students are statistically equated on their entry characteristics and their college experiences.[1]

Thus it appears that the questions being asked by researchers have
changed in the past two or three decades. Questions of whether or not
students change and whether or not such change is consistent across

---

[1] The regression models that have commonly been used in studying college effects on
students are often analyses of covariance (ANCOVA) models based on the statistical general
linear model. This is particularly true when studies have attempted to examine the effects of
college majors. ANCOVA models attempt to assess group differences on an outcome after statistically controlling for variability accounted for by other theoretically relevant variables (the
covariates). An incorrect interpretation of ANCOVA in the presence of nonrandom assignment of subjects to groups, but a frequent one nonetheless, is that the procedure statistically
"equates" groups that differ on the covariate. This statistical "equating" of nonequivalent
groups is chosen as a mathematical convenience when random assignment to groups is not
feasible, but it fails to model the real situation (see Bryk & Weisberg, 1976; Cronbach &
Furby, 1970; Pedhazur, 1982, among many others for discussions of this misinterpretation of
ANCOVA). Anderson (1963) puts this approach in strong perspective by noting that "one
may well wonder what exactly it means to ask what the data would look like if they were not
what they are" (p. 170); and Smith (1957) suggests that the adjusted means resulting from
ANCOVA analyses in nonexperimental studies should more appropriately be referred to as
"fictitious means" (p. 291). Furthermore, the results from these regression models do not examine whether students change or not; instead they examine whether the groups differ on the
outcome after the statistical control for a prior measure of the outcome and other covariates.

That these ANCOVA models do not tell us whether or not students change is easily
seen in the interpretation of the estimates of the regression coefficients. Take, for example,
the following estimated regression equation: POST = -12.491 + .919 PRE + 10.724 GROUP.
These results indicate that after statistically controlling for initial differences on the premeasure, the two groups differ by 10.724 points on the adjusted postmeasure means. Also,
after controlling for group differences on the postmeasure, students who differed by 1 unit
on the premeasure, on average, differ by .919 on the postmeasure. There is no indication
from these results that students in the "treatment" group on average increased by approximately 4.4 units from pre- to postmeasure, while students in the "control" group actually decreased by approximately 5.7 units. This only becomes apparent by examining the group
means given below or by calculating the adjusted postmeasure means (Group 1: 46.725;
Group 2: 57.449) and comparing them to the premeasure means:

		PRE	POST
Group 1:	Control	49.356	43.614
Group 2:	Treatment	56.123	60.559

To confound further our ability to examine whether or not groups changed across time when
the regression approach is taken, the general presentation of regression results includes only
the regression coefficients resulting from the estimation, and the only descriptive information, if presented at all, is for the entire sample and is not broken down for individual groups.

disparate departmental settings are no longer as central as they were in the past. Instead, perhaps in our rush to assist college officials and other policy makers with information useful for enhancing student learning, we have placed much less attention on the fundamental questions of whether students actually learn or change and whether their patterns of learning and change vary across departments and other relevant college settings. In so doing, academic departments and other group-level influences have assumed a secondary role in investigations, and our knowledge of their potential contributions to student learning and change may well have suffered accordingly.

Academic Disciplines and Academic Lives: A Theory-Based Inquiry of Academic Environments

As noted initially, our fundamental premise in this book is that knowledge of academic disciplines is a prerequisite to understanding variability in college faculty members' professional lives as well as change and stability in students that result from their undergraduate experiences. Whereas our review of the research findings based on the professional attitudes and behaviors of college faculty provides general support for this premise, such support is much less evident in the more recent research findings pertaining to college students. We suggest that this apparent inconsistency may be a function of the underlying assumptions of the research agendas and methods used by scholars in these two distinct domains of inquiry. Could it be that what one finds at the conclusion of an inquiry is partially contingent on what one expects to find at the outset?

Juxtaposing Research Findings on College Faculty and College Students

Research on the professional lives of college faculty largely assumes or accepts the centrality of academic disciplines. This fundamental assumption has important theoretical and methodological implications for those who conduct research by delimiting their research agendas and methods. Although we would not contend that research on college faculty has a strong theoretical foundation, major advances have been made in determining the conceptual, if not theoretical, underlying bases of disciplinary differences in faculty members' professional attitudes and behaviors. The evolving conceptual sophistication of research on disciplinary differences among college faculty may be seen in the efforts to distinguish disciplines in terms of their respective levels of codification (Zuckerman & Merton,

1971), paradigm development (Lodahl & Gordon, 1972; Biglan, 1973a), pure versus applied orientation (Biglan, 1973a), normative and functional integration (Hagstrom, 1964, 1965), knowledge domains and social features of knowledge communities (Becher, 1989), and consensus (Hargens & Kelly-Wilson, 1994). Although a unifying theory has not emerged from these inquiries, they clearly manifest a central focus on academic disciplines and the underlying bases of their differentiation.

The centrality of academic disciplines in the research agenda on college faculty also has important methodological implications. Given a focal concern on understanding differences among *groups* of academic disciplines, analyses of variance (ANOVAs) predominate. It is not that the use of analysis of variance is intrinsically significant, but that its use focuses attention of scholars on group differences and the underlying theoretical bases of these differences.

Our examination of the recent research literature on college students (since the mid 1960s) reveals a quite different research agenda and set of research methods. In terms of the research agenda, the centrality of academic disciplines appears to have declined substantially and to have been replaced by specific characteristics of *individuals* and their *interactions* with various aspects of their *institutional settings*. We base this perspective on the virtual omission of academic disciplines in the conceptual models that have guided much recent research on college students. None of the models, other than Weidman's (1989), even mentions academic disciplines as a potentially important influence on student learning, development, and other changes.

Thus we see broad differences in the research agendas and methods used by those who study college faculty and those who study college students. The first group of scholars and researchers assumes (based on evidence) that academic disciplines are a key element in the research design, focuses on exploring the underlying bases of academic disciplines and identifying the substantive nature of the differences among groups, and uses research methods (ANOVA-based procedures) to explore these anticipated differences. The second group has a different research agenda and set of acceptable or preferred research methods. Attention is on specific attributes of individuals and the interactions of these individuals with the more distal institutional environment rather than with the more proximal academic environment created by departmental faculty. The analytic and statistical methods used by this group seek to determine the relative influence of students' interactions with different aspects of the institutional environment rather than the pattern of stability and change on the focal (dependent) variable of interest. Given this overarching orientation, differential patterns of change and stability for students majoring in dissimilar academic programs is (at best) a secondary concern.

Theory-Based Inquiry into Differential Patterns of Change and Stability in College Students

Because of our fundamental interest in academic disciplines and the potentially different patterns of change and stability among college students, in our research agenda and methods we have more in common with researchers who study college faculty than with those who have studied college students in the past thirty years or so. We are specifically interested in discovering whether or not changes in students (resulting from their undergraduate experiences) vary as a function of the specific academic disciplines in which they major. This interest alone sets our inquiry apart from much of the recent research on college students, which is based on the common models currently used to study the effects of colleges on students. Our inquiry also differs from most research on both college students and faculty in its use of a strong theoretical framework that, while seldom used by higher education scholars, is highly appropriate for investigating differential patterns of change and stability among students resulting from their majoring in disparate academic departments. We refer to John L. Holland's (1966, 1973, 1985, 1997) theory of careers.

In the next chapter we provide an overview of Holland's theory and its fundamental assumptions. These assumptions form a theoretical and empirically defensible basis for the classification of academic disciplines/departments. They further provide a theoretical basis for our investigations about students' initial selection of academic majors, the differential socialization occurring in these disparate clusters of academic disciplines, and the consequences of the fit between students and their chosen academic disciplines on students' subsequent change and stability. In chapter 2, then, we fully explicate the fundamental assumptions of Holland's theory and their applicability to the study of both college faculty and students.

Summary

In this chapter we have provided a rationale for our belief that knowledge of academic disciplines is a prerequisite to understanding academic lives. We did so by contrasting the general perspectives of scholars who study college faculty with the general perspectives of those who study college students. In comparing these two streams of research, we noted that those who study the professional lives of faculty have largely assumed and accepted the centrality of academic disciplines; this has not been the case, especially in more recent years, for those who study change and stability of college students. We contend that this difference has both conceptual and methodological implications in terms of the research agendas and research methods evident in the two domains of research. Finally, although we have not yet presented the specifics of the theory of careers advanced by John L. Holland (1966, 1973, 1985, 1997), we have provided a rationale for our efforts in this book to assess the merits of Holland's theory as a theoretical framework for the study of faculty members' professional lives as well as the study of the patterns of change and stability in college students.

2

Holland's Theory and
Its Assumptions

IN THE previous chapter we noted the uneven attention given to the
potential influences of academic disciplines on the academic lives of
college faculty and the educational lives of college students. On the one
hand, research on the professional lives of college faculty has evidenced
much attention to the influences of academic disciplines, although that
research has commonly used dichotomous and simplistic classifications of
academic disciplines based on attributes such as levels of codification,
paradigm development, normative and functional integration, and consensus (Braxton & Hargens, 1996). On the other hand, current research
on the educational lives of students has shown an increasing lack of attention to the potential influences of academic disciplines.

We are less than sanguine about these tendencies in the respective research literatures on college faculty and students, and we believe that the
development of more systematic knowledge in either domain would be
enhanced by reliance on more comprehensive theories of human behavior. With this thought in mind, we have selected the theory of careers, developed by John L. Holland, as a primary focus of our book. In this
chapter we present a brief history of the evolution of Holland's theory,
offer an overview of its primary components and assumptions, and suggest its implications and appropriateness for research on both college
faculty and students.

29

Evolution of Holland's Theory

Holland's theory of careers was initially presented in the abbreviated format of a journal article; he sought to delineate a theory of vocational choice that was "comprehensive enough to integrate existing knowledge and at the same time sufficiently close to observables to stimulate further research" (Holland, 1959, p. 35). His efforts were in response to his concerns that existing theories of vocational choice at the time were either too broad (e.g., Ginzberg, Ginzberg, Axelrad, & Herma, 1951; Super, 1957) or too specialized (Hoppock, 1957; Roe, 1956, 1957). This initial statement provided a rudimentary elaboration of the six personality types and model environments that continue to be the foundation of the theory. Holland (1966) subsequently characterized this initial statement as a "heuristic theory of personality types and environmental situations" in that its primary objective was to stimulate "research and investigation by its suggestive character rather than by its logical or systematic structure" (pp. 8–9).

The first book-length elaboration of the theory, *The Psychology of Vocational Choice* (Holland, 1966), presented more explicit definitions of the main constructs. The author hoped to facilitate understanding, research, and practical application and to provide more comprehensive formulations of basic assumptions and premises in an effort to attract the assistance of other researchers in assessing the usefulness of the theory for understanding vocational choice, stability, satisfaction, and success. These first two statements spawned considerable research on the validity and usefulness of the theory and led to an even more comprehensive elaboration of the theory in 1973 focusing specifically on vocational problems encountered over a person's life span: vocational choice, work history, job changes, and occupational accomplishments. This iteration of the theory, *Making Vocational Choices: A Theory of Careers*, captured the attention of the research community—especially counseling psychologists. Holland (1973) noted that "this third statement offers a theory that better complies with scientific standards of logic and evidence, and suggests some concrete applications" (p. vii). The prominence in the scholarly community of this third statement of the theory was subsequently recognized through its selection by the Institute of Scientific Information (1980) as a Citation Classic by virtue of its high citation rates in the *Science Citation Index* (SCI) and the *Social Science Citation Index* (SSCI). Its specific usefulness for an understanding of vocational behavior is evident in the fact that Holland's theory received nearly twice as many citations as the second-ranked theory of careers by Donald E. Super (Watkins, Bradford, Lew, & Himmell,

1986). The applicability of this third statement of the theory to problems and concerns outside the specific domains of counseling psychologists is evident in Walsh's (1973) assessment of Holland's theory and five comparable person-environment theories based on six attributes of formal theories (comprehensiveness, clarity and explicitness, operational adequacy, incorporation of known findings, parsimony, and generation of empirical research). As based on Walsh's criteria, Holland's theory received the highest overall rating among the six general person-environment theories.

The fourth statement of the theory (Holland & Gottfredson, 1976) provided a brief clarification of the theory, especially in terms of its applicability to people of all ages. As Holland (1985) notes, the next iteration (the fifth statement) of the theory, *Making Vocational Choices: A Theory of Vocational Personalities and Work Environments*, closely resembles the 1973 version and its clarification (Holland & Gottfredson, 1976), and it continued the "tidying up process" of making the theory and its applications more comprehensive and explicit. This fifth statement of the theory differed from earlier statements in several respects, however. For example, Holland introduced the construct of identity "as another secondary construct to prop up the formulations for both types and environments" (p. x) and demoted the importance of the construct of consistency because of weak empirical evidence for its importance. These constructs—identity and consistency—are discussed later in this chapter. In addition, the assessment of personality types was modified to incorporate the contributions of Staats (1975; 1981), and the definitions of environments were supplemented with concepts derived from Barker's (1968) concept of behavior settings.

Holland (1997) noted in the sixth and most recent statement that "the theory has been extended by providing more explicit formulations for the types, the environments, and their interactions. My aim was to improve the internal structure so that the theory would have more explanatory power. In general, readers will find all parts of the theory to be more comprehensive, including more detail. In short, the main ideas are the same as before, but their exposition is more complete and, I hope, more satisfying" (p. 15). The 1997 edition of the theory also describes efforts to revise existing measures of the theory's central constructs and develop new ones. For example, the Self-Directed Search (SDS; Holland, Fritzsche, & Powell, 1994), a career-guidance device explicitly derived from the theory, has undergone two revisions since 1985. In addition, two new instruments have been developed to assist people in their choices of and adjustment to careers. The Career Attitudes and

Strategies Inventory (CASI; Holland & Gottfredson, 1994) was developed in 1994 to assess several career beliefs and experiences that are thought to influence career stability, satisfaction, and achievement. More recently, Gottfredson and Holland (1996b) have developed the Environmental Identity Scale to assess people's impressions of their work environments.

These efforts to develop measures of constructs central to Holland's theory of careers are distinctive in two respects. First, they reflect Holland's continuing dedication over a period of three decades to develop psychometrically robust measures of the key constructs so as to refine the theory and make it useful to researchers and others trying to understand vocational behavior. Second, they reflect Holland's abiding dedication to empirical evidence generated from tests of the propositions and hypotheses of the theory. Each iteration of the theory has contained refinements based on emerging findings from such inquiries.

Whereas Holland's theory has achieved considerable distinction within the broader social science research community, especially among psychologists, it has received little attention or use by higher education scholars who study college students or members of the academic profession. This neglect is evident from a virtual absence of citations to the theory in such general, main-line higher education journals as the *Journal of Higher Education, Research in Higher Education, Higher Education*, and *The Review of Higher Education*. Excluding the references of one of the present authors, there has been no more than a handful of citations to Holland's four books elaborating the fundamental premises of the theory in these higher education journals (as based on a citation search of the SSCI). This small number of citations clearly demonstrates the virtual lack of attention to Holland's theory by higher education scholars and illustrates the need for an elaboration of the basic tenets of the theory and their applicability to research on college faculty and students.

This chapter provides an overview of Holland's theory and its basic assumptions along with an elaboration of the applicability of the theory in higher educational settings and the specific research implications of each assumption for those who study college faculty and students. Thus, the introductory overview of the theory, which follows, provides the reader with a holistic understanding of the theory and its basic assumptions. The next section discusses the applicability of the basic assumptions to topics commonly addressed in efforts to understand both the professional lives of college faculty and the longitudinal patterns of change and stability in the abilities and interests of college students.

Overview of Holland's Theory

The underlying basis of Holland's theory is that human behavior is a function of the interaction between individuals and their environments (e.g., educational and work settings). Thus the theory focuses on an assessment of individuals, their environments, and the interaction or fit between individuals and their environments. Holland (1997) has characterized his theory as a structural-interactive or typological-interactive theory, noting that "it is structural or typological because it attempts to organize the vast sea of information about people and jobs" and that "it is interactive because it assumes that many careers and social behaviors are the outcome of people and environments acting on one another" (p. 12). The following subsections present an overview of each of these three components of the theory—individuals, environments, and the fit or congruence between individuals and environments—and the basic assumption associated with each component. The three specific assumptions associated with the three components are that (1) students choose academic environments compatible with their personality types, (2) academic environments reinforce and reward different patterns of student abilities and interests, and (3) students flourish in environments that are congruent with their dominant personality types.

Individuals: The Six Personality Types

A basic premise of Holland's theory is that an individual's selection of a vocation or academic major is an expression of personality since such preferences or choices tend to be moderately correlated with personality scales. This premise is distinctive in that other vocational behavior theories (e.g., Strong, 1943; Super & Crites, 1962) interpret people's occupational preferences or scores on vocational interest inventories to be "vocational interests." Holland (1985), however, assumes that individuals' occupational preferences or vocational interest scores "flow from their life history" and constitute "an expression of personality" (p. 7).

Instrumental to Holland's thinking were Forer's (1948) efforts to develop an inventory to assess personality from interests and activities and to show how an individual's preferences for, or aversions to, specific vocational interests and activities could be interpreted as expressions of selected dimensions of personality. Forer, however, did not subject his ideas to a direct scientific test, and this led Holland (1963) to develop a personality inventory, the Vocational Preference Inventory (VPI), composed entirely of occupational titles based on the rationale that preferences for occupations reflect an individual's personality. Holland (1966) provided the following elaboration of this rationale for the development of the VPI: "The choice of an occupation is an expressive act which reflects the person's motivation, knowledge, personality, and ability. Occupations represent a way of life, an environment rather than a set of isolated work functions or skills. To work as a carpenter means not only to use tools but also to have a certain status, community role, and a special pattern of living. In this sense, the choice of an occupational title represents several kinds of information: the S's motivation, his knowledge of the occupation in question, his insight and understanding of himself, and his abilities. In short, item responses may be thought of as limited but useful expressive or projective protocols" (p. 4).

In addition, Holland's theory posits that most people can be classified by their resemblance to one or more of six theoretical or ideal personality types (Realistic, Investigative, Artistic, Social, Enterprising, Conventional). Each of the personality types thus represents "a model against which we can measure the real person . . . [and is] the product of the characteristic interaction among a variety of cultural and personal forces including peers, biological heredity, parents, social class, culture, and the physical environment" (Holland, 1985, p. 2).

While Holland does not provide an extensive discussion of the longitudinal development of personality types, he does suggest two major influences: heredity and social experiences. Holland (1997) suggests that to some degree "types produce types" and that "parents create characteristic environments that include attitudes as well as a great range of obvious environmental experiences" (p. 17). Beyond parental influences, Holland suggests that "children create their own environments . . . by their demands upon parents and also by the manner in which parents react to and are influenced by their children" (p. 18). The demands of children are assumed to be a consequence of *both* their biological endowment and social learning. These complex interactions contribute to the development of preferences for selected activities, which foster the development of distinctive interests and ultimately lead to the acquisition of a special group of competencies. These unique sets of interests and competencies ultimately lead people to think, perceive, and act in special ways.

Holland's perspectives about the development of personality types was influenced by Staats's (1981) theory of social behaviorism: "The individual begins from birth to learn *systems* of 'skills,' according to the principles of conditioning, in three areas: language-cognitive processes, emotional-motivational processes, and sensori-motor acts. These systems are called . . . personality repertoires and are considered to be the basic constituents of personality in several ways. First, the way an individual *responds* to a situation is not only a function of the behaviorally significant acts of the situation but a function (in part) of the individual's personality repertoires. Second, this is true for what the person *experiences* in a situation as well as for what he or she *learns*. Each behavioral occurrence depends in part on the situation and in part on the individual's personality repertoires" (p. 244, emphases in original). Thus Holland views the six personality types as "models" of six common clusters of personality or behavioral repertoires that exist in society. Personality types are assumed not only to have a distinctive pattern of competencies, interests, and preferred activities but also to search for environments that reinforce and reward their distinctive attributes. This "searching" behavior is the basis for the "self-selection" assumption described later in this chapter; that is, it is assumed that college students, for example, choose academic environments/majors that are compatible with their dominant personality types.

Thorough definitions of the preferred activities and distinctive pattern of attitudes, interests, and competencies of each personality type have been developed by Holland (1997) "so that the validity of their formulations can be examined and so that the typology can be applied to everyday problems" (p. 28). The following is a summary of the distinctive profiles for the six personality types.

Realistic types prefer activities that involve the manipulation of machines, tools, and objects, and they have an aversion to educational, interpersonal, and therapeutic activities. They value material rewards for tangible accomplishments and have manual, mechanical, and agricultural competencies. They perceive themselves as being practical, conservative, asocial, and persistent, and they are seen by others as being normal and frank.

Investigative types prefer activities that entail the exploration, understanding, and prediction or control of natural or social phenomena and avoid those involving persuasion and sales. They value the development and acquisition of knowledge and scholarly and scientific achievements, and they have scientific and mathematical competencies. They perceive themselves as being critical, intelligent, and skeptical while lacking interpersonal skills, and they are seen by others as being asocial and intellectual.

Artistic types prefer literary, musical, and artistic activities and avoid activities associated with conformity to established rules. They value aesthetic qualities such as creative expression of ideas, emotions, and sentiments and have art, music, drama, and writing competencies. Artistic types perceive themselves as innovative, open to new experiences, emotional, sensitive, and often lacking in clerical and office skills. They are seen by others as unconventional, disorderly, and creative.

Social types prefer activities associated with helping other individuals through personal interaction, and they often avoid mechanical and technical tasks. They value social service and fostering the welfare of others and have interpersonal and educational competencies. Social types perceive themselves as cooperative, empathetic, helpful, understanding, and lacking in mechanical ability, and they are regarded by others as agreeable, nurturant, and extroverted.

Enterprising types prefer activities that entail persuading, manipulating, and directing others to attain organizational goals or economic gain, and they avoid engagement with scientific, intellectual, and abstruse topics. They value political and economic achievements and social status. Enterprising types perceive themselves as self-confident, pleasure-seeking, and sociable; they also see themselves as possessing public speaking and leadership competencies. They lack scientific abilities and are seen by others as energetic and gregarious.

Conventional types prefer activities associated with establishing and maintaining orderly routines and the application of standards to attain organizational or economic goals, and they have an aversion to ambiguous or unstructured activities. Their engagement in these activities leads to the development of clerical and numerical competencies and to a deficiency in artistic abilities. They value material or financial accomplishments and power in social, business, or political arenas and perceive themselves as conforming, orderly, methodical, and practical. Conventional types are seen by others as being careful and conforming.

Table 2.1 provides a summary of the distinctive pattern of competencies, interests, values, self-perceptions, and preferred activities of the six personality types that are central to Holland's theory.

Assessment of an individual's personality type. Holland (1997) notes that a variety of qualitative and quantitative methods may be used to assess a person's personality type. Among the *qualitative* methods is the observation of a person's expression of vocational preferences for, or actual employment in, an occupation that is characteristic of a type or a person's preference for, or actual engagement in, educational training that is characteristic of a type. For example, a person may want to become a chemical engineer or currently be employed as a chemical engineer, or plan to major in chemical engineering, or currently be enrolled as a chemical

Table 2.1

Salient Attributes of the Six Personality Types
from Holland's Theory [a]

REALISTIC people prefer activities that involve the explicit, ordered, and systematic manipulation of objects, tools, machines, and animals, and they avoid educational and interpersonal activities. These behavioral tendencies of Realistic people lead, in turn, to the acquisition of manual, mechanical, agricultural, electrical, and technical competencies and to a deficit in social and educational competencies. Realistic people perceive themselves as practical and conservative, having mechanical, technical, and athletic abilities, and as lacking ability in social skills. They value material rewards—money, power, and status—for tangible accomplishments.

INVESTIGATIVE people prefer activities that involve the observational, symbolic, systematic, and creative investigation of physical, biological, and cultural phenomena in order to understand and control such phenomena, and they avoid persuasive, social, and repetitive activities. These behavioral tendencies of Investigative people lead, in turn, to the acquisition of scientific and mathematical competencies and to a deficit in persuasive and leadership abilities. Investigative people perceive themselves as cautious, critical, complex, curious, independent, precise, rational, and scholarly, and they value the development or acquisition of knowledge.

ARTISTIC people prefer ambiguous, free, and unsystematized activities that involve the manipulation of physical, verbal, or human materials to create art forms or products, and they avoid routine activities and conformity to established rules. These behavioral tendencies of Artistic people lead, in turn, to the acquisition of artistic competencies—language, art, music, drama, writing—and to a deficit in clerical and business system competencies. Artistic people perceive themselves as expressive, original, intuitive, nonconforming, introspective, independent, emotional, and sensitive, and they value the creative expression of ideas, emotions, or sentiments.

continued

Table 2.1 *(continued)*

Salient Attributes of the Six Personality Types from Holland's Theory

SOCIAL people prefer activities that involve the manipulation of others to inform, train, develop, cure, or enlighten others, and they avoid explicit, ordered, systematic activities involving materials, tools, or machines. These behavioral tendencies of Social people lead, in turn, to the acquisition of human relations competencies (e.g., interpersonal and educational skills) and to a deficit in manual and technical ability. Social people perceive themselves as cooperative, empathetic, generous, helpful, idealistic, responsible, tactful, understanding, and warm, and they value fostering the welfare of others and social service.

ENTERPRISING people prefer activities that involve the manipulation of others to attain organizational goals or economic gain, and they avoid scientific, intellectual, and abstruse activities. These behavioral tendencies of Enterprising people lead, in turn, to an acquisition of leadership, interpersonal, speaking, and persuasive competencies and to a deficit in scientific ability. Enterprising people perceive themselves as aggressive, ambitious, domineering, energetic, extroverted, optimistic, popular, self-confident, sociable, and talkative, and they value material accomplishment and social status.

CONVENTIONAL people prefer activities that involve the explicit, ordered, systematic manipulation of data—such as keeping records, filing and reproducing materials, and organizing written and numerical data according to a prescribed plan—and they avoid ambiguous and unstructured undertakings. These behavioral tendencies of Conventional people lead, in turn, to the acquisition of clerical, computational, and business system competencies and to a deficit in artistic competencies. Conventional people perceive themselves as careful, conforming, orderly, and as having clerical and numerical ability. They value material and financial accomplishment and power in social, business, and political arenas.

[a] Adapted from J. L. Holland (1997) and G. D. Gottfredson (1991).

engineering major. Any one of these four kinds of information or combinations of them results in being classified as an Investigative type because "chemical engineering" is one of the occupations and academic majors that define the Investigative type.

Holland and his colleagues have developed a number of resources that may be used to identify occupations and academic majors that are associated with each personality type. For example, the *Dictionary of Holland Occupational Codes* (*DHOC*) developed by Gottfredson and Holland (1996a) may be used to identify the occupations associated with each personality type. The *DHOC* classifies all occupations included in the entire *Dictionary of Occupational Titles* (U.S. Department of Labor, 1977) into the six personality types included in Holland's theory. Similarly, *The College Majors Finder* (Rosen, Holmberg, & Holland, 1989), which classifies over nine hundred college majors according to their resemblance to the distinctive interests, skills, and abilities of the six personality types, may be used to identify academic majors associated with each personality type.

Among the *quantitative* methods that may be used to assess a person's personality type are scores on selected scales of personality and interest inventories such as the Self-Directed Search (SDS; Holland, Fritzsche, & Powell, 1994), the Vocational Preference Inventory (VPI; Holland, 1966), the Strong-Campbell Interest Inventory (SCII; Campbell & Hansen, 1981), and the Strong Vocational Interest Blank (SVIB; Campbell & Hansen, 1981). Specifically, the six theme scores of the SCII; the composite activities, competencies, occupations, and self-rating scales from the SDS; and the occupational preference scales of the VPI may be used to assess a person's resemblance to the six personality types.

Although Holland (1997) acknowledges that "no single assessment technique stands out as being the most advantageous for all purposes," he suggests that the use of selected scales of established personality and interest inventories and the use of current preferences for occupations and academic majors "have either produced more coherent results or have special advantages by virtue of their simplicity or theoretical construction" (p. 29). In sum, he suggests that it is preferable to use both inventory and occupational data.

Typological relations and secondary constructs. An important feature of Holland's theory is the hexagonal model (shown in Figure 2.1) reflecting the level of similarity among the six personality types. The personality types are arranged on the hexagon in the following clockwise order: Realistic, Investigative, Artistic, Social, Enterprising, and

Conventional. The relative similarity of the types is inversely proportional to the distance between any pair in the model (i.e., the shorter the
distance between any two personality types, the greater their psychological resemblance). For example, the Investigative type is most similar
to the Realistic and Artistic types (adjacent to it on the hexagon) and
least similar to the Enterprising type at the extreme opposite end of the
hexagon.

Figure 2.1

Hexagonal Model for Defining Psychological Resemblances among Personality Types and Academic Environments

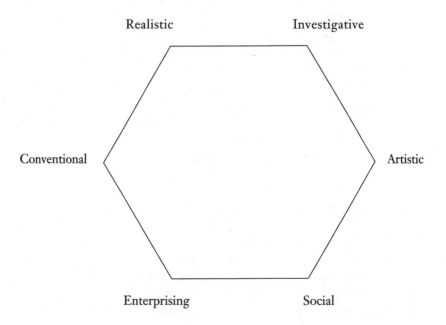

It is theoretically possible to assess a person's resemblance to all six
personality types, especially when using the SDS, VPI, SVIB, or SCII.
This six-level profile constitutes a person's "personality pattern."
Although people generally possess at least some attributes of all six

personality types, they tend to think and act in a manner consistent with one or two of these orientations more strongly than others. Thus, personality patterns may consist of anywhere from two to six variables or types where "the number of variables used is a matter of convenience, number of subjects, or judgment" (Holland, 1997, p. 31). For example, a person whose highest score is Social (S), whose second highest score is Artistic (A), and whose third highest score is Enterprising (E) would have a SAE personality pattern.

The hexagonal model in Figure 2.1 may be used to determine the *consistency* of a person's personality profile—that is, its internal coherence. For example, an R-I personality pattern is consistent because the dominant (R) and secondary (I) codes are adjacent on the hexagon, implying that they share many traits in common (unsociability, preference toward things rather than people, self-deprecation, and traditional masculinity). On the other hand, a C-A personality pattern is inconsistent because the two codes are at opposite ends of the hexagon, implying that these two dominant orientations share little in common (conformity versus originality, control versus expressiveness, and business versus aesthetic interests and abilities). Holland (1997) hypothesizes that the consistency of a personality pattern is positively related to educational and vocational stability, satisfaction, and success.

Personality patterns may also differ in terms of their *differentiation*—that is, the absolute difference between a person's highest and lowest scores across the six personality types. Spokane (1996) noted that differentiation "is a measure of the crystallization of interests and provides information about the relative definition of types in an individual's profile" (p. 45). A highly differentiated personality pattern has sharp peaks and low valleys, while an undifferentiated personality pattern is relatively flat. While differentiation itself may resemble a consistent personality pattern, Holland (1985) notes that "differentiation is concerned more with the range of scores in the whole profile than with the consistency of the highest scores" (p. 26). Like consistent personality patterns, however, those that are highly differentiated are hypothesized to be positively related to educational and vocational stability, satisfaction, and success (Holland, 1997).

A third secondary construct in Holland's theory is *identity*, or the clarity of a person's vocational goals and self-perceptions. Identity is measured by the eighteen-item Identity Scale of "My Vocational Situation" (Holland, Daiger, & Power, 1980). Those with high scores on the Identity Scale have a "small number of occupational goals that belong to a small number of main categories. Persons with low scores have many goals belonging to many main categories" (Holland, 1997, p. 33). High identity scores are also hypothesized to be positively related to educational and vocational stability, satisfaction, and success (Holland, 1997).

The purpose of the three secondary constructs—consistency, differentiation, identity—is to aid understanding of conditional predictions made from the personality types; they essentially reflect the clarity, definition, and predictability of an individual's personality pattern. For example, all Artistic types are not equally likely to possess the same level of characteristics theoretically associated with that type and may respond to situations in a different manner. Those with highly consistent and differentiated personality patterns and high identity scores should resemble Artistic types more than do those with low consistency, differentiation, and identity. In the context of Staats's (1981) theory of social behaviorism, the three constructs are also estimates of the variety of personality repertoires a person will exhibit.

Environments: The Six Model Environments

In Holland's theory human behavior depends on both personality and the environment, and therefore knowledge about environmental settings is equally as important as that about personality types. The theory proposes six analogous model environments that reflect the prevailing physical and social settings in society. Holland (1997) defines a model environment as "the situation or atmosphere created by the people who dominate a given environment . . . [noting that] just as we can assess real people by comparing them with the personality types, we can assess real environments by comparing them with the models" (p. 41). Each of the six environments is dominated by its corresponding personality type; for example, an Artistic environment would be an environment dominated by Artistic types.

Holland's definition of a model environment is grounded in the idea—found in works by interactional psychologists such as Linton (1945), Gellerman (1959), Mischel (1968, 1973), Bowers (1973), and others—that educational and work environments are created by the people in them. Schneider (1987) summarized the guiding perspective of interactional psychologists as "the idea that environments and people are not separable, and that the people in an environment make it what it is" (p. 440). Thus both the general character and dominant features of an environment "reflect the typical characteristics of its members. If we know what kind of people make up a group, we can infer the climate that the group creates" (Holland, 1997, p. 42).

The descriptions of the model environments parallel those of the six personality types in terms of their focus on activities, competencies, perceptions, and values. In general the model environments are assumed to require, reinforce, and reward the characteristics of the analogous personality types who dominate them. For example, Investigative environments are assumed to recruit individuals who possess the salient characteristics of Investigative types (see Table 2.1) and to reinforce and reward those attributes further. This socialization process occurs through efforts of environmental members (1) to stimulate individuals to perform the preferred activities of the environment, (2) to foster their respective competencies, (3) to encourage them to see themselves in ways consistent with the preferred values of the environment, and (4) to reward them for the display of the preferred values of the environment.

These premises about environments are the bases for the "socialization" assumption described later in this chapter. To take an example from environments found in colleges and universities, this assumption would imply that different academic environments/disciplines reinforce and reward different talents in their students. The socialization assumption, as we will show in subsequent chapters, is manifested in disciplinary differences in faculty members' attitudes about undergraduate education and in patterns of change and stability in students' abilities and interest. The following is a summary of the distinctive profiles for the six model environments in terms of the kinds of activities preferred, competencies developed, self-perceptions encouraged, values and personal styles cultivated, and behaviors rewarded (Holland, 1997; Gottfredson, 1991).

Realistic environments are characterized by concrete, practical activities involving machines and tools. They foster the development of manual and mechanical competencies; they encourage their members to see themselves as having practical, productive, and concrete values and to see the world in simple, tangible, and traditional terms; and they reward their members for the display of conventional values and goods—money, power, and tangible possessions.

Investigative environments are characterized by analytical and intellectual activities that involve the creation and use of knowledge. They foster the development of analytical, technical, and scientific competencies; they encourage their members to see themselves as valuing the acquisition of knowledge through scholarship and investigation and to see the world in complex, abstract, independent, and original ways; and they reward their members for the display of skepticism, persistence in problem solving, and scientific values.

Artistic environments are characterized by creative activities and unstructured intellectual endeavors. They foster the development of innovative and creative abilities and emotionally expressive interactions with others; they encourage their members to see themselves as having aesthetic values and unconventional ideas or manners and to see the world in complex, independent, and flexible ways; and they reward their members for the display of imagination in literary, artistic, and musical accomplishments.

Social environments are characterized by activities that entail working with others in a helpful or facilitative way. They foster the development of interpersonal competencies, skills in mentoring, and treating or teaching others; they encourage their members to see themselves as having a concern for the welfare of others and to see the world in flexible ways; and they reward members for the display of empathy, humanitarianism, sociability, and friendliness.

Enterprising environments are characterized by leadership and manipulative activities that are oriented toward the attainment of personal or organizational goals. They foster the development of leadership and public speaking competencies; they encourage their members to see themselves as aggressive, popular, and self-confident and to see the world in terms of power, status, and responsibility; and they reward members for the display of self-confidence, dominance, and initiatives in the pursuit of material accomplishments.

Conventional environments are characterized by activities with things, numbers, or machines to meet predictable organizational requirements or specified standards. They foster the development of clerical skills and the ability to meet precise performance standards; they encourage members to see themselves as having a traditional outlook and a concern for orderliness and routines and to see the world in constricted, simple, and dependent ways; and they reward members for dependability, conformity, and organizational talents.

Table 2.2 presents a summary of the distinctive patterns of activities, competencies, perceptions, and values of the six model environments.

The distinctive orientations of the environments and their respective sets of requirements and rewards are assumed to lead to different outcomes in terms of people's interests and abilities. For example, Holland (1997) notes that people in Realistic environments become more susceptible to pragmatic and traditional influences and less adept at coping with

Table 2.2

Salient Attributes of the Six Model Environments from Holland's Theory [a]

REALISTIC environments emphasize concrete, practical activities and the use of machines, tools, and materials. These behavioral tendencies of Realistic environments lead, in turn, to the acquisition of mechanical and technical competencies and to a deficit in human relations skills. People in Realistic environments are encouraged to perceive themselves as having practical, productive, and concrete values. Realistic environments reward people for the display of conforming behavior and practical accomplishment.

INVESTIGATIVE environments emphasize analytical or intellectual activities aimed at the creation and use of knowledge. Such environments devote little attention to persuasive, social, and repetitive activities. These behavioral tendencies in Investigative environments lead, in turn, to the acquisition of analytical, scientific, and mathematical competencies and to a deficit in persuasive and leadership abilities. People in Investigative environments are encouraged to perceive themselves as cautious, critical, complex, curious, independent, precise, rational, and scholarly. Investigative environments reward people for skepticism and persistence in problem solving, documentation of new knowledge, and understanding solutions of common problems.

ARTISTIC environments emphasize ambiguous, free, and unsystematized activities that involve emotionally expressive interactions with others. These environments devote little attention to explicit, systematic, or ordered activities. These behavioral tendencies in Artistic environments lead, in turn, to the acquisition of innovative and creative competencies—language, art, music, drama, writing—and to a deficit in clerical and business system competencies. People in Artistic environments are encouraged to perceive themselves as having unconventional ideas or manners and possessing aesthetic values. Artistic environments reward people for imagination in literary, artistic, or musical accomplishments.

continued

Table 2.2 *(continued)*

Salient Attributes of the Six Model Environments from Holland's Theory

SOCIAL environments emphasize activities that involve the mentoring, treating, healing, or teaching of others. These environments devote little attention to explicit, ordered, systematic activities involving materials, tools, or machines. These behavioral tendencies in Social environments lead, in turn, to the acquisition of interpersonal competencies and to a deficit in manual and technical competencies. People in Social environments are encouraged to perceive themselves as cooperative, empathetic, generous, helpful, idealistic, responsible, tactful, understanding, and having concern for the welfare of others. Social environments reward people for the display of empathy, humanitarianism, sociability, and friendliness.

ENTERPRISING environments emphasize activities that involve the manipulation of others to attain organizational goals or economic gain. These environments devote little attention to observational, symbolic, or systematic activities. These behavioral tendencies in Enterprising environments lead, in turn, to an acquisition of leadership, interpersonal, speaking, and persuasive competencies and to a deficit in scientific competencies. People in Enterprising environments are encouraged to perceive themselves as aggressive, ambitious, domineering, energetic, extroverted, optimistic, popular, self-confident, sociable, and talkative. Enterprising environments reward people for the display of initiative in the pursuit of financial or material accomplishments, dominance, and self-confidence.

CONVENTIONAL environments emphasize activities that involve the explicit, ordered, systematic manipulation of data to meet predictable organizational demands or specified standards. The behavioral tendencies in Conventional environments lead, in turn, to the acquisition of clerical, computational, and business system competencies necessary to meet precise performance standards and to a deficit in artistic competencies. People in Conventional environments are encouraged to perceive themselves as having a conventional outlook and concern for orderliness and routines. Conventional environments reward people for the display of dependability, conformity, and organizational skills.

[a] Adapted from J. L. Holland (1997) and G. D. Gottfredson (1991).

others due to their simple and direct coping methods and repertoires; those in Investigative environments become more susceptible to abstract, theoretical, and analytic influences and cope with others in rational, analytic, and indirect ways; those in Artistic environments become more susceptible to personal, emotional, and imaginative influences and cope with others in personal, expressive, and unconventional ways; individuals in Social environments become more susceptible to social, humanitarian, and religious influences and are more apt to cope with others by being friendly, helpful, and cooperative; people in Enterprising environments become more susceptible to social, emotional, and materialistic influences and are prone to cope with others by dominance and talkativeness; and those in Conventional environments become more susceptible to materialistic influences and tend to cope with others in conforming and practical ways.

Assessment of environmental types. The distinguishing characteristics of educational and work environments can be discerned in a rather straightforward manner given Holland's (1997) assumption that "many of the psychologically important features of the environment consist of or are transmitted by the people in it" (p. 48). This straightforward manner is known as the Environmental Assessment Technique (EAT) and entails a simple census of the occupations, training preferences, and vocational preferences of individuals who constitute an environment.

The *Dictionary of Holland Occupational Codes* (*DHOC*) developed by Gottfredson and Holland (1996a) may be used to take a census of the distribution of individual personality types in work settings or organizations. The *DHOC* classifies all occupations included in the *Dictionary of Occupational Titles* (U.S. Department of Labor, 1977) into the six personality types included in Holland's theory. Similarly, *The College Majors Finder* (Rosen, Holmberg, & Holland, 1989), which classifies over nine hundred college majors according to their resemblance to the distinctive interests, skills, and abilities of the six personality types, may be used to determine the environmental profiles of educational settings such as colleges and universities.

In addition to the EAT census approach, Gottfredson and Holland (1991) have developed the Position Classification Inventory (PCI) to classify occupational environments. The PCI, which focuses on environmental demands and rewards rather than on a census of environmental inhabitants, is an eighty-four-item assessment of job requirements, skills, perspectives, values, personal characteristics, talents, and key behaviors commonly performed in a job. This instrument yields a total of nine scales, including estimates of the extent to which an environment resembles each of the six hypothesized environmental models.

Typological relations and secondary constructs. As with the personality types, the hexagonal model shown in Figure 2.1 reflects the level of similarity among the six model environments. The environments, like the personality types, are arranged on the hexagon in the following clockwise order—Realistic, Investigative, Artistic, Social, Enterprising, and Conventional—with the relative similarity of the environments being inversely proportional to the distance between any pair in the model.

The constructs of consistency, differentiation, and identity, described earlier for the personality types, are similarly applicable to the assessment of an overall pattern of an environment. The hexagonal model can be used to determine the level of *consistency* of an environmental pattern. For example, an R-I environment would be dominated primarily by Realistic and Investigative personality types and would be considered to be a consistent environment because the two predominant personality types are adjacent on the hexagon, implying that they share reasonably similar activities, competencies, and rewards. On the other hand, a C-A environment would be dominated primarily by Conventional and Artistic personality types and would be considered to be inconsistent because the two codes are at opposite ends of the hexagon, implying that these two dominant orientations demand different interests, competencies, and values. Holland (1985) hypothesizes that the level of consistency in the profiles of environments is positively related to stability, involvement, satisfaction, and performance of environments.

Environmental *differentiation* is also defined in the same way as the differentiation of a personality pattern—that is, the percentage difference between the most and least common personality types in the environment. Because of the dominance of a single personality type in a highly differentiated environment, such an environment is characterized by its encouragement of "a narrow range of behavior in explicit ways"; undifferentiated environments, by contrast, have a greater balance among the personality types and tend to "stimulate a broad range of behavior and provide ambiguous guidance" (Holland, 1985, p. 42). Like consistent environmental profiles, those that are highly differentiated are hypothesized to be more stable and productive and to have higher levels of involvement and satisfaction.

The concept of *identity* refers to the extent to which the goals of an environment are consistent and explicit. Gottfredson and Holland (1996b; see also Holland, 1997) have developed an experimental scale, the Environmental Identity Scale, to assess people's perceptions of the relative

explicitness and consistency of an environment's goals, work rules, and rewards for performance. Environments "with a high (clear) identity would
have a focused set of consistent and explicit goals . . . [whereas those] with
a low (diffuse) identity would have a larger set of conflicting and poorly
defined goals" (Holland, 1997, p. 50). The concept of environmental identity was developed because of the neglect in earlier versions of the theory
to two important organizational conditions—size and structure. High
identity scores are expected to be associated not only with small size and
simple structure of environments but also with higher levels of stability,
involvement, satisfaction, and performance of those environments.

Congruence between Individuals and Environments

Holland's theory assumes that each personality type is most likely to flourish in the environment having the same label because such an environment
would provide opportunities, activities, tasks, and roles congruent with the
competencies, interests, and self-perceptions of its parallel personality
type. Specifically, it is assumed—other things being equal—that congruence of person and environment is related to higher levels of stability, satisfaction, and achievement of the person. By the same token,
incongruence of person and environment leads to educational or vocational instability, dissatisfaction, and low performance of the person.

These premises are the bases for the "congruence" assumption described in the following section of this chapter; that is, students, for example, are more likely to flourish in environments congruent with their
personality types. The hexagonal model in Figure 2.1 may be used to determine the degree of congruence or fit between people and their environments. Four levels of congruence can be derived for each of the personality
types. The highest level of congruence occurs when a given personality
type (for instance, Artistic) is in a matching environment (Artistic). The
next highest level of congruence is that of a given personality type—
Artistic—in an adjacent environment—Investigative or Social. An Artistic
person in either a Realistic or an Enterprising environment represents a
third and lower degree of congruence or fit. The lowest level of congruence occurs when a person is in an environment at the opposite end of the
hexagon—for example, an Artistic person in a Conventional environment.

The preceding descriptions of the salient characteristics of the personality types and model environments provide a basis for understanding
why Holland's theory assumes that congruence between people and their
environments is positively related to educational and vocational stability,

satisfaction, and success. When people are in matching environments they are provided opportunities to engage in their preferred activities, to use their strongest competencies, to engage in services and activities they value, to see themselves in ways consistent with their self-perceptions, and to exhibit the personality traits associated with their respective types. For instance, Enterprising types in an Enterprising environment would have the opportunity to engage in Enterprising activities, to use their distinctive Enterprising competencies, to perform services they value, to see themselves as aggressive, popular, and self-confident, and to exhibit personality traits such as ambitiousness, extroversion, and sociability. Equally important, Holland (1997) notes that a high level of congruence enables people to "avoid the activities they dislike, the demands for competencies they lack, the tasks and self-images they do not value, and the situations in which their personality types are not encouraged" (p. 56).

The outcomes—educational and vocational stability, satisfaction, and achievement—of congruence between personality type and environment are also assumed to be influenced by the consistency and differentiation of both a person's personality pattern and the environmental pattern. For instance, Holland (1997) suggests that "interactions of consistent people and consistent environments will result in more predictable outcomes, and that these outcomes will influence both the people and their environments to a greater degree" (p. 57) because people with consistent personality patterns have a higher level of integration of similar interests, competencies, values, and perceptions and because environments with consistent patterns usually exert pressures for similar behaviors. Similarly, he suggests that greater "differentiation of the personality or environment pattern increases both the possibility that the hypothesized behavior in the formulations will occur and the magnitude of the hypothesized behavior . . . [because] a well-defined . . . person is interacting with a well-defined environment that has a focused influence" (pp. 57–58).

Implications of Holland's Theory for Research on College Faculty and Students

The three essential components of Holland's theory—individuals, environments, congruence—and the three basic assumptions associated with them provide a theory-based framework for research on college students and faculty. We illustrate in this section the appropriateness of Holland's theory for exploring multiple aspects of the professional lives of faculty and for analyzing both college students' choices of academic majors and their subsequent patterns of change and stability in abilities and interests. Such elaboration is necessary because Holland's theory is intended primarily to explain vocational behavior; moreover, most research on the validity of the basic assumptions of the theory has been derived from studies of employed adults. Yet Holland (1997) has noted repeatedly that the basic assumptions of the theory are equally valid in educational settings.

Self-Selection Assumption: Students Choose Academic Environments Compatible with Their Personality Types

Perhaps used in higher education settings more than any other of the Holland basic assumptions is the assumption of self-selection—that people can be classified according to their resemblance to six personality types and that people search for environments affording them opportunities to take on agreeable roles (and to engage in preferred activities) as well as respecting and rewarding their values, self-perceptions, and personality traits. This assumption has primarily been used to assist students in their initial selection of academic majors and in clarifying their long-term career aspirations. Given the validity and stability of people's perceptions of academic majors and occupations noted earlier, the scores of individuals on vocational interest inventories have been used widely to assist college students in making career choices that are the most compatible with their distinctive patterns of interests and abilities, thereby presumably enhancing the likelihood of their long-term educational and career stability, satisfaction, and success. Considerable effort has also been expended to link specific academic majors with individuals' interests and abilities as well as with specific careers. Such efforts are especially valuable to the immediate needs of college students in selecting specific academic majors most likely to provide satisfaction and success and to increase the probability of entrance into chosen occupational fields. *The College Majors Finder* (Rosen, Holmberg, & Holland, 1989), when used in conjunction with established interest and personality inventories (for example, the SDS, VPI, SCII, and SVIB), is an especially valuable resource in this respect.

In addition to assisting students in choosing among an increasingly diverse array of academic majors and career options, the assumption that people search for environments that afford them opportunities to take on agreeable roles and engage in preferred activities and that respect and reward their values, self-perceptions and personality traits has major implications for assessing the impacts of educational environments on students' subsequent stability, satisfaction, and success. As Holland (1997) notes, although each personality type has a distinct pattern of attitudes and competencies for coping with environmental problems and tasks, all types "seek fulfillment by exercising characteristic activities, skills, and talents and by striving to achieve special goals" (p. 2). The implication, then, is that students are not passive participants in the search for academic majors and careers; rather, they actively search for and select academic environments that encourage them to develop further their characteristic interests and abilities and to enter (and be successful in) their chosen career fields.

Self-selection is thus an important consideration in longitudinal efforts to study college outcomes and the extent to which patterns of student change and stability vary across disparate educational environments. This is so because the different academic environments (college majors) initially attract students with different interests and talents. Longitudinal studies of how academic environments contribute to differential patterns of change and stability in college students must take into account this "self selection" of students to get a more accurate assessment of the actual influence of those environments on students.

Holland's theory provides a means for us to understand this self-selection into academic environments and has directed our own analyses of college students presented in chapter 5. Postulating six personality types and formulating the salient characteristics of these types allow a theory-based prediction of the basic kind of academic major that a student is most likely to enter and a fuller understanding of the student's choice. In our analysis we specifically examine the extent to which the characteristics of students entering the different academic environments proposed by Holland do, in fact, differ in accordance with this assumption of the theory. For example, students who major in Artistic fields would be expected to have stronger *initial* Artistic abilities and interests than do those who choose Investigative, Social, and Enterprising majors.

Socialization Assumption: Academic Environments Reinforce and Reward Different Talents

The basic assumption in Holland's theory of six environmental models that parallel the six personality types has important implications for our understanding of diversity in the professional attitudes and behaviors of faculty as well as our understanding of differential patterns of longitudinal change and stability in the abilities and interests of college students. Each academic environment (see Table 2.2) is assumed to provide opportunities for people to engage in a distinctive set of activities and to develop a distinctive set of competencies. Moreover, each academic environment presumably encourages people to see themselves in ways consistent with distinctive sets of values and differentially rewards them for their display of the distinctive set of competencies and values characterizing the environment. The disparate orientations of the six academic environments are described in Table 2.2 and provide a theory-based way of predicting and understanding differences in the professional attitudes and behaviors of college faculty and in the longitudinal change and stability of the abilities and interests of college students.

In chapter 4 we study college faculty in academic disciplines clustered according to the environmental models included in Holland's theory. We present the results of our own analyses to determine whether or not faculty in these disciplinary clusters differ in terms of their perceptions about various aspects of undergraduate education and whether or not these differences are consistent with the distinctive environmental patterns presented in Table 2.2. Specifically, we examine the extent to which there are differences among faculty members in these academic environments in terms of their goals for undergraduate education and their perceptions of undergraduate students and curricula.

Holland's theory assumes that the distinctive orientations of the environments and their respective sets of requirements and rewards lead to different outcomes in terms of people's interests and abilities. This assumption is our focus in chapter 6, where we examine (in the context of Holland's theory) the longitudinal patterns of change and stability in students' self-perceptions of their abilities and interests over a four-year period. Our specific interest focuses on similarities and differences in these patterns among students whose academic majors are classified in the different academic environments included in Holland's theory; we expect differences across the academic environments (due to their disparate character) that are consistent with the theoretical premises of Holland's theory. Our expectations derive from viewing major fields as socialization settings, whereby academic environments "induce" or encourage new members—that is, student entrants or "recruits"—to adhere to the prevailing ways of thinking, feeling, and behaving found in the group.

Congruence Assumption: People Flourish in Environments Congruent with Their Personality Types

Holland's theory assumes that each personality type is most likely to flourish in a congruent environment (that is, the environment having the same label) because such environments provide opportunities, activities, tasks, and roles that correspond to the competencies, interests, and self-perceptions of their parallel personality types. Specifically, it is assumed—other things being equal—that congruence of person and environment is related to higher levels of stability, satisfaction, and achievement. Educational stability (retention), satisfaction, and achievement clearly are central concepts in the larger study of college students; these concepts have important meaning to institutions of higher learning (which are seeking to promote student learning and to maintain or increase enrollments) as well as to their students (who are seeking to reach cognitive, affective, and career goals as a result of their psychological and economic investments in undergraduate education). And yet, as we have noted, use of Holland's theory in efforts to understand these and other important outcomes has been relatively rare.

In chapter 7 we focus specifically on the "congruence" hypothesis by examining longitudinal patterns of change and stability in the abilities and interests of students whose academic majors (environments) are and are not congruent with their dominant personality types at the time they began their undergraduate education. After first classifying entering students by their dominant personality types, we then find out whether the pattern of change and stability on selected ability and interest scales differs for those types who entered congruent academic environments (majors) rather than incongruent ones. According to Holland's theory, for example, students who enter college with a dominant Enterprising personality type and who major in an Enterprising environment should develop stronger Enterprising abilities and interests than their peers who also have an Enterprising personality type when they enter college but who subsequently major in other, incongruent academic environments. In chapter 8 we elaborate on the congruence assumption by tracing the effects of two different kinds of incongruence.

Distinctive Features of This Book

This book constitutes the first comprehensive assesment of the validity of the basic assumptions of Holland's theory as it applies to the study of college students and faculty. This aspect alone is perhaps the salient distinctive contribution of the book. Holland's theory is principally a theory of vocational behavior and the vast majority of extant research on the theory focuses on the choices of occupations by employed adults, and their subsequent satisfaction and success in occupational settings. Holland notes, however, that all of the assumptions are equally applicable in educational settings. While we have already noted the applicabiltiy of the theory in higher education settings in an abbreviated manner, the potential of Holland's theory to provide greater understanding of similarities and differences in the attitudes and behaviors of college faculty and students in disparate academic environments is a dominant focus in the remainder of this book.

Our work is also distinctive in two additional respects. First, the various literature reviews we present in chapters 4 through 7 provide the only available summary of empirical research evidence regarding the validity of the assumptions of Holland's theory as they pertain to the attitudes and behaviours of college faculty and students. Second, our empirical analyses assessing the validity of the primary assumptions of Holland's theory are distinctive in that they use the same sample of students for all analyses of student change and stability reported in chapters 5 though 8. Thus, the collective findings reported in subsequent chapters make a significant contrubution to the extant literature by comprehensively assessing the theory using a single sample of students.

Summary

Our overview of Holland's theory has highlighted the theory's three central components—individuals, environments, and congruence between the individuals and environments—and the three fundamental assumptions that flow from these components: (1) the self-selection assumption that individuals search for and select environments in which they can express their particular repertory of abilities and interests; (2) the socialization assumption that the respective environments require, reinforce, and reward different patterns of interests and abilities; and (3) the congruence assumption that individuals' stability in, satisfaction with, and success or achievement in educational or work environments are dependent on the congruence between their personality types and their environments. We have discussed the implications of each assumption for the study of college faculty and students to illustrate the potential of Holland's theory to provide a theoretical framework for studying the professional lives of college faculty and the patterns of stability and change in college students. The next chapter explicates how we went about using data from samples of both faculty and students to examine empirically Holland's theory.

3

Research Design and Sample

IN THIS chapter we present the full array of details concerning the data we collected and the statistical analysis of these data in an empirical examination of Holland's theory (as laid out in the previous chapter). By gathering together in one place this information about sampling, research design and statistical analysis, we are able in the chapters following this one to concentrate on the presentation and interpretation of the data themselves—referring the reader back to this chapter (when necessary) for certain details.

In our empirical examination of Holland's theory, we used data from samples of both faculty and students. The faculty data allow an examination of the environments (created by faculty and their disciplines) that are selected by students. In effect, faculty members not only create the opportunities for student choice but become the primary socialization agents for student change. The student data enable us to analyze the nature of that change and whether or not it is consistent with Holland's theory.

In our research, studying the role of faculty in the socialization of students involved an examination of differences of faculty members in the disparate academic environments (contained in Holland's theory) in alternative goal preferences for undergraduate education and in perceptions of undergraduate students and curricula. We used a sample of faculty drawn from the survey of college and university faculty conducted by the Carnegie Foundation for the Advancement of Teaching (1989) as part of a national study of the American professoriate. The complete sample, from which we obtained our subsample, consisted of 5,450 faculty from 306 two-year and four-year institutions. These faculty completed a multipurpose survey that obtained information concerning how they spend their time; their perceptions of their disciplines, departments, and students; and their goals for undergraduate education.

The validity of each of the three primary assumptions of Holland's theory discussed in chapter 2—self-selection, socialization, and congruence—was explored using longitudinal information on a sample of college students. Our analyses are based on data obtained from the 1986 and 1990 surveys of the Cooperative Institutional Research Program (CIRP) (Higher Education Research Institute, 1986) sponsored by the Higher Education Research Institute at the University of California, Los Angeles. The complete 1986–1990 sample, from which we obtained our subsample, consisted of 4,408 students attending 360 two-year and four-year institutions of higher education. Students completed the standard CIRP freshman survey upon entering college in the fall of 1986 and a follow-up survey in the winter of 1990. The initial survey obtained information regarding prior educational experiences of students, their expectations regarding their undergraduate careers, and self-perceptions of their abilities, interests, and goals. The follow-up survey obtained information about the actual college experiences of these students, perceptions of their growth during the intervening four years, and subsequent self-perceptions of their abilities, interests, and goals.

Faculty Sample and Variables
Faculty Sample

To examine Holland's socialization assumption, as evidenced in part by differing environments created by faculty and their disciplines, we analyzed data from a subsample of full-time faculty members in four-year institutions (institutions classified as Research and Doctorate-granting, Comprehensive, and Liberal Arts according to the Carnegie classification scheme) whose highest degrees were Ph.D., Ed.D., J.D., "other first professional," or medical (M.D., D.D.S., etc.). The selection of faculty in four-year institutions was necessary in order to have comparability between the types of institutions attended by students (see later remarks on restrictions of student sample) and those in which faculty work and teach. The degree restriction was based on our desire to include only those faculty members who had terminal degrees in their disiplines.

Additional restrictions to the sample were that each faculty member's discipline be included in *The College Majors Finder* (Rosen, Holmberg, & Holland, 1989) and that respondents have valid responses on the variables to be described. The analyses were based on a sample of 2,775 faculty.

Faculty Variables

Classification of faculty's academic departments (environments). The Carnegie faculty survey asked faculty to indicate the department of their teaching appointment from a list of twenty-nine academic disciplines (twenty-eight specific disciplines and one category of "other discipline"). If a faculty member's specific discipline did not appear in the list, instructions indicated selection of the most similar discipline. These departments were classified into five of the six academic environments (there were no Conventional disciplines) proposed by Holland using *The College Majors Finder* (Rosen, Holmberg, & Holland, 1989). A total of twenty-three of the twenty-nine disciplines could be classified (the generic categories of Education, Engineering, and Health Professions were unclassifiable because the individual specialties within the broad classifications represented multiple Holland types). Our analyses of the faculty data are limited to the Investigative, Artistic, Social, and Enterprising environments in order to match the environments represented by the student sample described below. The number of faculty in each of these four groups of disciplines is: Investigative (n = 835, 30 percent); Artistic (n = 390, 14 percent); Social (n = 1,150, 41 percent); and Enterprising (n = 400, 14 percent). The specific departments represented by the sample and their Holland classifications are shown in Table 3.1.

Goals for undergraduate education. The Carnegie survey asked faculty to rate the importance of each of seven goals for undergraduate education using the following scale: 1 = very important; 2 = fairly important; 3 = fairly unimportant; 4 = very unimportant; and 5 = no opinion. Five of the seven goals reflect characteristics associated with one of the four Holland environments represented by the faculty sample, as follows: "Provide an appreciation of literature and the arts" (Artistic); "Enhance creative thinking" (Artistic); "Provide a basic understanding in mathematics and science" (Investigative); "Provide knowledge of history and the social sciences" (Social); and "Prepare students for a career" (Enterprising). The items have been recoded such that a higher value represents greater importance and "no opinion" has a neutral value of 3.

Table 3.1

Holland Classification of Disciplines Represented by Faculty and Student Samples

REALISTIC

Faculty:

Industrial Arts
Military Science

Student:

Electrical Engineering
Mechanical Engineering
Marine Science
Drafting/Design
Military Science

INVESTIGATIVE

Faculty:

Allied Health (Medical Technologies)
Biological / Life Sciences
Economics
Geography
Mathematics/Statistics
Physical Sciences

Student:

General Biology

INVESTIGATIVE
(continued)

Biochemistry/Biophysics
Botany
Marine (Life) Science
Microbiology/Bacteriology
Zoology
Other Biological Science
Finance
Aeronautical/Astronautical Engineering
Civil Engineering
Chemical Engineering
Astronomy
Atmospheric Science
Chemistry
Earth Science
Mathematics
Physics
Statistics
Other Physical Science
Pharmacy
Premedical/Predental/Preveterinary
Anthropology
Economics
Ethnic Studies
Geography
Sociology

ARTISTIC

Faculty:

Architecture/Environmental Design
Fine Arts (Art, Drama, Music)
Foreign Languages

Student:

Arts
English
Language/Literature
Music
Speech
Theater/Drama
Music/Art Education
Architecture

SOCIAL

Faculty:

Area/Ethnic Studies
Home Economics
Humanities (Literature, History, Philosophy, Religion, Theology, Rhetoric)

continued

Table 3.1 *(continued)*

Holland Classification of Disciplines Represented by Faculty and Student Samples

SOCIAL *(continued)*	ENTERPRISING	NOT IN HOLLAND
	Faculty:	Faculty:
Library Science		
Physical and Health Education	Business/Management	Agriculture/Forestry/ Natural Resources
Psychology	Communications/ Journalism	Education (including Administration and
Social Sciences (Anthropology, Political Science, Social Work)	Computer/Information Science	Counseling)
	Law	Engineering
	Public Affairs	Health Professions (Dentistry, Medicine,
Student:	Student:	Nursing, Veterinary)
		Vocational/Technical Training
History	Journalism	Other Discipline
Philosophy	Business Administration	
Theology/Religion	Marketing	
Elementary Edu- cation	Management	Student:
Physical Education/ Recreation	Business Education Industrial Engineering	Other Humanities
Special Education	Communications	Other Business
Home Economics	Computer Science	Secondary Education
Library Science		Other Engineering
Nursing	CONVENTIONAL	Health Technology
Political Science		Therapy
Psychology	Faculty:	Other Professional
Social Work		Other Social Science
Women's Studies	none	Other Technical
Law Enforcement		Agriculture
	Student:	Other Fields
	Accounting	
	Secretarial Studies	
	Data Processing	

Perceptions of undergraduate students and curricula. We also selected a second set of items concerning the perspectives of faculty members on issues associated with the undergraduate curriculum, their preferences among alternative undergraduate teaching contexts, and their perspectives about undergraduate students. Unlike the first set of items, this second set is not related directly to Holland's theory. The intent of the analyses based on these items was not to test any specific premises that flow from Holland's theory, but rather to provide a descriptive profile of faculty in the four academic environments that could assist in understanding the differential patterns of change and stability of college students (chapters 6, 7, and 8).

We selected seven items from the Carnegie faculty survey that asked about such matters as the perspectives of faculty members on issues associated with the undergraduate curriculum, the preferences of these faculty for different undergraduate teaching contexts, and their perspectives about undergraduate students. We used a principal-components factor analysis (with an oblique rotation) to discern the underlying dimensionality of these seven items. Three factors with eigenvalues of 1.0 or greater were extracted. Table 3.2 presents the items and factor loadings. Because each variable loaded to some extent on each factor, for ease of interpretation of results only those coefficients with an absolute value of .3 or greater are given in the table.

The first factor is defined by two items reflecting faculty members' perspectives on the degree to which the undergraduate curriculum is too specialized. Those with higher scores on this factor, labeled "Curricular Specialization," tend to *disagree* with the perspectives that "the undergraduate curriculum has suffered from the specialization of faculty members" and that "undergraduate education in America would be improved if there were less emphasis on specialized training and more on broad liberal education." In essence, these faculty members are more comfortable with the current level of curricular specialization in academe than are their peers who have lower scores on this factor. The second factor is defined by three items reflecting faculty members' accessibility to students. Those with higher scores on this factor, labeled "Accessibility," tend to *agree* that "undergraduates should seek out faculty only during posted office hours" and that "most undergraduates expect too much attention"; they *disagree* with the statement that they "enjoy interacting informally with undergraduates outside the classroom." In general, they tend to be less accessible to undergraduates than are their colleagues who have lower scores on this factor. The third factor is defined primarily by two items about the

Table 3.2

Principal Components Analysis of Faculty Perceptions of Undergraduate Education, Perceptions of Undergraduate Students, and Preferences for Undergraduate Teaching [a]

Item	Curricular Specialization	Accessibility	Classroom/ Student Focus
The *typical* undergraduate curriculum has suffered from the *specialization* of faculty members.	- .873 (- .878)		
Undergraduate education in American would be improved if there were *less* emphasis on specialized training and *more* on broad liberal education.	- .751 (- .712)		- .397 (- .307)
Undergraduates should seek faculty *only* during posted office hours.		.764 (.758)	
I enjoy interacting *informally* with undergraduates outside the classroom.		- .698 (- .714)	
Most undergraduates expect too much attention.		.661 (.640)	
In my *undergraduate courses* I prefer teaching students who have a clear idea of the career they will be following.			.830 (.827)
I prefer teaching undergraduate courses *that focus on limited specialties* to those that cover wide varieties of material.			.701 (.680)

[a] Pattern coefficients are given in parentheses; only those coefficients with absolute value of .3 or greater are shown.

teaching preferences of faculty and is labeled "Classroom-Student Focus." Those faculty members with higher scores on this factor tend to *agree*—more so than do their peers with lower scores—that they "prefer teaching students who have a clear idea of the career they will be following" and that they "prefer teaching undergraduate courses that focus on limited specialties to those that cover wide varieties of material." In essence, they tend to prefer teaching more specialized courses and interacting with students who have more definite career plans. Factor scores from these three factors were used as dependent variables to examine differences in the attitudes of faculty toward undergraduate students and curricular issues in the four academic environments defined by Holland.

Student Sample and Variables
Student Sample

To assess the validity of the three fundamental assumptions of Holland's theory, we analyzed data from a subsample of students who attended four-year institutions (institutions classified as Research and Doctoral-granting, Comprehensive, and Liberal Arts according to the Carnegie classification scheme) and who had attended college for four years. The selection of students who attended an institution for all four years was based on our desire to control for variation in both types of institutions attended and the duration of students' exposure to those institutions. We had to delete from our sample students who began their college careers in two-year institutions because it was not possible from the data set to discern the types of institutions to which they transferred.

Additional restrictions to the sample were that students' intended (1986) and actual (1990) academic majors be included in *The College Majors Finder* (Rosen, Holmberg, & Holland, 1989) and that students have valid scores on the 1986 and 1990 ability and interests scales described below. Inclusion of students' intended and actual academic majors in *The College Majors Finder* was necessary because of our desire to distinguish between students who had similar and dissimilar academic environments over the four-year period; that is, students may have changed *majors* over the four-year period, but the Holland *environments* may or may not have remained the same. This interest was informed by the findings of Feldman and Weiler (1976) that longitudinal patterns of change and stability in students' personality profile scores and self-description indices are not necessarily the same for those with similar ("primary recruits") and dissimilar ("secondary recruits") initial and final academic environments. The majority of our analyses were based on a sample of 2,309 students. However, in some in-stances the sample size was slightly smaller because of students' movement between environments and the inclusion of new variables. These instances will be noted in the description of the individual analyses.

Student Variables

Classification of students' academic majors (environments). The 1986 fresh-man survey asked students to select their "probable field of study," and the 1990 follow-up survey asked them to select their "current/last field of study" from a list of eighty academic disciplines/majors (seventy-nine spe-cific majors and one classification of "other") and one option for "undecid-ed." Students in our sample, either initially in 1986 or subsequently in 1990, selected only seventy-six of the possible eighty disciplines/majors. These academic majors were classified into the six academic environments proposed by Holland using *The College Majors Finder* (Rosen, Holmberg, & Holland, 1989). A total of sixty-four of the seventy-six majors selected by our sample could be classified. However, the Realistic and Conventional categories had a combined total of only four academic majors with too few students to be useful in our analyses; consequently these two categories were not included in the analyses testing Holland's premises. We antici-pated this possibility prior to an examination of the data, for the major-ity of the Realistic and Conventional vocations are not represented by disciplines/majors within four-year institutions. The number of students in each of the remaining four groups of 1990 academic majors was: Investigative (n = 672, 29 percent); Artistic (n = 334, 15 percent); Social (n = 788, 34 percent); and Enterprising (n = 515, 22 percent).

The one exception to our exclusion of students in Realistic and Conventional majors as well as those undecided and in majors not classi-fied in a Holland category was in our examination of the fluidity in stu-dents' selections of majors between 1986 and 1990. While our primary focus was on students whose 1990 majors were Investigative, Artistic, Social, and Enterprising, a number of those students' 1986 majors were Realistic, Conventional, undecided, or not in a Holland category. Thus, in examining students' movement among environments between 1986 and 1990, it was necessary to include all categories of 1986 majors. The spe-cific disciplines/majors selected by the sample and their Holland classifi-cations are shown in Table 3.1.

1986 and 1990 ability and interest scales. The 1986 and 1990 CIRP sur-veys asked students to rate themselves, compared with the average person their age, on twelve different abilities (e.g., intellectual self-confidence, social self-confidence, leadership ability) on a scale with 1 = lowest 10 percent, 2 = below average, 3 = average, 4 = above average, and 5 = highest 10 percent. Students were also asked to indicate the importance of eighteen general goals and values (e.g., creating artistic work, being very well off financially) using a scale of 1 = not important, 2 = somewhat important, 3 = very important, and 4 = essential. Of these thirty items, twenty-six were characteristic of adjectives used to describe the four Holland personality types (Holland, 1997) considered in our analyses.

We used these twenty-six items to create precollege (1986) and follow-up (1990) scales reflecting the distinctive pattern of abilities and interests that each of the four groups of academic majors (environments) were assumed initially to attract and subsequently to reinforce and reward. For instance, Artistic academic environments were assumed to attract, reinforce, and reward Artistic abilities and interests, whereas Social academic environments were assumed to attract, reinforce, and reward Social abilities and interests. According to Holland, interests related to scholarly and scientific activities are reflective of Investigative traits; interests in aesthetic experiences and the arts are reflective of Artistic traits; interests in social and ethical activities are reflective of Social traits; and interests in economic and political enterprises are reflective of Enterprising traits. Thus, there was a total of eight scales, which represented four kinds of students' self-reported abilities and interests at the time students began college (1986) and four years later (1990). Each scale was created by standardizing the items and computing the average across the items. Student scores were converted to T-scores with a mean of 50 and a standard deviation of 10. The items constituting each scale and reliability estimates of those scales are presented in Table 3.3. As can be seen from an examination of the items constituting each scale, these abilities and interests do not reflect content specific to a discipline but rather broad traits that multiple disciplines value and emphasize to a greater or lesser degree.

Classification of students' dominant personality types. Holland (1997), in noting that a variety of methods may be used to assess a person's dominant personality type, acknowledges that "no single assessment technique stands out as being the most advantageous for all purposes" (p. 20). Nonetheless, he suggests that the use of scales of personality and interest inventories and the use of expressed preferences for occupations and academic majors "have either produced more coherent results or have special advantages by virtue of their simplicity or theoretical construction" (p. 29).

Table 3.3
1986 and 1990 Student Ability and Interest Scales [a]

1986 and 1990 Investigative Scales	Reliability
Self rating: Self-confidence (intellectual)	α = .682 (1986)
Self-rating: Academic ability	α = .630 (1990)
Self-rating: Mathematical ability	
Self-rating: Drive to achieve	
Goal: Making a theoretical contribution to science	

1986 and 1990 Artistic Scales	Reliability
Self-rating: Artistic ability	α = .683 (1986)
Self-rating: Writing ability	α = .697 (1990)
Goal: Becoming accomplished in one of the performing arts (acting, dancing, etc.)	
Goal: Writing original works (poems, novels, short stories, etc.)	
Goal: Creating artistic work (painting, sculpture, decorating, etc.)	
Goal: Developing a meaningful philosophy of life	

1986 and 1990 Social Scales	Reliability
Goal: Influencing the political structure	α = .750 (1986)
Goal: Influencing social values	α = .794 (1990)
Goal: Helping others who are in difficulty	
Goal: Becoming involved in programs to clean up the environment	
Goal: Participating in a community action program	
Goal: Helping to promote racial understanding	

continued

Table 3.3 *(continued)*
1986 and 1990 Student Ability and Interest Scales

1986 and 1990 Enterprising Scales	Reliability
Self-rating: Leadership ability	α = .752 (1986)
Self-rating: Popularity	α = .762 (1990)
Self-rating: Self-confidence (social)	
Goal: Become an authority in my field	
Goal: Obtaining recognition from my colleagues for contributions to my special field	
Goal: Having administrative responsibility for the work of others	
Goal: Being very well off financially	
Goal: Being successful in a business of my own	
Goal: Becoming an expert on finance and commerce	

[a] For the Self-Rating items, students responded to the prompt "Rate yourself on each of the following traits as compared with the average person your age" using a scale of 1 = Lowest 10 percent; 2 = Below average; 3 = Average; 4 = Above average; 5 = Highest 10 percent. For the Goal items, students responded to the prompt "Indicate the importance to you personally of each of the following" using a scale of 1 = Not important; 2 = Somewhat important; 3 = Very important; 4 = Essential.

The four 1986 ability and interest scales just described were used to determine the dominant personality type of each student in the sample. This determination was accomplished in a simple and straightforward manner, one consistent with scoring of students' responses to established occupational and personality inventories such as the Vocational Preference Inventory and the Strong-Campbell Interest Inventory. Specifically, a student's dominant personality type was determined by his or her highest score on the four 1986 ability and interest scales. For example, a student whose highest score was on the 1986 Investigative ability and interest scale was classified as an Investigative personality type, while a student whose highest score was on the 1986 Enterprising scale was classified as an Enterprising personality type. The number of students in each of the four categories of personality type was: Investigative (n = 789, 34 percent); Artistic (n = 377, 16 percent); Social (n = 553, 24 percent); and Enterprising (n = 590, 26 percent).

Self-reported growth. The CIRP 1990 follow-up survey to the 1986 freshman asked students to report their growth (in the intervening four-year period) in twenty different areas by responding to the overall question, "Compared with when you entered college as a freshman, how would you now describe your. . . ." Students rated change in each area on a scale of 1 = "much weaker," 2 = "weaker," 3 = "no change," 4 = "stronger," and 5 = "much stronger." Seventeen of these items tap characteristics of the four personality types and academic environments central to Holland's theory. For example, given Holland's (1997) descriptions of the salient characteristics of the four academic environments, students in Investigative environments would be expected to report more growth than would other students in problem-solving skills, those in Artistic environments would be expected to report greater growth in writing skills, those in Social environments would be expected to grow more in tolerance of people with different beliefs, and those in Enterprising environments would be expected to report more growth on leadership abilities. The seventeen items used in the analyses are listed in Table 3.4.

The items used to construct the ability and interest scales and the items about students' growth during college are based on students' self-reports. Pike (1995, 1996) has presented considerable evidence showing the relationships between students' self-reports and objective measures of abilities based on the use of confirmatory factor analysis and multitrait-multimethod analytical procedures. While he cautions that further research on the relationships between content correspondence and convergence is needed before self-reported data can be fully accepted as "valid proxies or policy indicators" (Pike, 1995, p. 19), he concludes that "using self-reports as general indicators of achievement can be justified . . . [because] self-reports and test scores based on the same set of specifications do represent the same education outcome domains (i.e., they are con-generic)" (Pike, 1996, p. 110).

Gender and consistency in choice of academic majors (environments). To trace possible conditional effects of gender and consistency or stability of decisions about academic environment relative to Holland's assumptions, we obtained information on the gender of students and whether their actual major in 1990 was the same or different from their major in 1986. Gender differences emerged in both Feldman and Weiler's (1976) study and Smart and Feldman's (1998) study of accentuation effects of academic departments. Likewise, as noted earlier, Feldman and Weiler also presented some (indirect) evidence that longitudinal patterns of change and stability in students' personality profile scores and self-description indices

Table 3.4
Student Self-Reported Growth Items [a]

Analytical and problem-solving skills

Ability to think critically

Interest in pursuing a graduate/professional degree

Preparation for graduate or professional school

Ability to work independently

Confidence in your academic abilities

Foreign language ability

Cultural awareness and appreciation

Writing skills

Public speaking ability

Tolerance of persons with different beliefs

Acceptance of people from different races/cultures

Job-related skills

Leadership abilities

Interpersonal skills

Competitiveness

Ability to work cooperatively

[a] Students responded to the prompt "Compared with when you entered college as a freshman, how would you now describe your . . ." using a scale of 1 = Much weaker; 2 = Weaker; 3 = No change; 4 = Stronger; 5 = Much stronger.

differed for students with similar and dissimilar initial and final academic majors. The total sample (n = 2,309) comprised 1,217 female students (52.7 percent) and 1,092 male students (47.3 percent). Of the full sample, 1,128 students (48.9 percent) had similar academic majors/environments in 1986 and 1990 (and thus, in our terminology, were "primary recruits" to their 1990 majors) and 1,181 students (51.1 percent) had dissimilar or different academic majors/environments over the four-year period (and thus were "secondary recruits" to their 1990 majors).

Analytical Procedures

We used a variety of both univariate and multivariate statistical analyses and descriptive statistics in examining the validity of the three assumptions that together form the basis of Holland's theory (chapter 2). In the chapters that present and discuss the actual findings of the analyses (chapters 4–8), the statistical results examining the validity of each assumption are presented in appendixes while the descriptive statistics (e.g., means, effect sizes, frequencies) are included in tables within the chapters themselves. Given our relatively large sample size, we used a .01 probability level for analyses involving the full sample of students, but when selecting subsets based on students' personality types in chapters 7 and 8 we used a .05 probability level. Moreover, our interpretations of the statistical findings are strongly determined by the effect sizes we found. These effect sizes convert mean differences between groups of faculty or students to standard-deviation units. When we found indication of interactive effects, we examined effect sizes separately for the groups involved in the interactions.

Exploratory analyses of the data were conducted prior to each statistical analysis. These analyses included examination of the distributions of all variables, testing for potential outliers or influential data points, and tests of the assumptions underlying the utilization of each particular statistical method. We tested for homogeneity of variance for between-subjects factors (or of variance/covariance matrices in the multivairate analyses) whenever analysis of variance procedures were used. When this assumption was violated, we adjusted the nominal alpha, a procedure recommended by Stevens (1996). When large variances were associated with groups containing larger numbers of subjects, the conservative nature of the test was overcome by using a slightly higher alpha. When large variances were associated with groups containing smaller numbers of subjects, the liberal nature of the test was overcome by using a slightly lower alpha. When large variances were spread across the large and small group sizes, no adjustment was made. The test for sphericity was not applicable for within-subjects analyses since there were only two levels for each within-subject factor.

As noted in chapter 2, examining self-selection of students (into environments) is an important consideration in our efforts to assess the validity of Holland's theory (and any research focusing on longitudinal change in college students). The theory itself implies that students actively search for and select academic environments relevant to their abilities and interests and that the different academic environments (e.g., college majors) attract students with different interests and talents. Theoretically, as well as empirically, we do not have the experimental condition of random assignment of either faculty or students to disciplinary clusters. Rather, we are dealing with intact groups and have an ex-post-facto design.

We do not believe that the lack of random assignment creates a threat to internal validity. The nonequivalence of the groups in our comparisons of faculty and student disciplinary groups is *expected*. In accordance with Holland's theory, the disciplinary clusters should differ in theoretically meaningful ways, and it is these differences that we examine in testing the validity of the theory. We examine them for faculty at one point in time. For students, we examine initial differences at college entry and then examine whether these differences remain stable or change after four years of college. Thus, given the theoretical assumption that students *do* differ at entry and four years later, we purposefully did not use in our analyses of student data the more common analysis-of-covariance approach that statistically equates the disciplinary groups at college entry. A central purpose of our analyses is to examine the validity of the assumption of self-selection, which would be manifested by initial group differences. We chose an analytical approach using repeated measures which allows the examination of initial and subsequent group differences as well as the direction and magnitude of the change of each group across two points in time (see footnote 1 in chapter 1, p. 24, for problems of interpretation associated with the use of analysis of covariance in the absence of random assignment).

When we initially examined the student data, we found negative correlations between students' scores on the four 1986 ability and interest scales and their *change* on these scales between 1986 and 1990 (Investigative, -.439; Artistic, -.387; Social, -.509; Enterprising, -.466). This result indicated to us the presence of regression-to-the-mean (Rogosa, 1988), which would confound our attempts to assess change in students' abilities and interests as a function of their Holland environments. There are many differing opinions in the literature about the causes of regression-to-the-mean as well as about methodological approaches to deal with the problem. We adapted a procedure developed by Roberts (1980) that adjusts initial scores for regression-to-the-mean bias (see Roberts for an excellent discussion of the historical background of problems associated with regression-to-the-mean). This procedure was used by the RMC

Research Corporation in their Title I Evaluation and Reporting System (Tallmadge, Wood, & Gamel, 1981). We note that although this procedure reduces the bias associated with regression-to-the-mean, it does not eliminate it (Linn, 1980; Reisner, Alkin, Boruch, Linn, & Millman, 1982; Roberts, 1980; Tallmadge, 1982). It should be noted that this adjustment does *not* statistically equate the groups.

The adjustments to the 1986 ability and interest scale scores were made using the following:

$$X' = X + (1 - r_{XX})(50 - X), \text{ where}$$

X' = adjusted 1986 scale score
X = unadjusted 1986 scale score
r_{XX} = test-retest reliability (correlation between 1986 and 1990 scores)
50 = mean of the scale scores (each scale was converted to T-scores with a mean of 50 and a standard deviation of 10)

The test-retest reliabilities used for these adjustments were: Investigative, .643; Artistic, .691; Social, .461; and Enterprising, .592. These adjusted scores were used in all analyses that examined patterns of change among students between 1986 and 1990. Unadjusted scores were used in analyses assessing differences among students at a single point in time.

Self-Selection Assumption: Students Choose Academic Environments Compatible with Their Personality Types

As background for assessing the validity of the self-selection assumption, we examined the patterns of change in and stability of students' selections of college environments in 1986 and 1990. Students' initial choices of academic majors as freshmen were classified according to the six academic environments proposed by Holland and two additional categories: one for those who were "undecided" on their academic majors; and the other for those whose intended academic majors were not included in *The College Majors Finder* (Rosen, Holmberg, & Holland, 1989). Students' actual majors in 1990 were classified using only the Investigative, Artistic, Social, and Enterprising academic environments in Holland's theory because of our focus on these four academic environments in subsequent analyses. The patterns of change and stability between the 1986 and 1990 academic environments were determined by cross-tabulating the eight categories of the 1986 environments and the four categories of the 1990 environments. We included the 1986 Realistic, Conventional, Undecided, and Not in Holland categories in order to examine student mobility over the four-year period.

As one way of examining the validity of the self-selection assumption, we determined whether or not students who initially intended to major in a specific academic environment (e.g., Investigative) possessed stronger abilities and interests associated with that environment than did students who initially intended to major in other academic environments (e.g., Artistic, Social, Enterprising) and whether or not results were similar for males and females. Four 2 x 2 ANOVAs were used to examine this assumption, one for each of the 1986 ability and interest scales used as dependent variables. We did not adjust the scale scores used in these analyses for regression-to-the-mean bias since no assessment of change was made. The independent variables were gender and 1986 academic environment. No post hoc analyses were necessary when significant main effects were found since there were only two categories in each independent variable. When a significant interaction was found, effect sizes were calculated seperately for males and females to illustrate the interaction between gender and academic environment. Only the Investigative, Artistic, Social, and Enterprising environments were considered in these analyses.

The sample size for this analysis was reduced to 1,739 from the full sample of 2,309 because 570 of the intended majors of students in 1986 were classified as either Realistic, Conventional, Undecided, or Not in Holland. For each 1986 ability and interest scale used as the dependent variable, we coded the independent variable of academic environment into two categories: one category for students selecting the academic environment equivalent to the scale; and the second category for students selecting any of the other three academic environments. For example, when examining differences in 1986 Investigative abilities and interests, we compared students initially selecting Investigative majors with the combined group of students initially selecting Artistic, Social, and Enterprising majors.

A second approach used to assess the validity of the self-selection assumption was to determine whether or not students of a dominant personality type as freshmen were more likely initially to select majors comparable to their personalities than to choose dissimilar majors, and whether or not this would be equally true for males and females. Additionally, we sought to find greater stability in 1986 and 1990 environments for students who initially selected majors consistent with their dominant personality types than for those who did not; moreover, we believed there would be a tendency for those not selecting parallel majors to shift to such majors in 1990. We tested these hypotheses by cross-tabulating the eight categories of 1986 academic environments with the four categories of the 1990 academic environments separately for each personality type and within each type separately for males and females. These analyses were based on the full sample of 2,309 students.

Socialization Assumption

We tested the validity of the socialization assumption in Holland's theory for both students and faculty. We first examined socialization by focusing on the academic environment defined by certain faculty characteristics since faculty, as the primary socialization agents for student change, presumably differ in their expectations of students and their goals for undergraduate education. We then examined the effects of these academic environments on students.

Faculty in different environments reinforce and reward different patterns of thought and action. Each academic environment is assumed to provide different opportunities for students' growth and development, and faculty within those environments are assumed to have differing expectations of students and to promote the development of differing abilities and interests. Our specific interests were on faculty's goals for undergraduate education and their perceptions of undergraduate students and curricula and how these perspectives might differ across academic environments. We expected, for example, that faculty in Artistic academic environments (disciplines) would emphasize goals related to art and literature to a greater extent than would faculty in the other environments and that emphasis on career development would be more pronounced for faculty in Enterprising environments. The Tukey HSD (Honesty Significant Difference) test was used for all post hoc comparisons.

To determine whether or not faculty in different Holland environments held differing perceptions of students and curricula, we conducted separate one-way analyses of variance using the five goals for undergraduate education and the three factor scores measuring faculty perceptions of students and curricula as the dependent variables, and the Holland classification of faculty's academic environment was used as the independent variable. The four categories of the independent variable were the Investigative, Artistic, Social, and Enterprising academic environments.

Longitudinal patterns of change in college students are dependent upon their academic environments. We also tested the validity of the socialization assumption by examining whether or not students exhibited differential patterns of change and stability as a result of their differing academic environments. We first looked at students' self-ratings of their abilities and interests to determine if changes between 1986 and 1990 in students' abilities and interests varied as a result of their academic environments irrespective of their dominant personality types. Given Holland's socialization assumption, for example, we expected that regardless of the dominant personality of students, those majoring in Investigative fields would exhibit greater growth in Investigative abilities and interests than would those students majoring in non-Investigative environments. Thus the primary hypothesis tested is one of interaction—changes in abilities and interestes between 1986 and 1990 will be different for the two focal groups of students. In the context of our analyses this differential change is manifested by the interaction of year and Holland environment.

We conducted four 2 x 2 x 2 x 2 split-plot analyses of variance, using each of the four 1986 and 1990 ability and interest scales (previously described) as dependent variables. For these analyses the 1986 scores were adjusted for regression-to-the-mean bias since we were examining change between 1986 and 1990. Three of the four independent variables were between-subjects factors. One of these, students' final academic environments in 1990, was the primary independent variable of interest. The other two between-subjects factors were included to test for the possibility of interactions between the Holland environments and (1) the gender of the student and (2) similarity or dissimilarity of the student's environment in 1986 and 1990 (an indicator of whether the student was a primary recruit or a secondary recruit into the environment). The fourth factor was a within-subjects repeated measure of abilities and interests in 1986 and 1990. We took a significant interaction between Holland environment and year to indicate that change in abilities and interests between 1986 and 1990 depended on the Holland environment of the student's 1990 major.

Each analysis had two levels for each factor. The two gender levels were males and females. The two levels for similarity of students' 1986 and 1990 academic environments were primary recruits (similar environments in 1986 and 1990) and secondary recruits (dissimilar environments in 1986 and 1990). The two levels of students' final academic environments distinguished between students who majored in and those who did not major in an academic environment analogous to the specific ability and interest scale of the particular analysis. For instance, the two levels of students' academic environments in the analysis of students' change in Social abilities and interests distinguished between students who were in Social environments and those who were in other environments, while in the assessment of change and stability in Investigative abilities and interests, the two levels of students' academic environments distinguished between those who were and those who were not in Investigative environments.

When we found significant interactive effects of Holland environment and year (supporting the socialization assumption), we plotted and interpreted the interactive effects. In each instance the graphical illustration of the interaction shows differences between the two focal groups of students (those who were and those who were not in an academic environment analogous to the scale being tested) at the two points in time (1986 and 1990), with the lines of the graph indicating the direction of change for each group. Effect sizes were calculated indicating the magnitude of the difference between the two groups at each time point. These effect sizes were calculated using the error mean squares from the between-subjects analyses; they convert the differences between students in the two types of academic environments in both 1986 and 1990 to standard-deviation units. For socialization to have occurred there should be greater differences between the two groups in 1990 than the initial differences present in 1986. We also calculated effect sizes indicating the magnitude of change for each group between 1986 and 1990. These latter effect sizes, which were calculated using the error mean squares from the within-subjects analyses, convert the difference between the 1986 and 1990 means for each group to standard-deviation units. When interactions were found between Holland environment and gender or type of recruit, the graphs were plotted separately for the subgroups of students.

We further tested the socialization assumption by analyzing students' self-reported growth during their four years of college. The validity of the socialization assumption would be evidenced by variance in the areas of students' perceived growth as a function of their academic environments, since academic environments are presumed to reinforce and reward different educational values and behaviors. For example, we would expect that students majoring in Investigative environments would report greater growth in areas consistent with descriptions of Investigative environments, while those majoring in Artistic environments would report greater growth in areas consistent with Artistic environments. Again, we expected these sorts of findings regardless of the students' dominant personality types.

Using the seventeen self-reported growth items described earlier, we conducted four separate three-factor 2 x 2 x 2 multivariate analyses of variance to determine if the patterns of growth were consistent with the academic environment and if these patterns were essentially the same for male and female students and for primary and secondary recruits. Thus, the three independent variables in each analysis were academic environment, gender, and type of recruit; the dependent variables were the seventeen growth items. Each of the analyses compared a particular environment to the other three environments combined. For example, to assess whether or not the self-reported growth of students in Investigative environments was in areas consistent with Investigative traits and different from those in other environments, we classified students' academic environments as Investigative or Non-Investigative (and similarly for the other three types of environments).

We used discriminant analysis as the post hoc procedure when a significant main effect was found in order to examine the differential patterns of perceived growth between the academic environments. Discriminant analysis allows the identification of the most important variables that contribute to group differentiation; it is preferable to univariate analyses of variance in that it stays within the multivariate context and examines the underlying dimension differentiating the groups (Bray & Maxwell, 1982; Huberty, 1998; Huberty & Morris, 1989). We used correlations greater than .20 between an item and the discriminant function as the criteria for the identification of items differentiating between the Holland groups. When significant interactions were found for gender or type of recruit, the discriminant analyses were conducted separately for the subgroups of students. The sample size for these analyses was reduced to 2,270 from the full sample of 2,309 because of missing data on the growth items.

Congruence Assumption: People Flourish in Environments That Are Congruent with Their Dominant Personality Types

As noted earlier, when considering the validity of the socialization assumption we examined differential patterns of change and stability associated with differing academic environments *regardless* of the students' dominant personality types. The congruence assumption, however, explicitly considers the match or fit between the chosen academic environment and the student's dominant personality type. The assessment of the validity of this assumption parallels the approach used in examining the socialization assumption but considers each of the four personality types separately. We sought to determine whether or not the enhancement of the initial dominant personalities of students was dependent on their choice of academic environments that fit their dominant personality types. Again, we first looked at students' self-ratings of their abilities and interests. The validity of the congruence assumption would be evidenced by greater growth in initially dominant characteristics for those students who selected academic environments matching their dominant interests than for similar students who selected other environments. For example, there should be greater growth in Artistic abilities and interests for Artistic students entering Artistic academic environments than for Artistic students who selected non-Artistic environments. Thus, we have an interaction hypothesis similar to that described in the test of the socialization assumption with the difference being the selection of students based on their personality types. In our analyses this differential change by the two groups of students is manifested in the year-by-Holland-environment interaction.

Again we conducted four 2 x 2 x 2 x 2 split-plot analyses of variance using each of the four 1986 and 1990 ability and interest scales as dependent variables, with the 1986 scales adjusted for regression-to-the-mean bias. The analysis of each scale was conducted only for the subset of students whose dominant personality type was associated with that scale. Thus, the full sample of 2,309 was broken down into the following subsamples based on the students' personality types: Investigative (n = 789); Artistic (n = 377); Social (n = 553); and Enterprising (n = 590). Each of the four independent variables was the same as that used for testing the socialization assumption, and the students' final academic environments in 1990 constituted the primary independent variable of interest. In each analysis the two levels of students' final academic environment distinguished between students who majored in and those who did not major in an academic environment analogous to the specific ability and interest scale used as the dependent variable. A significant interaction between Holland environment and year would indicate that growth in the initially prominent abilities and interests between 1986 and 1990 depended on the Holland environment of the student's major. These interactive effects were plotted indicating differences between students in the two categories of Holland environment at the two time points, with lines of the graph indicating the direction of change for each group of students. As before, effect sizes were calculated using the between-subjects error mean squares, converting both the 1986 and 1990 mean differences between the two focal groups of students to standard deviation units. A second set of effect sizes was calculated using the within-subjects error mean squares, which thus converted the change in abilities and interests between 1986 and 1990 for each group of students to standard-deviation units. When interactions were found between Holland environment and gender or type of recruit, the Holland-by-year interactions were plotted separately for the subgroups of students.

As before, we also used discriminant analyses of the seventeen self-reported growth items to examine patterns of growth and development preceded by multivariate analyses of variance to determine whether the patterns of growth were the same for male and female students and for primary and secondary recruits. These analyses were conducted four times, once for each of the four types of personalities. In each of the four analyses we compared students whose academic environments matched their dominant personalities to students whose environments did not match their personality types. Thus, the total group of students with complete data (n = 2,270) was divided into the four separate personality-type groups: Investigative (n = 778); Artistic (n = 370); Social (n = 544); and Enterprising (n = 515).

We now move to our analyses, turning first to faculty perceptions of undergraduate students, curricula, and teaching where results pertaining to one aspect of the socialization assumption of Holland's theory are presented. Chapter 4 is followed by four chapters that present the results obtained from our analyses of the student data examining the validity of all three assumptions of Holland. Chapter 5 presents results pertaining to the self-selection assumption, chapter 6 to a second aspect of the socialization assumption, and chapters 7 and 8 to the congruence assumption. Where appropriate, we embed our particular findings and interpretations in those of existing research.

4

Academic Environments
and Faculty

GAINING INCREASED knowledge of academic environments is important for developing a fuller understanding of students' selection of these environments as well as the consequences of these choices on longitudinal patterns of change and stability in student abilities, interests, and reports of self-growth. In this chapter we present information about faculty members in the various academic environments (as categorized according to Holland's theory), since faculty presumably are the primary representatives of the academic environments and the primary contributors to differential patterns of change and stability in students who choose those environments as majors.

Our intentions in this chapter are twofold. We begin by reviewing extant research findings concerning the variability in professional attitudes and behaviors of faculty members whose academic disciplines have been classified according to the six kinds of academic environments posited in Holland's theory. This review is followed by the presentation of findings from our original analyses of data derived from the national survey of the academic profession by the Carnegie Foundation for the Advancement of Teaching (CFAT). We have been guided in both intentions by the basic premise of Holland's theory that the six academic environments require, reinforce, and reward the characteristics of the analogous personality types who dominate them (as described in chapter 2).

There is not an extensive body of empirical evidence about environments categorized by Holland's schema or about the validity of the premise that they require, reinforce, and reward the prevalent characteristics of the personality types dominating them. As Holland (1997) noted, "the environmental models are only occasionally studied" (p. 160); and Walsh and Holland (1992) concluded that the theory emphasizes "person variables . . . [and is] lean on the concept of reinforcement" (p. 63) by the respective environments. Fortunately for our purposes, however, the majority of studies conducted in this domain focus specifically on academic environments in colleges and universities.

Extant Evidence Relevant to the Socialization Assumption

Because faculty create the respective norms and values of academic environments, we believe that variations in faculty's professional attitudes and behaviors across disparate clusters of academic disciplines are important prerequisites to understanding differential change and stability in the abilities, interests, and reports of self-growth of students in those disciplines. Our belief is consistent with the perspectives of Parsons and Platt (1973), Vreeland and Bidwell (1966), and Weidman (1989), who regard academic departments (environments) as a potentially important influence on students since they possess powerful normative and utilitarian sanctions for the socialization of students. These authors suggest, for example, that the influence of faculty is guided by their differential preference for and emphasis on alternative goals for undergraduate education and is manifested in their ability to reward students differentially for their performances through the assignment of grades. Our belief is also consistent with the perspectives of Kelly and Hart (1971) and Lipset and Ladd (1971), who suggest that the strong influence of academic departments on student change and stability is a result of an underlying selective recruitment process of distinctive personality types into academic disciplines that have prevailing orthodoxies, biases, and definitions of "the right way" to think and act.

Thus we initially seek a greater understanding of the systematic differences among the academic environments that are an integral component in Holland's theory by reviewing the extant empirical evidence on variations in the professional attitudes and behaviors of faculty, for faculty are the primary agents of those environments and are largely responsible for creating the prevailing orthodoxies, biases, and definitions of "the right way" to think and act in those environments (Kelly & Hart, 1971;

Lipset & Ladd, 1971). Such knowledge serves two primary purposes. First, it represents an indirect assessment of the socialization assumption: we anticipate the presence of systematic differences among faculty in the distinctive academic environments that will be consistent with the characterization of those environments in Holland's theory (see Table 2.2, p. 45). Second, the review of extant empirical evidence provides a portrait of what is known of each academic environment. Collective evidence of differential patterns of importance and emphasis among faculty in academic environments can thus aid our understanding of students' choices of these environments and the subsequent patterns of change and stability in the abilities, interests, and reports of self-growth among students enrolled in them.

Most investigations of differential professional attitude and behavior patterns of faculty members in the six Holland-defined academic environments can be classified according to one of two broad areas of interest. The first includes studies of the *overall institutional environments* of colleges and universities; the intent of this research is to determine if perceptions of the overall campus environment differ in terms of the distribution of the six personality types. This line of inquiry is predicated on the idea that both the general character and the dominant features of an environment "reflect the typical characteristics of its members. If we know what kind of people make up a group, we can infer the climate that the group creates" (Holland, 1997, p. 42). The second line of inquiry focuses on *distinct academic environments within institutions* and more specifically on differences in the importance faculty in the six academic environments (departmental groups) attach to selected educational goals and values. If these academic environments are distinct, their faculties should manifest the characteristics of their analogous personality types (described in chapter 2). Because our interest is decidedly on the second concern, our overview of broader institutional environments is brief; we focus in greater depth on findings derived from studies of distinct academic environments within the larger institutional context.

Campus Environments

A. W. Astin and J. M. Richards have been the primary scholars investigating the extent to which the overall environments of undergraduate institutions vary in proportion to the distribution of student and faculty (personality) types at those institutions. Most of their studies were conducted in the 1960s and 1970s. In this research the Environmental

Assessment Technique (EAT) (described in chapter 2) is commonly used to assign students and faculty to one of the six personality types based on their academic fields or majors; the proportion of students and faculty in the six personality categories is then correlated with commonly used measures of college environments (for example, the College Characteristics Index, or CCI [Pace, 1969], and the College and University Environment Scales, or CUES [Pace & Stern, 1958]).

Based on a series of related studies, Astin and Richards (and their colleagues) have shown that the distribution of students and faculty according to the six personality types is related to the perceptions of the overall college environments (Astin & Holland, 1961; Astin, 1963, 1965a, 1965b, 1968; Richards, Rand, & Rand, 1966; Richards & Seligman, 1969; Richards, Seligman, & Jones, 1970). For example, Astin (1963) found fourteen of the eighteen college environment items to be significantly related to EAT variables in the predicted direction, and Richards et al. (1970) found the EAT variables to be significantly related in the predicted direction to scales from the CUES. Because the prevailing interest of our book is on distinct academic environments within broader institutional settings, an extended consideration of research findings in this area is not presented. Those interested in specific findings can consult the series of studies just noted as well as Baird's (1988) comprehensive review of theories and research on college environments.

Academic Environments and Faculty Attitudes

Abundant evidence exists that faculty in academic departments, classified according to the six academic environments proposed by Holland, differ in ways theoretically consistent with the postulates of Holland's theory. Six studies conducted by Smart and his colleagues directly apply. One of these studies (Smart & McLaughlin, 1974) examined the goals of academic departments and found variations generally consistent with postulates of the theory. For example, Investigative and Realistic departments placed more emphasis than other departments on research and graduate education goals, while Social, Artistic, and Conventional departments placed more emphasis than other departments on goals related to the provision of a congenial work environment for faculty. A second study (Smart, 1976b) found similar variability in the duties performed by department chairs, and the findings from a third study (Smart, 1975) showed wide variability in the relative importance of fifteen specific sources of job satisfaction to the overall job satisfaction of chairs of academic departments classified according to the six academic environments. The three remaining studies by Smart (and colleagues) are given extended consideration below since they are particularly applicable to the context of this book in that they focus on variation in the overall educational orientations and specific teaching goals of faculty in the six academic environments. The findings from all three of these studies are supportive of the assumptions of Holland's theory.

The first of the three remaining studies examined the educational orientations of a sample of faculty members in a large doctoral-granting public university (Morstain & Smart, 1976). Faculty, who were assigned to five of the six academic environments (the Conventional environment was not included) based on their departmental affiliations, were asked to complete the Faculty Orientations Survey (FOS) (Morstain, 1973). The FOS is a forty-item instrument that yields six scales assessing faculty attitudes toward alternative curricular-instructional strategies, grading policies, and preferred student-faculty roles in educational decision making. The results of the study suggested the existence of three broad disciplinary clusters among the five academic environments under consideration. Realistic and Investigative faculty were distinctive in terms of their high mean scores on the Achievement, Assignment Learning, and Assessment scales. These findings suggest that Realistic and Investigative faculty are more oriented than their colleagues in other academic environments toward student achievement of career-related, a priori goals and student acquisition of specific skills and credentials (Achievement scale); prefer more formal and structured teaching-learning arrangements and feel that students learn best by meeting specific, clear-cut requirements (Assignment Learning scale); and place a high value on grades and examinations (Assessment scale). These orientations are not shared by Artistic and Social faculty, who have decidedly lower mean scores on these three scales. Rather, Artistic and Social faculty are best characterized by their mean scores on the Independent Study and Interaction scales of the FOS, which are higher than the scores of their colleagues in Realistic and Investigative environments. In general, Artistic and Social faculty prefer more informal, unstructured teaching-learning arrangements in which students set their own goals and pursue their own interests. They appear to place a high value on student freedom and independence in the learning process and believe that students do their best work when they are on their own (Independent Study scale). Further, Artistic and Social faculty tend to consider students fully competent to share educational decision making, to believe students should participate with faculty in planning courses and academic programs, and to prefer a collegial mode of interaction with students (Interaction scale). Enterprising faculty were distinctive in that their profile of scores on the five FOS scales was essentially undifferentiated: their scores tended to be in the middle of the scales with few peaks and valleys.

The Inquiry scale of the FOS did not differentiate among faculty in the five academic environments, implying that faculty, in general, tend to share a common belief that learning is its own reward and that an intrinsic interest in learning should be the primary motivation for a student's undergraduate education. They further tend to share the overarching importance of insight, perception of relationships among fields, and placing high value on knowing how to learn. Finally, they were uniformly supportive of students who are intellectually curious and who enjoy the intrinsic satisfaction of learning, irrespective of utilitarian or practical considerations (Morstain & Smart, 1976).

These broad educational orientations of faculty in the different academic environments were also evident in the specific teaching goals of faculty in a second study by Smart (1982), which examined the relative importance attached to sixteen undergraduate teaching goals by faculty in the six academic environments across five distinct types of institutions. His findings not only provide general support for the distinctiveness of the six academic environments but further demonstrate that such differences are consistent across decidedly different types of colleges and universities. For example, faculty in Realistic, Conventional, and Enterprising environments place much greater emphasis than do their peers in other environments on undergraduate education goals associated with the vocational development of students (e.g., to prepare students for employment after college and to provide the local community with skilled human resources). Faculty in Artistic and Social environments, on the other hand, place much greater emphasis than do their peers in other environments on undergraduate education goals related to the character development of students (e.g., to provide for students' emotional development, to achieve deeper levels of students' self-understanding, to develop moral character). Faculty in Investigative environments were distinctive in terms of their low scores on both vocational and character development. Comparable to the findings obtained by Morstain and Smart (1976), the importance attributed to undergraduate education goals associated with students' intellectual development (e.g., to develop creative capacities, to increase the desire and ability to undertake self-directed learning, to develop the ability to think clearly) did not differentiate among faculty in the six academic environments.

The third and most recent study by Smart presents further evidence of the distinctive classroom climates provided by faculty members in disparate academic environments (Thompson & Smart, 1999). This study examined the relative emphasis that faculty members in Investigative, Artistic, Social, and Enterprising academic environments placed on the development of alternative student competencies in their classes at a large doctoral-granting university, and the findings fully support the premise of Holland's theory that faculty in the four academic environments reinforce and reward students for the development of different patterns of competencies in their classes. Faculty members in Investigative academic environments attached a greater emphasis to competencies involving mathematical, analytical, and scientific skills and abilities than did their colleagues in the three other environments. These findings indicate that Investigative faculty tended to have a greater preference for more rational and systematic methods of inquiry. Investigative faculty encouraged students to rely on thinking, gathering information, and careful, objective analytical skills. Faculty members in Artistic academic environments attached a greater emphasis to competencies involving innovation, creativity, and literary skills than did colleagues in other environments. These findings indicate that Artistic faculty tended to place greater importance on using imagination and emotions in their work. Artistic students are encouraged to be original, expressive, and intuitive when solving problems. Faculty members in Social academic environments emphasized humanitarian, teaching, and interpersonal skills, while faculty in Enterprising academic environments placed greater importance on managerial, leadership, and persuasive competencies. These findings indicate that Social faculty placed a greater emphasis on students' abilities to help and understand others. They encouraged their students to use social beliefs, empathy, and patience in their work while perceiving problems in a social context. Enterprising faculty, however, placed greater importance on leadership, status, and power. They encouraged their students to be ambitious, assertive, and domineering and to regard social influence (e.g., power and status) in considering alternative problem-solving strategies.

In addition to the series of studies undertaken by Smart and colleagues, a number of other studies have examined differences in the attitudes and activities of faculty classified according to the six academic environments. Peters's (1974) findings illustrate that the subject matter faculty teach (i.e., academic environments) is related to the instructional techniques they use in a manner consistent with expectations from Holland's theory. Her results support her contention that the use of more formal instructional techniques, such as the lecture-discussion approach, is most common in Realistic and Conventional environments and least prevalent in Artistic and Social environments. These findings are generally consistent with those reported by Morstain and Smart (1976) discussed earlier.

Richards et al. (1970) examined the relationships between the proportion of faculty in the six academic environments and five scales from the College and University Environment Scales (CUES), as well as eighteen measures of college environments developed by Astin (1965b, 1968). The majority of his findings were consistent with expectations from Holland's theory, although some of the correlations were moderate in magnitude. For example, the proportion of faculty in Investigative environments was positively correlated with the CUES Scholarship scale and Astin's (1965b) Intellectualism scale; the proportion of faculty in Realistic environments was positively related to Astin's (1965b) Pragmatism scale; the proportion of faculty in Conventional environments was positively related to the CUES Propriety scale; and the proportion of faculty in Enterprising environments was positively correlated with Astin's (1965b) Status scale. At the same time the nonsignificant correlations between the proportion of faculty in Social environments and the CUES Community scale and the proportion of faculty in Artistic environments and Astin's (1965b) Estheticism scale provided little support for expectations derived from Holland's theory.

Because, as noted earlier, research on work and academic environments is relatively sparse, any overall conclusions about findings in this area must be regarded as tentative. What appears evident from the findings reviewed here, however, is that there are wide differences in the broad educational orientations and specific teaching goals and instructional methods used by faculty in the six academic environments and that these differences are generally consistent with the environmental descriptions provided by Holland (1997).

Empirical Findings on Differences among Faculty

We now present the findings based on our original analyses of data obtained from the national survey of the academic profession by the Carnegie Foundation for the Advancement of Teaching (CFAT). We selected two sets of items from the CFAT survey to examine potential differences in the attitudes of faculty classified according to four of the six academic environments (Investigative, Artistic, Social, Enterprising).

Realistic and Conventional environments were not selected because there were too few faculty in these environments in the CFAT data set. A complete description of the procedures used to investigate the differences among these academic environments was provided in chapter 3. We have organized the following discussion according to the two sets of items: the relative importance to faculty of a series of goals for undergraduate education; and faculty members' perspectives on undergraduate education, their perceptions of undergraduate students, and their teaching preferences among alternative kinds of undergraduate courses and students.

Importance of Alternative Goals for Undergraduate Education

The first set of items, measuring the relative importance faculty members attach to five selected goals for undergraduate education, pertains directly to Holland's theory. The goals represent distinct areas of knowledge (based on subject matter) and associated competencies that are theoretically linked to the four academic environments of interest in this chapter on faculty (and in the following four chapters on college students). Based on the requirements and patterns of reinforcement and reward of academic and

Table 4.1

Expected Relationships between Importance of Goals for Undergraduate Education and Academic Environments

Specific Goals for Undergraduate Education	Academic Environment Assumed to Place Highest Importance on the Specific Goal
Provide a basic understanding in mathematics and science	Investigative
Provide an appreciation of literature and the arts	Artistic
Enhance creative thinking	Artistic
Provide knowledge of history and the social sciences	Social
Prepare students for a career	Enterprising

work environments, as described by Holland (1997) and Gottfredson (1991), we expected the pattern of findings described in Table 4.1 to emerge.

Straightforward one-way analyses, with Tukey HSD post hoc pairwise comparisons, of variance, described in chapter 3, were used to examine differences in importance attached to these goals by faculty members classified according to their membership in the four academic environments (based on departmental affiliation). The complete results of these analyses are presented in Appendix 4.A at the end of this chapter. Table 4.2 presents the means and standard deviations of faculty in the four academic environments on these five goals for undergraduate education.

Inspection of the information in Table 4.2 and Appendix 4.A shows that the findings conform to expectations based on Holland's theory with

Table 4.2

Means and Standard Deviations of Goals for Undergraduate Education of Faculty [a]

Goals for Undergraduate Education	Academic Environments			
	Investigative	Artistic	Social	Enterprising
Provide a basic understanding in mathematics and science	4.648 (0.567)	4.480 (0.712)	4.537 (0.645)	4.503 (0.592)
Provide an appreciation of literature and the arts	4.283 (0.820)	4.787 (0.510)	4.577 (0.665)	4.178 (0.966)
Enhance creative thinking	4.692 (0.560)	4.800 (0.552)	4.626 (0.708)	4.658 (0.625)
Provide knowledge of history and the social sciences	4.406 (0.742)	4.608 (0.627)	4.597 (0.616)	4.390 (0.714)
Prepare students for a career	3.437 (1.213)	3.303 (1.283)	3.212 (1.272)	3.745 (1.168)

[a] Standard deviations are given in parentheses.

a single exception. As expected, faculty in Investigative academic environments have a higher mean score than their peers in the other three environments on the importance of providing students with a basic understanding in mathematics and science; faculty in Artistic academic environments have a higher mean score than other faculty on goals concerning the importance of an appreciation of literature and the arts and enhancing students' creative thinking; and faculty in Enterprising academic environments have a higher mean score than their colleagues on the importance of preparing students for careers. The single exception to our expectations based on Holland's theory is that faculty in Social academic environments do not judge the importance of providing knowledge of history and the social sciences to be greater than the importance attached to this specific goal by faculty in Artistic environments. Even here, however, there is partial support for Holland's theory in that faculty in Social academic environments (along with faculty in Artistic environments) rate this goal to be more important than do faculty in Investigative and Enterprising environments.

The *magnitude* of the differentiation among faculty in the four academic environments on the five undergraduate education goals is indicated by the effect sizes reported in Table 4.3, in which the mean differences are converted to standard-deviation units. Effect sizes are presented only for pairwise differences found to be statistically significant. Inspection of the effect sizes in this table shows that the mean differences among the academic environments generally range from one-quarter to one-half a standard deviation. The strongest differentiation is between Artistic and the other academic environments on the goal pertaining to an appreciation of literature and the arts, with the differences between Artistic and Investigative and Enterprising environments especially pronounced. Otherwise, there is a rather consistent pattern in the magnitude of differentiation among faculty in the four academic environments.

Perspectives of Undergraduate Curriculum, Teaching, and Students

A second set of items concerns the perspectives of faculty members on issues associated with the undergraduate curriculum, their preferences among alternative undergraduate teaching contexts, and their views of undergraduate students. Unlike the first set of items, the second set is not related directly to Holland's theory. Thus, our intent at this point is not to test any specific propositions that flow from Holland's theory, but rather to provide a descriptive profile of faculty in the four academic environments that

Table 4.3

Relative Importance of Selected Goals for Undergraduate Education: Effect Sizes

Provide a basic understanding in mathematics and science (Investigative goal)

	Investigative
Artistic	.269
Social	.194
Enterprising	.232

Provide an appreciation of literature and the arts (Artistic goal)

	Artistic
Investigative	.675
Social	.281
Enterprising	.816

Enhance creative thinking (Artistic goal)

	Artistic
Investigative	.171
Social	.275
Enterprising	.224

Provide knowledge of history and the social sciences (Social goal)

	Artistic	Social
Investigative	.301	.284
Social	(n.s.)	
Enterprising	.324	.308

Prepare students for a career (Enterprising goal)

	Enterprising
Investigative	.248
Artistic	.356
Social	.429

may assist in understanding the differential patterns of change and stability of students presented in chapters 6, 7, and 8. Moreover, establishing faculty differences across the four academic environments helps support the chain of logic embedded in the various formulations of Holland's theory.

As reported in chapter 3, we conducted a factor analysis of seven items in the Carnegie faculty survey—measuring faculty views on undergraduate curriculum, teaching contexts, and undergraduate students. Three factors were found. The first factor has been given the title of Curricular Specialization; those with high scores on this factor tend to *disagree* with the perspectives that the undergraduate curriculum has suffered from the specialization of faculty members and that undergraduate education in America would be improved if there were less emphasis on specialized training and more emphasis on broad liberal education. In essence, these faculty are more comfortable with the current level of curricular specialization in academe than are their peers with lower scores on this factor. The second factor has been called Accessibility to Students; those with high scores on this factor tend to *agree* that undergraduates should seek out faculty only during posted office hours and that most undergraduates expect too much attention and to *disagree* with the statement that they enjoy interacting informally with undergraduates outside the classroom. In general, these faculty tend to be less accessible to undergraduates than their colleagues who have lower scores on this factor. The third factor has been labeled Classroom-Student Focus; those with high scores tend to *agree* that they prefer teaching students who have a clear idea of the careers they will be following and that they prefer teaching undergraduate courses that focus on limited specialties as opposed to those that cover wide varieties of material. In essence, they tend to prefer teaching more specialized courses and interacting with students who have more definite career plans.

Once again we used straightforward one-way analyses of variance (described in chapter 3) with Tukey HSD post hoc pairwise comparisons to examine differences in the perspectives of faculty members—classified according to their membership in the four academic environments based on their departmental affiliations—on these three dimensions of faculty perspectives on undergraduate education. The complete results of these analyses are presented in Appendix 4.B at the end of this chapter. Table 4.4 presents the means and standard deviations of the four academic environments on these three dimensions.

Our results indicate significant variation among the groups of faculty members in their satisfaction with the current level of Curricular Specialization (see Appendix 4.B). In general, faculty in Investigative and

Enterprising academic environments are more comfortable with the current level of curricular specialization than are their peers in Artistic and Social environments. That is, the first set of faculty tends to *disagree* that the undergraduate curriculum has suffered from too much specialization of faculty members and does not believe that undergraduate education would be improved by a stronger emphasis on broad liberal education, whereas the second set tends to *agree* with such perspectives.

Table 4.4

Means and Standard Deviations of Faculty's Perspectives on Undergraduate Curriculum, Teaching, and Students [a]

	Academic Environments			
Dimensions	Investigative	Artistic	Social	Enterprising
Curricular Specialization	0.247	-0.267	-0.165	0.214
	(1.008)	(0.950)	(0.956)	(0.993)
Accessibility to Students	-0.031	-0.020	-0.006	0.099
	(0.982)	(0.973)	(1.005)	(1.019)
Classroom-Student Focus	0.069	0.102	-0.206	0.355
	(0.931)	(1.045)	(0.982)	(1.008)

[a] Standard deviations are given in parentheses.

Significant variability is also evident in the Classroom-Student Focus of faculty in the four academic environments. Faculty in Enterprising environments, more so than their peers in any of the three other environments, prefer to teach specialized undergraduate courses and to teach undergraduate students who have definite career plans; at the same time, faculty in Social environments prefer to teach undergraduate courses that are less specialized and undergraduate students who do not necessarily have clear career plans. The teaching preferences of faculty in Investigative and Artistic environments fall between these two extremes—being less focused than those in Enterprising environments and more focused than those in Social environments.

The significant variability evident in the perspectives of faculty in the four academic environments in terms of Curricular Specialization and Classroom-Student Focus is not evident in terms of their accessibility to students. The results of our analyses indicate no differences in the responses of the four groups of faculty on the Accessibility to Students scale, indicating that faculty in the four academic environments report being equally accessible to students.

The magnitude of differentiation among the four academic environments on the Curricular Specialization and Classroom-Student Focus factors is indicated by the effect sizes reported in Table 4.5, in which the mean differences are converted to standard-deviation units. Effect sizes are presented only for pairwise differences found to be statistically significant. As with the previous findings pertaining to the five goals for undergraduate education, we again find effect sizes generally ranging from

Table 4.5

Relative Importance of Faculty's Perspectives on Undergraduate Curriculum, Teaching, and Students: Effect Sizes

	Curricular Specialization		
	Investigative	Artistic	Social
Investigative			
Artistic	.527		
Social	.422	n.s.	
Enterprising	n.s.	.493	.388

	Classroon-Student Focus		
	Investigative	Artistic	Social
Investigative			
Artistic	n.s.		
Social	.280	.314	
Enterprising	.292	.258	.573

one-quarter to one-half a standard deviation. The effect sizes tend to be somewhat greater in terms of variability among the four academic environments concerning faculty perceptions of the Curricular Specialization than for their preferences concerning Classroom-Student Focus; the magnitude of differences on the former hover around one-half a standard deviation, the latter around one-fourth of a standard deviation.

Comparison of Findings with Those in the Extant Literature

While extant research findings commonly portray wide differentiation in the prevailing attitudes and values of faculty in the six academic environments, the findings of Morstain and Smart (1976) and Smart (1982) suggest that at the same time faculty members in general have a common, collective interest in students' broad academic and intellectual development—irrespective of their particular affiliations in academic environments. This similarity is evident in the absence of significant differences across the academic environments regarding the Inquiry scale in Morstain and Smart and the "intellectual development" scale in Smart. Our findings concerning undergraduate goals suggest that faculty members' overall collective emphasis on students' general intellectual development coincides with staunch adherence to the differential importance of their respective subject matters. Thus, although broad student intellectual development seems to be important to faculty members in all academic environments, faculty differ decidedly on the relative importance of their respective subject-matter areas. In addition, this diversity is highly consistent with the postulates of Holland's theory, thereby providing a foundation for understanding the different intellectual traditions of the different academic environments and the bases for their differential requirement, reinforcement, and rewarding of various abilities and interests in their students.

The broad differences in relative importance ascribed to subject-matter-based goals by undergraduate education faculty members among the four academic environments is consistent with the findings of Lattuca and Stark (1994), who analyzed the results of a dozen separate disciplinary task forces appointed by the Association of American Colleges (AAC). Their findings revealed that "the task forces from all disciplinary groupings called for autonomy in goal setting . . . [and] tended to treat goals as departmental objectives to be articulated locally" (Lattuca & Stark, 1994, p. 410). In essence, all twelve AAC disciplinary task forces agreed that the right to define the content of the undergraduate curriculum should be determined on the basis of the distinctive perspectives of their respective academic disciplines (environments).

Our findings suggest that when left to the "pull" of their distinctive perspectives, faculty members place greater value on undergraduate education goals consistent with their own academic environments. Thus, faculty create academic environments inclined to require, reinforce, and reward the distinctive patterns of abilities and interests of students in a manner consistent with Holland's theory. For instance, Investigative academic environments are dominated by Investigative people who have strong mathematical and scientific abilities, and faculty in Investigative environments, not surprisingly, assign a decidedly greater importance to providing a basic understanding in mathematics and science than do their colleagues in other environments. By the same token, Artistic academic environments are dominated by Artistic people who have strong cultural interests and creative talents, and faculty in these environments assign a decidedly greater importance to providing an appreciation of literature and the arts and enhancing students' creative thinking than do their colleagues in other environments.

These differences in values faculty members in disparate academic environments place on broad undergraduate-education goals are also highly consistent with variations in the relative emphases faculty place on the development of different student competencies, as found by Thompson and Smart (1999). For instance, the greater importance ascribed by faculty in Investigative academic environments to developing a basic understanding in mathematics and science in this study parallels the finding by Thompson and Smart that Investigative faculty attach greater emphasis on the development of mathematical, analytical, and scientific competencies in their students. Similarly, the greater importance attributed to the goals of developing an appreciation of literature and the arts and enhancing students' creative thinking by faculty in Artistic academic environments parallels the finding by Thompson and Smart that Artistic faculty place more emphasis on the development of student competencies involving innovative, creative, and literary skills.

We also discovered broad differences in faculty groups' satisfaction with the current levels of specialization in the undergraduate curriculum and in their preferences among alternative undergraduate teaching contexts. That faculty in Artistic and Social academic environments believe the current curriculum suffers from overspecialization is generally consistent with the findings of Morstain and Smart (1976) that faculty in these two environments place higher value than do their peers in other

environments on student freedom and independence in the learning process. Their findings show that Artistic and Social faculty, compared to
other faculty, have a stronger conviction in the beliefs that students do
their best work when they are on their own and that students are fully
competent to share in educational decision making. Similarly, our finding
that faculty members in Enterprising academic environments have a
stronger preference for teaching undergraduate courses in which students have a clear idea of the careers they will be following than do their
colleagues is consistent with Smart's (1982) finding that this group of
faculty—as well as faculty in Realistic and Conventional environments—
places greater emphasis in the classroom on students' vocational development.

The fact that faculty in Enterprising environments generally accept
the current level of specialization in the undergraduate curriculum
(Curricular Specialization factor) and prefer undergraduate classes that
focus on limited specialties rather than covering a wide variety of material
(an item in the Classroom-Student Focus factor) is somewhat surprising,
however, since Morstain and Smart (1976) did not find that Enterprising
faculty scored high on either the Achievement scale or the Assessment scale
from the FOS, which together assess the extent to which faculty prefer
teaching contexts characterized by efforts to convey specific skills and credentials (Achievement scale) and specific, clear-cut course requirements
(Assessment scale). Given the limited number of studies of academic environments, we are unable to explain this apparent inconsistency.

Our findings show that preferences about the accessibility of faculty
members to students do not vary across the four academic environments
we studied. This finding seems potentially important given extensive research findings over the past two decades that students' involvement with
faculty, both within and outside formal classroom settings, is an important
contributor to numerous outcomes of benefit to students (Pascarella &
Terenzini, 1991). Because of the similarities we discovered in terms of the
accessibility of faculty members to students across the four academic environments, it appears that this attribute is not a major contributor to efforts to explain and understand differential patterns of change and stability
in students' abilities and interests, the purview of chapters 6, 7, and 8.

Vignettes of Academic Environments Created by Faculty

It is clear from the extant literature as well as our own empirical findings
in this chapter that faculty create distinctive academic environments in a

manner generally consistent with the postulates of Holland's theory. While Holland (1997) notes that there has been decidedly less research— within the context of his theory—on these environments than on the personal attributes of individuals, academic environments are an essential component of his theory. It is from among these environments that students ultimately select specific academic majors; and we assume that these environments are the primary mechanism by which students further their distinctive patterns of abilities and interests during their collegiate careers.

The following vignettes of each of the four focal academic environments should aid an understanding of the distinctive academic environments that students choose and that ultimately influence which abilities and interests are strengthened, maintained, and diminished throughout their undergraduate education. The statements in each of these vignettes are based on specific findings from the extant research literature and our original analyses as presented in this chapter, although we do not indicate specific references to document each statement. Before presenting the vignettes portraying the distinctive professional attitudes and behaviors of faculty in the respective academic environments, we remind the reader of two attributes that appear to be common to all four environments, as discussed earlier. First, faculty in all four academic environments appear to share a common emphasis on the intellectual development of students. Second, faculty in the four academic environments appear to be equally accessible to and express the same level of comfort in their informal interactions with students.

Investigative Academic Environments

These environments, which emphasize a basic understanding of mathematics and science, have a strong general orientation toward scholarship, intellectualism, and conventional notions of academic rigor. These broad orientations and emphases are in direct contrast to the relatively little attention given by faculty to students' character and career development. Rather, faculty in Investigative environments place primary attention on the development of students' analytical, mathematical, and scientific competencies.

In seeking to instill these broad orientations and specific competencies in their students, faculty in Investigative environments use a distinctive pattern of classroom strategies. They rely more heavily than others on formal and structured teaching-learning strategies (e.g., lecture-discussion) that are strongly subject-matter centered, believing that students learn best by meeting specific, clear-cut a priori course requirements. They also place high value on examinations and grades and seek to develop specific skills and competencies in their students that are consistent with their general orientation to scholarship, intellectualism, mathematics, and science. Specifically, they place great importance on the development of students' analytical, mathematical, and scientific competencies.

Whereas faculty in Investigative environments, like their counterparts in Enterprising environments, are satisfied with the current level of curricular specialization, they, like their colleagues in Artistic environments, do not express a decided preference for teaching either specialized or general courses or for interacting with students who have either clear or indefinite career plans.

Artistic Academic Environments

These environments are best characterized by a strong commitment to aesthetics and an emphasis on emotions and sensations as well as on the mind. This broad orientation or emphasis is reflected in their curricula, which stress acquisition of an appreciation of literature and the arts and enhancing students' creative thinking. Faculty in Artistic environments place primary attention on the development of students' literary abilities and competencies associated with innovation and creativity. In addition, faculty in Artistic environments, like their counterparts in Social environments, place strong emphasis on values and the character development of their students.

Faculty in Artistic environments employ a distinctive set of classroom strategies in their efforts to develop the unique pattern of abilities, interests, and values of their students just described. Like their colleagues in Enterprising environments, they use a blending of formal, structured, subject-matter-centered instructional strategies and informal, unstructured, and student-centered teaching approaches. While utilizing this blending of both subject-matter-centered and student-centered instructional approaches faculty in Artistic environments, like their colleagues in Social environments, place high value on student freedom and independence in the learning process, prefer a collegial mode of interaction with students, and believe that students do their best work when they are on their own.

Faculty in Artistic environments share a similar concern with their peers in Social environments that the current level of curricular specialization is too strong. Their orientation here is not one-sided for they, like their counterparts in Investigative environments, do not express a decided preference for teaching either specialized or general courses or for interacting with students who have either clear or indefinite career plans.

Social Academic Environments

These environments have a strong community orientation with a particular emphasis on creating a faculty workplace climate characterized by warmth and friendliness. Social and Artistic academic environments share some similar characteristics. The curricular offerings in both environments stress student acquisition of knowledge of history and the social sciences, and the faculties of both environments place emphasis on values and the character development of students. While they share these common orientations, the faculty in Social environments place a distinctly greater emphasis on the development of humanitarian, teaching, and interpersonal competencies in their students.

The general nature of student-faculty interaction in Social environments is also similar to that of Artistic environments in that their respective faculties place a high value on student freedom and independence in the learning process, prefer a collegial mode of interaction with students, and believe that students do their best work when they are on their own. In addition, both faculties also share a concern that the current level of curricular specialization is too strong.

There are, however, differences in the specific teaching-learning strategies used by faculties of Social and Artistic environments. Unlike the more balanced approach of their counterparts in Artistic environments, faculty in Social environments place strong reliance on informal, student-centered teaching strategies (e.g., small-group discussions) and prefer to teach less specialized undergraduate courses to students who do not have clear career plans. Thus, while Social and Artistic environments share a number of similar broad orientations, they differ in more specific instructional approaches and teaching-learning strategies.

Enterprising Academic Environments

The defining orientation of these environments is their strong emphasis on the career preparation of students and status acquisition. This orientation is clearly evident in the uncommonly high emphasis their faculty place on the vocational and career development of their students as well as their efforts to develop students' leadership competencies, to motivate them to strive to be successful in terms of common indicators of career and organizational status, and to acquire and use power to attain organizational and career goals. It is also evident in the preferences of their faculty to teach students who have definite career plans and to teach specialized undergraduate courses. These faculty, like their colleagues in Investigative environments, are satisfied with the current level of curricular specialization in their institutions.

The nature of student-faculty interaction and the specific teaching-learning strategies used by faculty in Enterprising environments are the most balanced or undifferentiated of any of the four environments. For example, faculty in Enterprising environments, like their counterparts in Artistic environments, use (to a similar extent) formal, structured, subject-matter centered instructional strategies (e.g., lecture-discussion) and informal, unstructured, and student-centered teaching (e.g., small-group discussion) approaches. In addition, faculty in Enterprising environments have the most balanced, undifferentiated profile in terms of alternative approaches to student-faculty interactions in the teaching-learning process. That is to say, they place equivalent emphasis on student-faculty interactions characterized by a faculty-centered orientation (in which there is a strong emphasis on grades, examinations, and students meeting specific clear-cut requirements) and those characterized by a student-centered orientation (which places a high value on student freedom and independence in the learning process, a collegial mode of interaction with students, and a belief that students do their best work when they are on their own).

The four vignettes just described clearly illustrate the distinctive norms and values of the four academic environments as manifested in the typical professional attitudes and values of their respective faculties. These academic environments are a key component in Holland's theory since they constitute the available choices from which students initially select their academic majors and presumably are a primary influence on students' subsequent growth and development throughout their college careers. In the next chapter we examine student choices from among these academic environments to assess the assumption of Holland's theory that students choose environments consistent with their personality types and associated abilities and interests.

Analysis of Variance Results: Goals for Undergraduate Education

	ANOVA			Tukey HSD		

Understanding of Mathematics and Science

Source	df	Mean Square	F	Environment	Mean	A E S
Holland	3	3.624	9.267***	Artistic	4.480	
Within	2771	.391		Enterprising	4.503	
				Social	4.537	
				Investigative	4.648	* * *

Appreciation of Literature and Arts

Source	df	Mean Square	F	Environment	Mean	E I S
Holland	3	38.517	69.136***	Enterprising	4.178	
Within	2771	.557		Investigative	4.283	
				Social	4.577	* *
				Artistic	4.787	* * *

Enhance Creative Thinking

Source	df	Mean Square	F	Environment	Mean	S E I
Holland	3	3.072	7.657***	Social	4.626	
Within	2771	.401		Enterprising	4.658	
				Investigative	4.692	
				Artistic	4.800	* * *

Knowledge of History and Social Sciences

Source	df	Mean Square	F	Environment	Mean	E I S
Holland	3	9.098	20.134***	Enterprising	4.390	
Within	2771	.452		Investigative	4.406	
				Social	4.597	* *
				Artistic	4.608	* *

Career Preparation

Source	df	Mean Square	F	Environment	Mean	S A I
Holland	3	30.143	19.562***	Social	3.212	
Within	2771	1.541		Artistic	3.303	
				Investigative	3.437	*
				Enterprising	3.745	* * *

*statistically significant pairwise difference

*** $p < .001$

Analysis of Variance Results: Faculty's Perspectives on
Undergraduate Curriculum, Teaching, and Student Perspectives

	ANOVA			Tukey HSD		

Curricular Specialization

Source	df	Mean Square	F	Environment	Mean	A S E
Holland	3	42.809	44.912***	Artistic	- .267	
Within	2771	.953		Social	- .165	
				Enterprising	.214	* *
				Investigative	.247	* *

Accessibility to Students

Source	df	Mean Square	F	Environment	Mean
Holland	3	1.643	1.658	Investigative	- .031
Within	2771	.991		Artistic	- .020
				Social	- .006
				Enterprising	.099

Classroom-Student Focus

Source	df	Mean Square	F	Environment	Mean	S I A
Holland	3	35.716	37.196***	Social	- .206	
Within	2771	.960		Investigative	.069	*
				Artistic	.102	*
				Enterprising	.355	* * *

*statistically significant pairwise difference
*** $p < .001$

5

Students' Self-Selection into Academic Environments

CHOOSING AN academic major is not a simple matter for most college students. This choice involves many different components, including students' perceptions of their own interests and abilities, their career aspirations, the availability of desired majors at specific institutions, the influence and encouragement of family and friends, and students' assessments of educational and employment opportunities following completion of their undergraduate studies. Such complexity not only makes the initial choice and subsequent persistence in academic majors somewhat problematic for students; it also makes these matters difficult for researchers to study and understand. We begin our investigation of the self-selection assumption in Holland's theory by exploring the nature and patterning of students' initial and subsequent choices of academic majors.

Choice of Academic Environments

Feldman and Newcomb (1969) reviewed nearly three dozen studies, conducted primarily in the 1950s and 1960s, containing data on the percentage of students changing either their career choices or their major fields (see vol. 1, pp. 36–38 and vol. 2, Table 2). Although the investigators found that across these studies the percentage of students who changed either choice of career or choice of major field ranged from a low of 20 percent to a high of 66 percent, most of the percentages were in the range of 30 percent to 49 percent. They pointed out that such percentages necessarily reflect the particular classification of occupations or major fields used in each study. The finer and more detailed the classification system the more likely it is that slight shifts in choice of occupation or major field will register, thereby increasing the percentage of students who show changes in their choices. Most categorizations in the studies they reviewed, however, were rather broad ones; therefore, shifts among these categories represented rather major changes in educational and career plans.

Our own examination of the fluidity in students' choices of academic majors focused on the distribution of majors chosen by the students in our sample when they were in their freshman year (1986) and the patterns of change and stability in these choices between 1986 and 1990. As described in chapter 3, students' initial freshman preferences for some eighty specific possible academic majors (and their actual majors four years later) have been classified into the academic environments of Holland's theory to yield theoretically meaningful clusters of academic majors. Thus, the following presentations do not consider individual academic majors but rather the broader categories of academic majors that parallel Holland's academic environments. One consequence of this procedure is that students might actually change specific academic majors but remain within the broader categories. For example, in comparing students' initial and subsequent choices of academic majors, a student who chose mathematics as a freshman and subsequently selected civil engineering would not be considered as having changed academic environments since both specific majors are classified in Holland's theory as being examples of Investigative academic environments. One implication of the use of broad categories is that our examination of patterns of change and stability in students' academic majors underestimates the magnitude of change relative to instances in which others have used individual majors as the unit of analysis.

Our selection of the sample for this study was determined by the distribution of the 1990 majors. We selected only students whose 1990 majors were classified as Investigative, Artistic, Social, or Enterprising because too few students picked Realistic and Conventional majors. We then examined the initial choices of students in the four focal groups when they were freshmen in 1986. These initial choices of academic majors were classified according to the six academic environments proposed by Holland and two additional categories: one for those who were undecided on their academic majors and the other for those whose intended academic majors were not included in *The College Majors Finder* (Rosen, Holmberg, & Holland, 1989). We included all of these classifications in

1986 so that we could examine more fully any movement into the four environments (between 1986 and 1990) on which our study is focused.

Table 5.1 presents the distribution of initial selection of academic environments when the students in our sample were freshmen and their actual distribution in the four focal academic environments four years later. The row totals in this table show a fairly balanced tendency for students in our sample to begin college with the intention to major in fields associated with Investigative, Social, and Enterprising academic environments in that each of these three categories of students includes between 20 percent and 25 percent of the total sample. The same row totals also show that decidedly fewer students in our sample began college with the intention to major in fields associated with the Artistic academic environment (7.8 percent).

The distribution of students in our sample four years later was somewhat different, as reflected in the column totals in Table 5.1. In general, the proportion of students in Enterprising environments remained rather constant over the four-year period (21.1 percent in 1986 and 22.3 percent in 1990), while there was a small to moderate increase in the proportion of students in the three other academic environments of focal interest. This increase is most evident in Social environments where the proportion of students grew from 21.9 percent in 1986 to 34.1 percent in 1990. Smaller, but still substantial, increases are evident in the proportions of students who majored in fields associated with Investigative and Artistic environments; the former increased from 24.6 percent to 29.1 percent, and the latter nearly doubled from 7.8 percent to 14.5 percent. Table 5.1 also shows the relatively small percentage of our sample of students whose freshman majors were undecided, not classified, or associated with the Realistic and Conventional academic environments in Holland's theory. They collectively account for slightly less than one-fourth of all students in the sample.

Inspection of the marginal totals in Table 5.1 masks considerable variability in the stability of students' initial choices of academic environments as freshmen and the composition of students in the respective academic environments four years later, as shown in the internal cells of Table 5.1. Discernible from these cells, for example, is the proportion of students (in our sample) who selected a particular academic environment and "persisted" in this selection during their college years. Throughout this book we call these "persisters" the *primary recruits* to an academic environment (cf. Feldman & Weiler, 1976). Of interest here is any variation in the proportion of these persisters or primary recruits across aca-

Table 5.1

Distribution of Students' Intended (1986) and Final (1990) Academic Environments [a]

| | 1990 Academic Environments | | | | |
1986 Academic Environments	Investigative	Artistic	Social	Enterprising	Row Totals
Realistic	28 (48.3) [4.2]	5 (8.6) [1.5]	6 (10.3) [0.8]	19 (32.8) [3.7]	58 [2.5]
Investigative	365 (64.4) [54.3]	34 (6.0) [10.2]	109 (19.2) [13.8]	59 (10.4) [11.5]	567 [24.6]
Artistic	8 (4.4) [1.2]	116 (64.4) [34.7]	34 (18.9) [4.3]	22 (12.2) [4.3]	180 [7.8]
Social	40 (7.9) [6.0]	49 (9.7) [14.7]	385 (76.2) [48.9]	31 (6.1) [6.0]	505 [21.9]
Enterprising	85 (17.5) [12.6]	50 (10.3) [15.0]	90 (18.5) [11.4]	262 (53.8) [50.9]	487 [21.1]
Conventional	28 (31.8) [4.2]	5 (5.7) [1.5]	10 (11.4) [1.3]	45 (51.1) [8.7]	88 [3.8]
Undecided	59 (25.4) [8.8]	46 (19.8) [13.8]	84 (36.2) [10.7]	43 (18.5) [8.3]	232 [10.0]
Not in Holland [b]	59 (30.7) [8.8]	29 (15.1) [8.7]	70 (36.5) [8.9]	34 (17.7) [6.6]	192 [8.3]
Column Total	672 (29.1)	334 (14.5)	788 (34.1)	515 (22.3)	2,309

[a] Row percentages are in parentheses; column percentages are in brackets.
[b] Intended academic major not included in *The College Majors Finder* (Rosen, Holmberg, & Holland, 1989).

demic environments. As shown in Table 5.1—when looking at row percentages—over three-fourths (76.2 percent, n = 385) of the 505 students who initially selected majors in a Social academic environment were in that environment four years later, whereas slightly over half (53.8 percent, n = 262) of the 487 students who initially selected majors in an Enterprising environment remained in that environment after four years. Slightly less than two-thirds (64.4 percent) of students who initially selected majors in either an Investigative (n = 567) or Artistic (n = 180) academic environment persisted in those majors throughout the four-year period (n = 365 and 116, respectively). Thus, students in our sample who initially selected a Social academic environment were the most likely to remain with their choices, those choosing an Enterprising academic environment were least likely to do so, and those choosing an Investigative or Artistic academic environment were somewhere in between. Overall, approximately two-thirds (64.9 percent)[1] of these students persisted in majors in the academic environments they chose as freshmen, while 35.1 percent changed to majors in the three other academic environments. Note that the percentage of changers falls within the range of percentage changers most often found in the studies reviewed by Feldman and Newcomb (1969).

The internal cells of Table 5.1 also show the distribution of *secondary recruits* to each academic environment—that is, the distribution of students who were located in academic environments in their fourth year of college that were *not* their initial freshman choices. Note, for example (again, as shown by row percentages), that of the students who did not persist in their choice of a Social academic environment, some subsequently chose an Investigative academic environment (7.9 percent of those initially choosing the Social environment), an Artistic academic environment (9.7 percent of those initially choosing the Social environment), or an Enterprising academic environment (6.1 percent of those initially choosing the Social environment)—a fairly even distribution among these three environments. Note further that the Social academic environment was the most likely new choice for those who changed from their initial choices of Investigative, Artistic, or Enterprising environment (19.2 percent, 18.9 percent, and 18.5 percent respectively).

---

[1] This percentage was derived by dividing the total number of students whose 1986 *and* 1990 majors were in Investigative, Artistic, Social, and Enterprising academic environments (365 + 116 + 385 + 262) by the total number of students who initially (1986) intended to major in those four academic environments (567 + 180 + 505 + 487).

The information in Table 5.1 can be looked at in another way by examining the column (rather than the row) percentages in the cells. To do
so is instructive, for these percentages reflect the extent to which each of
the four academic environments in 1990 was populated by students who
did or did not initially intend to be in that environment. It is conceivable
that these two groups of students—the primary and secondary recruits—
in an environment differ somewhat in their abilities and interests and that
the proportion of each of these groups in an academic environment determines in part the success of the environment in socializing students.
Because the socialization assumption to be tested in the following chapter
is that the four focal academic environments reinforce and reward different sets of student abilities and interests, it is useful to know something
about the composition of the student bodies of these environments.

Inspection of the column percentages in the cells of Table 5.1 reveals
that only a third to slightly more than a half of the students in the four academic environments were primary recruits to those environments. The
percentages hover around a half for students in Investigative (54.3 percent), Enterprising (50.9 percent), and Social (48.9 percent) academic environments, whereas only about a third (34.7 percent) of students who
ultimately majored in fields associated with the Artistic environment intended to major in that environment as freshmen four years earlier. These
four academic environments, then, were populated by a large proportion
of secondary recruits; overall, not quite one-half (48.9 percent)[2] of the students in our sample who ultimately majored in the four focal academic environments began college with the intention of majoring in fields
associated with these specific environments. These percentages clearly illustrate the overall fluidity in students' initial selection of academic majors
and the heterogeneous composition of students (in terms of their initial
selection) within each of the four academic environments after a lapse of
four years.

Artistic academic environments are clearly the most distinctive in that
almost two-thirds of their students entered college with the intention of
majoring in fields in other academic environments. Nearly half of the students who ultimately majored in an Artistic academic environment intended to major in fields within the Enterprising (15.0 percent) or Social
(14.7 percent) academic environments or were undecided (13.8 percent)

[2] This percentage was derived by dividing the total number of students whose 1986 *and*
1990 majors were in Investigative, Artistic, Social, and Enterprising academic environments
(365 + 116 + 385 + 262) by the total number of students in the sample (2,309).

about their major fields as freshmen. As for students who ultimately majored in fields within the Social academic environment, over a third of them intended as freshmen to major in Investigative (13.8 percent) or Enterprising (11.4 percent) environments or were undecided about their majors (10.7 percent). The migration of students to fields in the Investigative academic environment appears to have been predominantly by students who initially selected Enterprising majors (12.6 percent), while the Enterprising academic environment tended primarily to attract students who initially selected Investigative majors (11.5 percent) in 1986.

In sum, the four focal academic environments to be studied more closely in later chapters are populated by many students who did not intend to be there when they first entered college, and the magnitude of variability ranges from about two-thirds of the students in Artistic environments to about half of the students in the three other academic environments. This fluidity of students' choices has potential implications for the cohesiveness of the peer culture of each academic environment and for the capacity of the several environments to be successful in their efforts to reinforce and reward different sets of abilities and interests in their students. At a minimum, this overall fluidity provides a context within which to interpret and understand the findings of studies on the self-selection assumption of Holland's theory. We turn first to the findings from existing empirical research on this assumption and then present the results from our own analyses.

Self-Selection Assumption: Evidence from the Research Literature

Literally dozens of studies have examined the assumption that college students and employed adults prefer and select educational and occupational settings that parallel their dominant personality types. In general, the findings of these studies provide clear support for the assumption. Because these studies have been reviewed elsewhere in comprehensive reviews of research findings based on Holland's theory (see, for example, Hackett & Lent, 1992; Osipow & Fitzgerald, 1995; and Walsh & Holland, 1992), we consider here only some illustrative examples of these findings (especially those pertaining to college students).

Reflective of the research on college students concerning the self-selection assumption of Holland's theory are the findings that students tend to prefer college subcultures that parallel their own personality types (Apostal, 1970), expect to like other students who have similar interests

(Hogan, Hall, & Blank, 1972), actually become attracted to students like themselves (Holland, 1964), and select academic environments that value the interests and competencies they possess (Holland & Nichols, 1964). In addition, Smart (1976a) examined the relative importance of twelve job characteristics for a sample of freshmen in a large research university and obtained results consistent with expectations from Holland's theory. For example, those enrolled in Artistic academic majors were best characterized by the high importance they attached to the opportunity to "work with ideas" and having a "great deal of independence"; those enrolled in Social academic majors were distinctive in terms of the importance they attached to being "able to work with people" and the opportunity to "be helpful to others"; and those in Enterprising and Conventional majors placed greater importance than others on such status attributes as "high anticipated earnings," the "chance for steady progress," and the possibility of "rapid career advancement."

In a recent study Huang and Healy (1997) found that college freshmen select academic environments (majors) that are consistent with their career goals and aspirations. Their findings, based on a sample of 18,137 students who completed the Cooperative Institutional Research Program (CIRP) freshman survey in 1985, revealed, for example, that students who initially selected Enterprising and Conventional majors placed higher importance on such values as "having administrative responsibility for the work of others" and "being very well-off financially" than did their peers who selected other academic environments, while those selecting Social majors attached greater importance to "helping others who are in difficulty" than did others. Students selecting Artistic majors were distinctive in terms of the high importance they placed on "creating artistic work." In related research also based on the 1985 CIRP freshman survey, Antony (1998) found that premedical (Investigative) students had stronger Investigative abilities and interests than nonpremedical students, as would be predicted from Holland's theory.

The findings by Smart and Feldman (1998) demonstrated a clear-cut selection effect for entering male and female students in Investigative, Artistic, Social, and Enterprising academic environments. Their study of self-reported abilities and interests of college freshmen showed a consistent pattern: students who intended to major in one of the four environments perceived themselves as possessing stronger abilities and interests in their chosen academic environment than in the other environments. For instance, freshmen who chose to major in an Enterprising academic environment perceived themselves as having stronger Enterprising abilities and interests than did their peers who chose to major in any of the three other environments.

As in their selection of academic majors, college students also tend to become involved in cocurricular activities that correspond to their personality types. Much of the considerable evidence showing this tendency is based on assessments of the kinds of voluntary activities of students. For example, Sergent and Sedlacek (1989) found that Social types were more likely to become involved in peer counseling activities while Enterprising students were more likely to volunteer for campus recruiting activities. O'Brien, Sedlacek, and Kandell (1994) also found that Social type students were more inclined to participate in counseling-center and campus hotline activities than were other personality types.

Hearn and Moos (1976) used the University Residence Environmental Scale (URES) to examine the social climates of residence halls, and their results were generally in accord with expectations from Holland's theory, though they did obtain some contrary findings. As expected, for example, residence halls with a high proportion of Conventional majors tended to emphasize a traditional social orientation, competition, order, and organization; but contrary to expectations, residence halls with a high proportion of Investigative majors tended to emphasize involvement and were not high on academic achievement.

The preceding are but illustrative examples from the rich research literature regarding the extent to which college students as well as employed adults prefer, seek, and select educational and work environments that parallel their personality types. Comprehensive reviews of this broader literature consistently have concluded that there is clear support for the self-selection assumption of Holland's theory. Thus, Hackett and Lent (1992) concluded that "studies involving either college students or employed workers have found that [personality] types generally aspire to, or inhabit, fields that match their primary interests" (p. 423). Similarly, Osipow and Fitzgerald (1995) noted that "a systematic relationship existed between the predictions and the actual choices and, furthermore, that where the predictions were wrong, a large proportion of the careers chosen were in the level adjacent to the actual choice" (p. 91). Finally, Walsh and Holland (1992) concluded that "an overwhelming amount of research does . . . indicate that college students tend to select and enter college major environments congruent with their personality types" (p. 51) and that, though there have been fewer studies, the extant findings "suggest that employed men and women tend to enter and remain in occupational environments congruent with their personality types" (p. 52).

Clearly substantiated by extant findings, then, is the assumption that college students and employed adults are not passive in their search for academic majors and careers, but rather are active in searching for and selecting educational and occupational settings that encourage them to develop further their dominant characteristic interests and abilities and to enter (and be successful) in their chosen occupational careers or academic major fields. Given that students across the six academic environments differ at the time they enter college, efforts to assess the validity of the subsequent assumption of differential socialization patterns of the respective environments and the assumed positive outcomes accruing from person-environment fit must take account of these precollege differences in order to disentangle the interaction of self-selection and socialization.

We turn now to the results of our own analyses of the validity of the self-selection assumption. We examined the initial choices of academic environments of students in our sample along with change and stability patterns in those choices over a four-year period. Results are presented for each of the four dominant personality types in our sample as well as for the four corresponding focal environments—Investigative, Artistic, Social, and Enterprising. The research procedures used in our investigations were described fully in chapter 3.

Empirical Findings on Student Self-Selection

The initial basic assumption of Holland's (1997) theory is that people "search for environments that will let them exercise their skills and abilities, express their attitudes and values, and take on agreeable problems and roles" (p. 4). This assumption implies that people "are not passive victims of the environments they encounter but are rather *active seekers* of potentially compatible situations and *active avoiders* of potentially incompatible situations" (Holland, 1997, p. 98, emphasis added). Of course, people are not entirely free to exercise this normal inclination because of their varied experiences, marketplace considerations, employment opportunities, and other such circumstances. Moreover, people have varying degrees of knowledge about their own distinctive abilities and interests.

The validity of Holland's initial assumption may be examined in at least two ways when studying college students and their choices of academic majors (environments). First, those students who initially intend to major in a specific academic environment (e.g., Investigative) should possess stronger abilities and interests that are reinforced and rewarded by that particular environment than do students who initially intended to major in other academic environments (e.g., Artistic, Social, Enter-prising). In the context of our investigation this possibility would be man-ifested if, for instance, those who initially intended to major in Investigative academic environments possessed higher scores on the 1986 Investigative ability and interest scale (see chapter 3) than those who ini-tially intended to major in Artistic, Social, and Enterprising academic en-vironments. Second, the validity of this assumption would be supported if those students with a particular dominant personality type at the time of college entry (e.g., Social) show a greater propensity to major in a parallel academic environment (i.e., Social) than in dissimilar academic environ-ments (i.e., Investigative, Artistic, Enterprising). In our investigation this possibility would be manifested if, for example, those with a dominant Social personality type when they entered college in 1986 were more like-ly to major in a Social academic environment than were their peers with dominant Investigative, Artistic, and Enterprising personality types at col-lege entry. We examined both of these possibilities for students in our sample.

1986 Ability and Interest Scores Based on Initial Major

We based our initial assessment of the validity of the self-selection as-sumption in Holland's theory on an analysis of the unadjusted 1986 abili-ty and interest scale scores of students (see chapter 3) who intended to major in each of the four academic environments. Our expectation, given the self-selection assumption, was that students who initially intended to major in a particular academic environment would score higher on the parallel ability and interest scale than those who initially intended to major in the other three academic environments.

A 2 x 2 analysis of variance was used to explore this possibility with separate analyses for each of the four 1986 ability and interest scales de-scribed in Table 3.3. In each case the independent variables were the in-tended academic major (environment) of students when they entered college in 1986 (2 levels: major was in the parallel environment for the specific scale or was not) and gender (2 levels: males, females). The de-pendent variable in each analysis was the particular ability and interest scale score. The means, standard deviations, and effect sizes for students intending to major in each of the four academic environments on each of the four 1986 ability and interest scales are shown in Table 5.2, and the ANOVA results are given in Appendix 5.A.

Table 5.2

Self-Selection Effects: Means, Standard Deviations, and Effect Sizes for Unadjusted 1986 Ability and Interest Scales [a]

1986 Ability and Interest Scales	Equivalent Academic Environment	Nonequivalent Academic Environment	Effect Size
Investigative [b]			
Males and females combined	56.014 (9.753)	47.290 (8.974)	0.952
Artistic [b]			
Males and females combined	60.228 (9.910)	49.345 (9.577)	1.132
Social			
Males	54.913 (10.223)	49.080 (9.895)	0.587
Females	52.066 (10.061)	50.252 (9.841)	0.182
Enterprising [b]			
Males and females combined	53.222 (10.280)	49.073 (9.635)	0.426

[a] Standard deviations are in parentheses.
[b] Intended major by gender interaction was not significant.

The overall results in Table 5.2 provide strong support for the self-selection assumption in Holland's theory: in contrast to the relevant comparison groups, students who intended to major in a particular academic environment generally perceived themselves as having decidedly stronger abilities and interests commensurate with those that their chosen environment tended to reinforce and reward. With a single exception (students initially intending to major in Social environments), our findings are similar for males and females in the four academic environments.

In more specific terms, Table 5.2 shows both that students who intended to major in fields associated with Investigative, Artistic, and Enterprising academic environments scored significantly higher on the parallel 1986 ability and interest scale (than those who declared majors associated with other academic environments) and that the differences are similar for males and females in the three environments. To give one example, students who initially selected majors in Artistic academic environments had stronger Artistic abilities and interests (60.228) than did their peers who chose majors in the three other environments (49.345). The magnitude of differences across these three academic environments—as shown in the column of effect sizes—differs considerably, however. For instance, the differences (approximately one standard deviation) between Investigative and non-Investigative majors on the 1986 Investigative ability and interest scale and between Artistic and non-Artistic majors on the 1986 Artistic ability and interest scale are about twice the size of the difference (about half a standard deviation) between Enterprising and non-Enterprising majors on the 1986 Enterprising ability and interest scale.

The results for students who initially selected majors associated with Social academic environments are different for males and females. While both male and female students who initially chose majors in Social environments had significantly higher scores on the 1986 Social ability and interest scale than did those who selected majors in non-Social academic environments, the differences are more pronounced for males than females. The magnitude of the difference for males (effect size = .587) is about three times greater than the equivalent effect size for females (.182).

In sum, the overall pattern of findings presented in Table 5.2 shows a strong self-selection tendency consistent with expectations from Holland's theory in that students who intended to major in each of the four academic environments had higher scores on the parallel ability and interest scales than did those who initially selected the three other academic environments. This pattern is especially strong for those who selected Artistic and Investigative academic environments and, while still substantial, is somewhat weaker for those who selected Enterprising academic environments and males who selected Social environments. The weakest pattern is for females on the 1986 Social ability and interest scale where the difference between those who initially selected Social and non-Social academic environments is much less pronounced.

Personality Types and Academic Environments

The analysis just presented did not consider differences in the personality types of students in their selection of academic majors. A second way, then, to examine the validity of the self-selection assumption of Holland's theory is to examine explicitly the relationship between a student's dominant personality type—as defined in chapter 3—and the student's intended (1986) major and actual (1990) major classified according to Holland's academic environments. We examined this relationship separately for each of the four dominant personality types comprised by our focal interest. For each of the four personality types we also examined the relationship separately for males and females. In the following presentation of our results, as organized by the four personality types under consideration, we first discuss students' initial choices of academic majors/environments at the time they entered college as freshmen and then turn to their actual majors four years later.

Investigative personality types. Table 5.3 shows the distributions of the initial and subsequent academic environments (see Appendixes 5.B and 5.C for the full cross-tabulations) for male and female students with a dominant Investigative personality type (as defined in chapter 3). In 1986 both gender groups entered college with a greater likelihood of wanting to major in fields associated with the Investigative academic environment than any other environment. This likelihood was somewhat stronger for males (45.8 percent) than for females (34.1 percent). Investigative males were three times more likely to choose majors in an Investigative environment than to choose the second most popular major environment (Enterprising, 15.3 percent). For Investigative females this prevailing orientation was not as strong, with some 22 percent of the females intending to major in fields associated with Social academic environments. Nonetheless, there was a rather strong tendency (a weighted average of 40.3 percent) for the combined sample of male and female Investigative students to select majors in Investigative academic environments at the time they entered college.

This pattern became slightly stronger four years later: 43.2 percent (weighted average) of the combined sample of male and female students with

Table 5.3

Distribution of Intended (1986) and Final (1990) Academic Environments of Students with a Dominant Investigative Personality Type [a]

Academic Environments	1986			1990		
	Males (n=417)	Females (n=372)	Combined (n=789)	Males (n=417)	Females (n=372)	Combined (n=789)
Realistic	26 (6.2)	9 (2.4)	35 (4.4)			
Investigative	191 (45.8)	127 (34.1)	318 (40.3)	210 (50.4)	131 (35.2)	341 (43.2)
Artistic	32 (7.7)	21 (5.6)	53 (6.7)	51 (12.2)	51 (13.7)	102 (12.9)
Social	29 (7.0)	82 (22.0)	111 (14.1)	72 (17.3)	137 (36.8)	209 (26.5)
Enterprising	64 (15.3)	43 (11.6)	107 (13.6)	84 (20.1)	53 (14.2)	137 (17.4)
Conventional	11 (2.6)	9 (2.4)	20 (2.5)			
Undecided	37 (8.9)	39 (10.5)	76 (9.6)			
Not in Holland [b]	27 (6.5)	42 (11.3)	69 (8.8)			

[a] Percentages are in parentheses.
[b] Intended academic major not included in *The College Majors Finder* (Rosen, Holmberg, & Holland, 1989).

a dominant Investigative personality type were in majors associated with Investigative academic environments. This pattern was again somewhat stronger for male (50.4 percent) than female (35.2 percent) Investigative students. The tendency for a substantial portion of Investigative females to select majors in Social fields as freshmen became even stronger four years later; in fact, virtually an equal number ultimately chose Investigative (35.2 percent) and Social (36.8 percent) majors.

Thus, the overall results for students with a dominant Investigative personality type are generally consistent with the self-selection assumption of Holland's theory at the time they entered college and four years later. There is a clear tendency, however, for this pattern to be more representative of male Investigative students. Female Investigative students showed a stronger than expected tendency as freshmen to select majors associated with Social academic environments, and this tendency showed up even more strongly four years later for essentially as many of them majored in Social environments as Investigative environments.

Artistic personality types. Table 5.4 shows the distributions of the initial and subsequent academic environments for male and female students with a dominant Artistic personality type (see Appendices 5.D and 5.E for the full cross-tabulations). The combined results for male and female Artistic students do *not* support the self-selection assumption of Holland's theory in that only 18.8 percent (weighted average) of the combined sample began college with the expectation of majoring in fields associated with Artistic academic environments; this pattern was similar for both males (17.2 percent) and females (20.0 percent). Nearly twice as many males with a dominant Artistic personality type intended to major in Enterprising (32.5 percent) as in Artistic academic environments. There was a fairly even balance for females with a dominant Artistic personality type to select majors in fields associated with Artistic (20.0 percent), Enterprising (22.7 percent), and Social (26.8 percent) academic environments.

There was a somewhat stronger tendency for both male and female students with a dominant Artistic personality type to select majors associated with Artistic academic environments four years later, but the results still do not support the self-selection assumption of Holland's theory. This somewhat stronger tendency is indicated by the additional 10 percent of male (27.4 percent compared with 17.2 percent) and female (31.4 percent compared with 20.0 percent) Artistic students who were in Artistic environments, but the Artistic environment was still not the primary major/environment for either male or female students with a dominant

Table 5.4

Distribution of Intended (1986) and Final (1990) Academic Environments of Students with a Dominant Artistic Personality Type [a]

Academic Environments	1986			1990		
	Males (n=157)	Females (n=220)	Combined (n=377)	Males (n=157)	Females (n=220)	Combined (n=377)
Realistic	4 (2.5)	1 (0.5)	5 (1.3)			
Investigative	19 (12.1)	17 (7.7)	36 (9.6)	32 (20.4)	16 (7.3)	48 (12.7)
Artistic	27 (17.2)	44 (20.0)	71 (18.8)	43 (27.4)	69 (31.4)	112 (29.7)
Social	26 (16.6)	59 (26.8)	85 (22.6)	35 (22.3)	89 (40.5)	124 (32.9)
Enterprising	51 (32.5)	50 (22.7)	101 (26.8)	47 (29.9)	46 (20.9)	93 (24.7)
Conventional	4 (2.5)	3 (1.4)	7 (1.9)			
Undecided	19 (12.1)	30 (13.6)	49 (13.0)			
Not in Holland [b]	7 (4.5)	16 (7.3)	23 (6.1)			

[a] Percentages are in parentheses.
[b] Intended academic major not included in *The College Majors Finder* (Rosen Holmberg, & Holland, 1989).

Artistic personality type. There was a fairly even distribution across the four academic environments for males, whereas for females there remained a strong tendency to major in fields associated with the Social (40.5 percent) academic environment.

These findings for students with a dominant Artistic personality type must be considered in the context of the rather small proportion of students overall who initially (7.8 percent) or at some point after matriculation subsequently (14.5 percent) selected majors associated with Artistic academic environments (see Table 5.1). One explanation for the tendency of students not to choose majors affiliated with Artistic academic environments may be the lack of clear employment opportunities for graduates of such fields and the growing "vocationalism" of higher education.

Social personality types. The distributions of the initial and subsequent academic environments for male and female students with a dominant Social personality type, which are presented in Table 5.5, generally support the self-selection assumption of Holland's theory (see Appendices 5.F and 5.G for the full cross-tabulations). For the combined sample of male and female Social types, 40.1 percent (weighted average) initially intended to major in fields affiliated with Social academic environments, and this percentage increased to 48.3 (weighted average) four years later.

This overall pattern, however, differs substantially for males and females with a dominant Social personality type and is much more characteristic of females than males. The findings for females clearly support the self-selection assumption of Holland's theory both when they entered college and subsequently. For females with a dominant Social personality type, an intended major in a Social academic environment (48.6 percent) was nearly four times as prevalent as the second most prevalent environment (Investigative, 12.6 percent). The pattern remained strong four years later when a larger majority of females with a dominant Social personality type were in majors affiliated with Social academic environments (54.6 percent), although the percentage of students in Investigative environments (the second most prevalent environment) had also risen (18.1 percent). The findings for males with a dominant Social personality type do not reveal such distinctiveness in selection, especially at the time males entered college as essentially equal proportions of them intended to major in fields associated with Social (25.9 percent) and Investigative (26.8 percent) academic environments. However, the findings for these males four years later are more in accord with the self-selection assumption of Holland's theory in that being in a major field affiliated with Social academic environments was decidedly more likely (37.6 percent) than being in any of the

Table 5.5

Distribution of Intended (1986) and Final (1990) Academic Environments of Students with a Dominant Social Personality Type [a]

Academic Environments	1986			1990		
	Males (n=205)	Females (n=348)	Combined (n=553)	Males (n=205)	Females (n=348)	Combined (n=553)
Realistic	3 (1.5)	1 (0.3)	4 (0.7)			
Investigative	55 (26.8)	44 (12.6)	99 (17.9)	59 (28.8)	63 (18.1)	122 (22.1)
Artistic	10 (4.9)	21 (6.0)	31 (5.6)	25 (12.2)	46 (13.2)	71 (12.8)
Social	53 (25.9)	169 (48.6)	222 (40.1)	77 (37.6)	190 (54.6)	267 (48.3)
Enterprising	34 (16.6)	39 (11.2)	73 (13.2)	44 (21.5)	49 (14.1)	93 (16.8)
Conventional	5 (2.4)	9 (2.6)	14 (2.5)			
Undecided	27 (13.2)	36 (10.3)	63 (11.4)			
Not in Holland [b]	18 (8.8)	29 (8.3)	47 (8.5)			

[a] Percentages are in parentheses.
[b] Intended academic major not included in *The College Majors Finder* (Rosen, Holmberg, & Holland 1989).

three other environments. The "migration" of males with a dominant Social personality type to majors in Social environments over the four-year period does not appear to be from any single source but rather from most all of the other academic environments—other than Artistic—at the time they entered college (see the internal cells of the table in Appendix 5.F).

Enterprising personality types. The distributions of the initial and subsequent academic environments for male and female students with a dominant Enterprising personality type, which are presented in Table 5.6, provide somewhat mixed support for the self-selection assumption of Holland's theory for both males and females (see Appendixes 5.H and 5.I for the full cross-tabulations). Both males and females with a dominant Enterprising personality type entered college with a prevailing tendency to select majors in fields affiliated with Enterprising academic environments. While not overwhelmingly so, majors in Enterprising environments are the most common for both males (37.1 percent) and females (32.5 percent) with a dominant Enterprising personality type. Gender differences for freshmen are most evident in the prevalence of the second most frequently intended majors of male and female Enterprising students. Intended majors in fields associated with Investigative (25.6 percent) academic environments were the second most prevalent for male Enterprising students, whereas fields affiliated with Social (21.3 percent) environments were the second most prevalent for female Enterprising students. Still, for both groups during the freshman year a clear tendency to select majors in Enterprising environments can be seen.

This pattern, however, is less clear for subsequent selection of both males and females evidenced by data four years later. For males with a dominant Enterprising personality type there is a rather even balance among the selection of majors in fields affiliated with Investigative (33.9 percent), Enterprising (31.3 percent), and Social (27.5 percent) academic environments. For females with a dominant Enterprising personality type, the proportion who majored in Enterprising environments remained more or less constant (33.9 percent compared with 32.5 percent), but there was a substantial increase in the proportion of these women who moved to majors associated with Social academic environments. This movement resulted in a fairly similar proportion of females with a dominant Enterprising personality type who ultimately majored in fields affiliated with Social (36.8 percent) and Enterprising (33.9 percent) academic environments. Thus, the findings for both male and female Enterprising

Table 5.6

Distribution of Intended (1986) and Final (1990) Academic Environments of Students with a Dominant Enterprising Personality Type [a]

Academic Environments	1986			1990		
	Males (n=313)	Females (n=277)	Combined (n=590)	Males (n=313)	Females (n=277)	Combined (n=590)
Realistic	13 (4.2)	1 (0.4)	14 (2.4)			
Investigative	80 (25.6)	34 (12.3)	114 (19.3)	106 (33.9)	55 (19.9)	161 (27.3)
Artistic	10 (3.2)	15 (5.4)	25 (4.2)	23 (7.3)	26 (9.4)	49 (8.3)
Social	28 (8.9)	59 (21.3)	87 (14.8)	86 (27.5)	102 (36.8)	188 (31.9)
Enterprising	116 (37.1)	90 (32.5)	206 (34.9)	98 (31.3)	94 (33.9)	192 (32.5)
Conventional	24 (7.7)	23 (8.3)	47 (8.0)			
Undecided	17 (5.4)	27 (9.7)	44 (7.5)			
Not in Holland [b]	25 (8.0)	28 (10.1)	53 (9.0)			

[a] Percentages are in parentheses.
[b] Intended academic major not included in *The College Majors Finder* (Rosen, Holmberg, & Holland 1989).

students four years later provide somewhat ambiguous support for the self-selection assumption of Holland's theory.

Self-Selection Assumption: Summary Comments

The fluidity of college students' initial and ultimate selections of academic majors is clearly evident in our finding that approximately one-third of the students in our sample changed among the broad classification of academic disciplines or environments in Holland's theory over the four-year period. Moreover, the use of such broad classifications actually underestimates students' movement among specific academic major fields. These results support (but of course do not prove) Holland's (1997) contention that students "are not passive victims of the [academic] environments they encounter but are rather active seekers of potentially compatible situations and active avoiders of potentially incompatible situations" (p. 98).

The fluidity of students' choices of majors has implications for the "peer cultures" that characterize—in part—the respective academic environments in which they are members in their fourth year of college. Overall, approximately half of the students (in our sample) in Investigative, Social, and Enterprising academic environments are primary recruits—that is, students who intended to be there when they initially enrolled in college as freshmen—while slightly over a third of those who ultimately majored in Artistic environments began in those environments. Put otherwise, one-half to two-thirds of the students who constituted the "student bodies" of these respective academic environments were secondary recruits who did not anticipate being there as freshmen. Such a high proportion of "migrants" into these academic environments conceivably might make problematic the efforts of faculty members in these environments to socialize students to the respective environments' prevailing norms. The extent to which the respective academic environments are successful in socializing students to their respective norms and values is the topic of the following chapter. The point here is to show the diversity and variety in the composition of students who constituted the "peer cultures" of the four academic environments.

Our findings suggest that Holland's theory has much to offer in terms of understanding students' choices of academic environments by demonstrating that the initial choices of these environments are consistent with strengths in students' patterns of abilities and interests. We found that in all instances students who initially selected a major in any of the four focal academic environments of our study had higher scores on the commensurate ability and interest scale than did those who majored in the three other academic environments. We interpret such results as showing that students tend to select initially majors in those academic environments that are assumed to reinforce and reward their stronger abilities and interests and that they tend to avoid those academic environments that reinforce and reward their relatively weaker abilities and interests. This is clearly evident for males and females who initially chose to major in Investigative, Artistic, and Enterprising environments and for males who initially selected majors associated with Social environments. The evidence for females who initially intended to major in fields affiliated with Social environments is much weaker, though the findings are in the proper direction and are statistically significant.

Additional evidence from our examination of the relationship between students' dominant personality types and their initial and subsequent choices of academic environments also provides general support for this basic assumption of Holland's theory, though the results of these analyses suggest gender differences in the magnitude of the relationship. In essence, there is reasonably strong evidence that students with dominant Investigative, Social, and Enterprising personality types tend to select majors, both initially and subsequently, in parallel academic environments. This tendency is strongest for students with Investigative and Social personality types, somewhat weaker for students with Enterprising personality types, and not at all evident for students (either male or female) with a dominant Artistic personality type. The percentages of initial or subsequent selections for Investigative, Social, and Enterprising personality types are usually the highest for personality types in corresponding academic environments; when they are not, they are more or less tied with another academic environment. These percentages are generally in the 30s and 40s, which means that the majority of the students with any particular dominant personality type do not enter an academic environment that presumably is most supportive of their abilities and interests. The largest percentage of students selecting congruent fields either initially or subsequently are males with dominant Investigative personalities selecting Investigative environments (45.8 percent of them in 1986 and 50.4 percent by 1990) and females with dominant Social personalities selecting Social environments (48.6 percent, 54.6 percent). (In chapters 7 and 8 we track the effects on students of whether or not they entered congruent environments.)

As mentioned, the findings for students' initial and subsequent choices of academic environments reveal several instances of differing patterns for males and females. Gender differences are apparent in both of our analyses pertaining to the Social academic environment. Men who chose Social environments as freshmen perceived themselves to have much stronger Social abilities and interests than did men who chose the three other academic environments, but this clear pattern of differentiation is not as evident in the comparison of women who selected Social and other environments (see Table 5.2). Nonetheless, women with a dominant Social personality type were nearly twice as inclined as men with a dominant Social personality type to select majors in fields associated with Social academic environments as freshmen (see Table 5.5). Gender differences are also evident in the selection of Investigative academic environments. Men with a dominant Investigative personality type were decidedly more likely than women with this dominant personality type to choose initially a major in an Investigative academic environment as freshmen, and this difference became even more apparent four years later (see Table 5.3). This disparity between men and women in the selection of Social and Investigative majors may well be the result of differences in the nature of the Social and Investigative disciplines. Investigative majors are more likely to be quantitative in nature, related to the sciences and mathematics, and the socialization experiences of women appear to lead them away from the selection of such disciplines (Eccles, 1994). The Social majors are less quantitative in nature and tend to be those with higher concentrations of women.

That less than an absolute majority of students with any particular dominant personality type actually entered parallel academic environments most supportive of their abilities and interests might be regarded by some as raising questions about Holland's assumptions of how people self-select themselves into environments congruent with their abilities and interests. We think such concerns are largely unfounded given the complexities of students' choices of academic majors noted at the outset of this chapter and the totality of our findings reported in this chapter. In the context of these complexities, our evidence clearly shows that students who initially selected a major in any of the four focal environments had higher scores on the commensurate ability and interest scale than those who majored in the three other academic environments. Furthermore, while less than an absolute majority of students with any particular dominant personality type actually entered parallel academic environments most supportive of their abilities and interests, those with dominant Investigative, Social, and Enterprising personality types did enter parallel academic environments in much higher percentages than nonparallel environments. For instance, 43.2 percent of males and females with a dominant Investigative personality type ultimately selected majors in Investigative environments while 26.5 percent of them selected Social majors, the second most prevalent environment (see Table 5.3); and 48.3 percent of males and females with a dominant Social personality type ultimately selected majors in Social environments while 22.1 percent of them selected Investigative majors, the second most prevalent environment (see Table 5.5). We interpret the totality of this evidence as basically supporting the self-selection assumption of Holland's theory, though the strength of this support varies, as we have acknowledged, by the dominant personality type of the student.

It is instructive to sort certain of the major findings of this chapter by academic environment. When this is done, the differing "profiles" of the academic environments (in terms of student selection) become clear. Conceivably, these different patterns of student selection in part create conditions that differentially affect the ease and success of faculty efforts to socialize students. As a speculation, and assuming all else equal, it would seem that students in Investigative academic environments would be the most open to influence from faculty in such environments. Students initially selecting an Investigative environment are already rather highly differentiated (with respect to their Investigative abilities and interests) from students initially selecting other environments. Moreover, compared to the students in other academic fields, they form the largest percentage of primary recruits. Finally, those students who have a dominant Investigative personality (males in particular) are more likely than most other dominant personality types to select an environment that presumably supports their interests and abilities.

The profile of student selection for the other academic environments suggests—again as a speculation on our part—that faculty in each of them will have somewhat less success in socializing students (or, if equally successful, will have had to exert more effort). Consider the Artistic academic environment. It is true that students initially selecting such an environment are highly differentiated from students initially selecting other environments with respect to the students' Artistic abilities and interests. Yet this environment contains the lowest proportion of primary recruits, which is to say that it has the largest proportion of secondary recruits; moreover, students with a dominant Artistic personality are not particularly likely to select this environment either initially or subsequently. For males selecting Social environments and both males and females selecting Enterprising environments, the situation is different again. Here students who have a dominant personality type either as Social (females) or Enterprising (males and females) evidence a certain likelihood of seeking congruent environments, but the percentages involved are modest at best; and students who actually select these environments (whatever their dominant personalities) are differentiated from students selecting other environments in their abilities and interests pertinent to these environments, but again only moderately so. Finally, perhaps most problematic with respect to the socialization efforts of faculty are females selecting the Social academic environment. Despite the likelihood of females with dominant Social personalities to select Social academic environments either initially or subsequently, females who initially select social environments (whatever their dominant personalities) are only slightly different in their Social abilities and interests from females selecting other environments. In this respect, faculty do not have a "special" or differentiated population of students with which to work.

In all, our findings generally support the presence of a self-selection in students' choices of academic majors in accord with Holland's theory; but these findings also give evidence of gender differences in some instances. These overall findings have broad implications for efforts to assess the subsequent socialization effects of academic environments, which is the concern of the following chapter. First, our findings illustrate the clear need to take account of initial differences among students in terms of their abilities and interests in order to obtain a more true or accurate estimate of the socialization effects of the academic environments. Second, they suggest the need to be attentive to the possibility that such effects may differ for male and female students in these environments. Finally, the fluidity of students' choices of academic environments emphasizes the need to be attentive to the possibility that the socialization effects of those environments may also differ for students who have similar (primary recruits) and dissimilar (secondary recruits) initial and subsequent academic majors.

Analysis of Variance Results: 1986 Ability and Interest Scales

Investigative Abilities and Interests

Source	df	Mean Square	F
Holland	1	25099.81	298.79***
Gender	1	1849.78	22.02***
Holland by Gender	1	40.96	.49
Residual	1735	84.01	

Artistic Abilities and Interests

Source	df	Mean Square	F
Holland	1	18876.21	204.10***
Gender	1	5.46	.06
Holland by Gender	1	.00	.00
Residual	1735	92.48	

Social Abilities and Interests

Source	df	Mean Square	F
Holland	1	4379.76	44.34***
Gender	1	210.10	2.13
Holland by Gender	1	1210.25	12.25***
Residual	1735	98.79	

Enterprising Abilities and Interests

Source	df	Mean Square	F
Holland	1	5451.09	57.51***
Gender	1	1164.71	12.29***
Holland by Gender	1	568.62	6.00
Residual	1735	94.79	

*** $p < .001$

Distribution of Intended (1986) and Final (1990) Academic Environments of Males with a Dominant Investigative Personality Type [a]

1986 Academic Environments	1990 Academic Environments				Row Totals
	Investigative	Artistic	Social	Enterprising	
Realistic	11 (42.3) [5.2]	2 (7.7) [3.9]	2 (7.7) [2.8]	11 (42.3) [13.1]	26 [6.2]
Investigative	152 (79.6) [72.4]	9 (4.7) [17.6]	18 (9.4) [25.0]	12 (6.3) [14.3]	191 [45.8]
Artistic	1 (3.1) [0.5]	24 (75.0) [47.1]	6 (18.8) [8.3]	1 (3.1) [1.2]	32 [7.7]
Social	3 (10.3) [1.4]	6 (20.7) [11.8]	19 (65.5) [26.4]	1 (3.4) [1.2]	29 [7.0]
Enterprising	13 (20.3) [6.2]	3 (4.7) [5.9]	12 (18.8) [16.7]	36 (56.3) [42.9]	64 [15.3]
Conventional	3 (27.3) [1.4]	0 (0.0) [0.0]	0 (0.0) [0.0]	8 (72.7) [9.5]	11 [2.6]
Undecided	13 (35.1) [6.2]	6 (16.2) [11.8]	10 (27.0) [13.9]	8 (21.6) [9.5]	37 [8.9]
Not in Holland [b]	14 (51.9) [6.7]	1 (3.7) [2.0]	5 (18.5) [6.9]	7 (25.9) [8.3]	27 [6.5]
Column Totals	210 (50.4)	51 (12.2)	72 (17.3)	84 (20.1)	417

[a] Row percentages are in parentheses; column percentages are in brackets.
[b] Intended academic major not included in *The College Majors Finder* (Rosen, Holmberg, & Holland, 1989).

Distribution of Intended (1986) and Final (1990) Academic Environments of Females with a Dominant Investigative Personality Type [a]

1986 Academic Environments	1990 Academic Environments				Row Totals
	Investigative	Artistic	Social	Enterprising	
Realistic	5 (55.6) [3.8]	1 (11.1) [2.0]	0 (0.0) [0.0]	3 (33.3) [5.7]	9 [2.4]
Investigative	86 (67.7) [65.6]	7 (5.5) [13.7]	24 (18.9) [17.5]	10 (7.9) [18.9]	127 [34.1]
Artistic	1 (4.8) [0.8]	18 (85.7) [35.3]	1 (4.8) [0.7]	1 (4.8) [1.9]	21 [5.6]
Social	2 (2.4) [1.5]	7 (8.5) [13.7]	72 (87.8) [52.6]	1 (1.2) [1.9]	82 [22.0]
Enterprising	11 (25.6) [8.4]	2 (4.7) [3.9]	5 (11.6) [3.6]	25 (58.1) [47.2]	43 [11.6]
Conventional	2 (22.2) [1.5]	1 (11.1) [2.0]	2 (22.2) [1.5]	4 (44.4) [7.5]	9 [2.4]
Undecided	13 (33.3) [9.9]	8 (20.5) [15.7]	15 (38.5) [10.9]	3 (7.7) [5.7]	39 [10.5]
Not in Holland [b]	11 (26.2) [8.4]	7 (16.7) [13.7]	18 (42.9) [13.1]	6 (14.3) [11.3]	42 [11.3]
Column Totals	131 (35.2)	51 (13.7)	137 (36.8)	53 (14.2)	372

[a] Row percentages are in parentheses; column percentages are in brackets.
[b] Intended academic major not included in *The College Majors Finder* (Rosen, Holmberg, & Holland, 1989).

Distribution of Intended (1986) and Final (1990) Academic Environments of Males with a Dominant Artistic Personality Type [a]

1986 Academic Environments	1990 Academic Environments				Row Totals
	Investigative	Artistic	Social	Enterprising	
Realistic	3 (75.0) [9.4]	1 (25.0) [2.3]	0 (0.0) [0.0]	0 (0.0) [0.0]	4 [2.5]
Investigative	7 (36.8) [21.9]	1 (5.3) [2.3]	7 (36.8) [20.0]	4 (21.1) [8.5]	19 [12.1]
Artistic	0 (0.0) [0.0]	18 (66.7) [41.9]	0 (0.0) [0.0]	9 (33.3) [19.1]	27 [17.2]
Social	4 (15.4) [12.5]	5 (19.2) [11.6]	16 (61.5) [45.7]	1 (3.8) [2.1]	26 [16.6]
Enterprising	8 (15.7) [25.0]	11 (21.6) [25.6]	7 (13.7) [20.0]	25 (49.0) [53.2]	51 [32.5]
Conventional	0 (0.0) [0.0]	0 (0.0) [0.0]	1 (25.0) [2.9]	3 (75.0) [6.4]	4 [2.5]
Undecided	8 (42.1) [25.0]	3 (15.8) [7.0]	3 (15.8) [8.6]	5 (26.3) 10.6]	19 [12.1]
Not in Holland [b]	2 (28.6) [6.3]	4 (57.1) [9.3]	1 (14.3) [2.9]	0 (0.0) [0.0]	7 [4.5]
Column Totals	32 (20.4)	43 (27.4)	35 (22.3)	47 (29.9)	157

[a] Row percentages are in parentheses; column percentages are in brackets.
[b] Intended academic major not included in *The College Majors Finder* (Rosen, Holmberg, & Holland, 1989).

Distribution of Intended (1986) and Final (1990) Academic Environments of Females with a Dominant Artistic Personality Type [a]

1986 Academic Environments	1990 Academic Environments				Row Totals
	Investigative	Artistic	Social	Enterprising	
Realistic	0 (0.0) [0.0]	0 (0.0) [0.0]	0 (0.0) [0.0]	1 (100.0) [2.2]	1 [0.5]
Investigative	5 (29.4) [31.3]	5 (29.4) [7.2]	6 (35.3) [6.7]	1 (5.9) [2.2]	17 [7.7]
Artistic	3 (6.8) [18.8]	26 (59.1) [37.7]	11 (25.0) [12.4]	4 (9.1) [8.7]	44 [20.0]
Social	3 (5.1) [18.8]	10 (16.9) [14.5]	45 (76.3) [50.6]	1 (1.7) [2.2]	59 [26.8]
Enterprising	1 (2.0) [6.3]	11 (22.0) [15.9]	11 (22.0) [12.4]	27 (54.0) [58.7]	50 [22.7]
Conventional	0 (0.0) [0.0]	0 (0.0) [0.0]	0 (0.0) [0.0]	3 (100.0) [6.5]	3 [1.4]
Undecided	3 (10.0) [18.8]	11 (36.7) [15.9]	9 (30.0) [10.1]	7 (23.3) [15.2]	30 [13.6]
Not in Holland [b]	1 (6.3) [6.3]	6 (37.5) [8.7]	7 (43.8) [7.9]	2 (12.5) [4.3]	16 [7.3]
Column Totals	16 (7.3)	69 (31.4)	89 40.5)	46 (20.9)	220

[a] Row percentages are in parentheses; column percentages are in brackets.
[b] Intended academic major not included in *The College Majors Finder* (Rosen, Holmberg, & Holland, 1989).

Distribution of Intended (1986) and Final (1990) Academic Environments of Males with a Dominant Social Personality Type [a]

1986 Academic Environments	1990 Academic Environments				Row Totals
	Investigative	Artistic	Social	Enterprising	
Realistic	3 (100.0) [5.1]	0 (0.0) [0.0]	0 (0.0) [0.0]	0 (0.0) [0.0]	3 [1.5]
Investigative	33 (60.0) [55.9]	5 (9.1) [20.0]	9 (16.4) [11.7]	8 (14.5) [18.2]	55 [26.8]
Artistic	0 (0.0) [0.0]	7 (70.0) [28.0]	2 (20.0) [2.6]	1 (10.0) [2.3]	10 [4.9]
Social	5 (9.4) [8.5]	6 (11.3) [24.0]	39 (73.6) [50.6]	3 (5.7) [6.8]	53 [25.9]
Enterprising	0 (0.0) [0.0]	2 (5.9) [8.0]	10 (29.4) [13.0]	22 (64.7) [50.0]	34 [16.6]
Conventional	2 (40.0) [3.4]	0 (0.0) [0.0]	0 (0.0) [0.0]	3 (60.0) [6.8]	5 [2.4]
Undecided	6 (22.2) [10.2]	5 (18.5) [20.0]	11 (40.7) [14.3]	5 (18.5) [11.4]	27 [13.2]
Not in Holland [b]	10 (55.6) [16.9]	0 (0.0) [0.0]	6 (33.3) [7.8]	2 (11.1) [4.5]	18 [8.8]
Column Totals	59 (28.8)	25 (12.2)	77 (37.6)	44 (21.5)	205

[a] Row percentages are in parentheses; column percentages are in brackets.
[b] Intended academic major not included in *The College Majors Finder* (Rosen, Holmberg, & Holland, 1989).

Distribution of Intended (1986) and Final (1990) Academic Environments of Females with a Dominant Social Personality Type [a]

1986 Academic Environments	1990 Academic Environments				Row Totals
	Investigative	Artistic	Social	Enterprising	
Realistic	1	0	0	0	1
	(100.0)	(0.0)	(0.0)	(0.0)	
	[1.6]	[0.0]	[0.0]	[0.0]	[0.3]
Investigative	25	4	12	3	44
	(56.8)	(9.1)	(27.3)	(6.8)	
	[39.7]	[8.7]	[6.3]	[6.1]	[12.6]
Artistic	2	12	5	2	21
	(9.5)	(57.1)	(23.8)	(9.5)	
	[3.2]	[26.1]	[2.6]	[4.1]	[6.0]
Social	13	12	133	11	169
	(7.7)	(7.1)	(78.7)	(6.5)	
	[20.6]	[26.1]	[70.0]	[22.4]	[48.6]
Enterprising	2	4	11	22	39
	(5.1)	(10.3)	(28.2)	(56.4)	
	[3.2]	[8.7]	[5.8]	[44.9]	[11.2]
Conventional	3	1	1	4	9
	(33.3)	(11.1)	(11.1)	(44.4)	
	[4.8]	[2.2]	[0.5]	[8.2]	[2.6]
Undecided	8	8	17	3	36
	(22.2)	(22.2)	(47.2)	(8.3)	
	[12.7]	[17.4]	[8.9]	[6.1]	[10.3]
Not in Holland [b]	9	5	11	4	29
	(31.0)	(17.2)	(37.9)	(13.8)	
	[14.3]	[10.9]	[5.8]	[8.2]	[8.3]
Column Totals	63	46	190	49	348
	(18.1)	(13.2)	(54.6)	(14.1)	

[a] Row percentages are in parentheses; column percentages are in brackets.
[b] Intended academic major not included in *The College Majors Finder* (Rosen, Holmberg, & Holland, 1989).

Distribution of Intended (1986) and Final (1990) Academic Environments of Males with a Dominant Enterprising Personality Type [a]

1986 Academic Environments	1990 Academic Environments				Row Totals
	Investigative	Artistic	Social	Enterprising	
Realistic	4 (30.8) [3.8]	1 (7.7) [4.3]	4 (30.8) [4.7]	4 (30.8) [4.1]	13 [4.2]
Investigative	46 (57.5) [43.4]	3 (3.8) [13.0]	17 (21.3) [19.8]	14 (17.5) [14.3]	80 [25.6]
Artistic	0 (0.0) [0.0]	3 (30.0) [13.0]	5 (50.0) [5.8]	2 (20.0) [2.0]	10 [3.2]
Social	4 (14.3) [3.8]	1 (3.6) [4.3]	18 (64.3) [20.9]	5 (17.9) [5.1]	28 [8.9]
Enterprising	32 (27.6) [30.2]	7 (6.0) [30.4]	22 (19.0) [25.6]	55 (47.4) [56.1]	116 [37.1]
Conventional	10 (41.7) [9.4]	3 (12.5) [13.0]	3 (12.5) [3.5]	8 (33.3) [8.2]	24 [7.7]
Undecided	4 (23.5) [3.8]	3 (17.6) [13.0]	5 (29.4) [5.8]	5 (29.4) [5.1]	17 [5.4]
Not in Holland [b]	6 (24.0) [5.7]	2 (8.0) [8.7]	12 (48.0) [14.0]	5 (20.0) [5.1]	25 [8.0]
Column Totals	106 (33.9)	23 (7.3)	86 (27.5)	98 (31.3)	313

[a] Row percentages are in parentheses; column percentages are in brackets.
[b] Intended academic major not included in *The College Majors Finder* (Rosen, Holmberg, & Holland, 1989).

Distribution of Intended (1986) and Final (1990) Academic Environments of Females with a Dominant Enterprising Personality Type [a]

1986 Academic Environments	1990 Academic Environments				Row Totals
	Investigative	Artistic	Social	Enterprising	
Realistic	1	0	0	0	1
	(100.0)	(0.0)	(0.0)	(0.0)	
	[1.8]	[0.0]	[0.0]	[0.0]	[0.4]
Investigative	11	0	16	7	34
	(32.4)	(0.0)	(47.1)	(20.6)	
	[20.0]	[0.0]	[15.7]	[7.4]	[12.3]
Artistic	1	8	4	2	15
	(6.7)	(53.3)	(26.7)	(13.3)	
	[1.8]	[30.8]	[3.9]	[2.1]	[5.4]
Social	6	2	43	8	59
	(10.2)	(3.4)	(72.9)	(13.6)	
	[10.9]	[7.7]	[42.2]	[8.5]	[21.3]
Enterprising	18	10	12	50	90
	(20.0)	(11.1)	(13.3)	(55.6)	
	[32.7]	[38.5]	[11.8]	[53.2]	[32.5]
Conventional	8	0	3	12	23
	(34.8)	(0.0)	(13.0)	(52.2)	
	[14.5]	[0.0]	[2.9]	[12.8]	[8.3]
Undecided	4	2	14	7	27
	(14.8)	(7.4)	(51.9)	(25.9)	
	[7.3]	[7.7]	[13.7]	[7.4]	[9.7]
Not in Holland [b]	6	4	10	8	28
	(21.4)	(14.3)	(35.7)	(28.6)	
	[10.9]	[15.4]	[9.8]	[8.5]	[10.1]
Column Totals	55	26	102	94	277
	(19.9)	(9.4)	(36.8)	(33.9)	

[a] Row percentages are in parentheses; column percentages are in brackets.
[b] Intended academic major not included in *The College Majors Finder* (Rosen, Holmberg, & Holland, 1989).

Socialization Effects of
Academic Environments

T HE PREVIOUS chapter focused on *college students* and the extent to
which they select academic environments (majors) consistent with
their perceptions of their own abilities and interests and with their dominant personality types. Holland (1997) notes that since "human behavior
depends upon both personality and the environment in which a person
lives and works, the personality types must be supplemented by environmental information" (p. 41). Thus, in this chapter we consider *academic
environments* of colleges and universities—in particular, certain consequences of being in one rather than another of these environments.

Although the educational or work environment is an absolutely essential component in Holland's theory, the research literature on such environments per se is not as abundant as that on other aspects of the theory.
The vast bulk of this literature concentrates instead on the validity of the
personality types and on the outcomes assumed to be the consequence of
the congruence or fit between individuals and their environments. In
essence, attention has been directed primarily to the educational and vocational choices of individuals and the significance of these choices for
their educational and vocational stability, satisfaction, and success. This
dominant focus on individuals may be understood as a consequence of the
primary focus of the theory itself and the scholarly interests of those who
have conducted most of the relevant research. Holland (1997) notes that
"the primary concern of the theory is to explain vocational behavior and

to suggest some practical ideas to help young, middle-aged, and older people select jobs, change jobs, and attain vocational satisfaction" (p. 1). Thus, as a theory of careers his theory is intended primarily to be of assistance to individuals in their search for satisfying and rewarding careers, and the research on the theory reflects this orientation toward individuals. Environments have not been a central concern; rather they serve as a necessary means to the ultimate end of assisting individuals in their choice of satisfying and rewarding careers.

The theory is thus psychological in nature (though by no means exclusively so) and intended for the use of counselors in their efforts to assist individuals in making educational and vocational decisions. Holland (1997) acknowledges that "the environmental models are only occasionally studied" (p. 160). As Walsh and Holland (1992) have put it: "We view the theory as primarily psychological in nature and one in which the personality variables are the most powerful and influential. . . . The theory tends to emphasize personal variables and lean on the concept of reinforcement" (p. 63). It is therefore not surprising, given the psychological orientations of Holland's theory and those who have conducted the bulk of the research on the theory, that educational and work environments, in general, and the interpersonal and social structural patterns of environmental reinforcement, in particular, have not been of central interest.

Nonetheless, that these environments require, reinforce, and reward the characteristics of the analogous personality types that dominate them is a basic assumption of Holland's theory, and this essential aspect of the theory has a more sociological view of environments implicit in it. This view is that the distinctive orientations of the faculty who constitute these environments and their respective expectations of students commensurate with their disciplines lead to different student outcomes. We refer to these differential patterns of student outcomes resulting from faculty influence as the socialization effects of academic environments and analyze them as such.

The extent to which the academic environments in Holland's theory differ in terms of the abilities, interests, and values they seek to develop or reinforce in students was discussed as part of the focus on faculty in chapter 4. Our attention in the present chapter is on the socialization effects of academic environments as manifested in longitudinal patterns of change and stability in students' interests and abilities; our assumption is that these patterns will be different for students who major in different academic environments. We begin with a review of existing research findings

on the validity of the socialization assumption and then present the findings of our own analysis of socialization effects.

Extant Evidence Concerning the Socialization Assumption

Of interest here are the patterns of change and stability in students' interests and abilities given the assumption that these patterns theoretically
should be different for students who major in different academic environments. We emphasize that, unlike the studies in the following chapter on
the congruence assumption, the studies included in this chapter consider
all students in the respective academic environments *irrespective of their
personality types.* The typical approach of these studies is to examine patterns of change and stability in students' abilities and interests while controlling for equivalent precollege measures. Because students tend to be
classified according to their final academic environments in these studies,
the students who constitute the "peer culture" of any one environment
have different personality types. (In contrast, in the following two chapters on the congruence assumption, students' personality types *and* their
academic environments are considered simultaneously.) As in the preceding chapter, we present only some illustrative examples of research findings because of the extant, comprehensive reviews of general research
findings on Holland's theory (see, for example, Hackett & Lent, 1992;
Osipow & Fitzgerald, 1995; and Walsh & Holland, 1992).

W. Bruce Walsh and his associates have conducted several studies assessing the impact of academic environments on students' perceptions of
change over time. Walsh and Lacey (1969) examined the premise that students' perceived patterns of growth over time should be consistent with
the norms and values of their respective academic environments. Their
study used the Perceived Change Inventory to assess perceptions of
growth and development for a sample of 150 male college seniors whose
majors were in each of the six academic environments included in
Holland's theory. Their findings provided mixed support for the socialization assumption of Holland's theory: students in Realistic, Investigative,
and Artistic environments reported changes consistent with the dominant
personality orientations of these three environments, but students in
Social, Enterprising, and Conventional academic environments did not.
In a parallel study Walsh and Lacey (1970) obtained relatively comparable
findings for college women. In general, women in Investigative, Artistic,
and Conventional academic environments reported changing in ways consistent with the modal personality types of their respective environments;

this consistency was not apparent for women in Social, Enterprising, and Realistic academic environments.

Walsh, Vaudrin, and Hummel (1972) investigated self-reports of growth over two quarters of an academic year for 154 male and 165 female freshmen enrolled in an undergraduate general psychology course. Their findings provide partial support—at best—for the premise that perceived growth in different domains varies for students whose expected academic majors are in the six academic environments. They did find that men and women who anticipated majoring in Investigative environments generally perceived more growth in Investigative traits than did those expecting to major in other environments; moreover, compared to those in other environments, men expecting to major in Artistic environments reported more growth in Artistic characteristics, and women anticipating to major in Conventional environments reported more growth in Conventional attributes. These investigators did not, however, find any differences associated with the students' academic environments concerning self-perceived growth in Realistic, Social, or Enterprising traits for either males or females. The small size and particular character of the sample on which the findings were based and the absence of any controls for precollege characteristics make their findings problematic. It is even questionable whether college freshmen in their initial two quarters of enrollment have sufficient involvement with the academic environments for the environments to have effects on their abilities and interests.

Smart (1985) examined changes in the intellectual, artistic, and leadership self-esteem of college students over a nine-year period. Equivalent measures of these three domains of self-esteem were obtained at the time students initially entered college and nine years later. The study was based on the responses of students attending eight distinct types of colleges and universities (as based on the Carnegie Commission typology of institutions). His findings were consistent with expectations from Holland's theory in that graduates of Investigative environments scored higher than graduates of other academic environments on intellectual self-esteem and graduates of Artistic environments scored higher than graduates of other environments on artistic self-esteem. Contrary to expectations, however, graduates of Enterprising environments did not score higher on leadership self-esteem than did their peers in Investigative and Artistic environments. His study also found that there were no differences among the graduates of the eight institutional types and that the differences among students in these academic environments were similar across the eight distinct types of colleges and universities.

The consistency of differences in the patterns of change and stability of students attending different types of institutions was also evident in Smart's (1997) study of students' self-reported career and leadership, artistic and cultural, and educational and social growth over a four-year period. Consistent with expectations from Holland's theory, students in Enterprising environments reported more growth than did those in other environments in terms of career and leadership development (e.g., job-related skills, leadership abilities); those in Artistic environments perceived more growth than did those in other environments in artistic and cultural development (e.g., cultural awareness and appreciation, ability to think critically); and students in Social environments reported more growth than did those in other environments in educational and social development (e.g., interest in graduate education, acceptance of people from different races and cultures).

A distinctive feature of the findings obtained in these two studies by Smart (1985, 1997) is that the differential pattern of change and stability in abilities, interests, and perceived growth for students in the different academic environments is similar for students enrolled in decidedly different types of colleges and universities. These findings suggest that the distinctive requirements, reinforcements, and rewards of the respective academic environments transcend specific institutional settings.

Huang and Healy (1997) found significant relationships over a four-year period between six work values of college students and their academic majors classified according to Holland's theory. In general, their findings are consistent with expectations derived from Holland's theory. After controlling for students' precollege scores on the six work values and a series of other student background and institutional characteristics as well as students' collegiate experiences, they found that majoring in Enterprising and Conventional environments was associated with high scores on "having administrative responsibility for the work of others" and "being very well-off financially"; majoring in Social environments was related to high scores on "helping others in difficulty"; and majoring in Artistic environments was associated with the importance of "creating artistic work." Moreover, Huang and Healy found an expected negative relationship between majoring in an Investigative environment and the work values that characterize majors in Enterprising, Conventional, Artistic, and Social academic environments.

Huang and Healy (1997) noted that, contrary to their expectations, students majoring in Investigative environments did not report higher scores on "becoming an authority in my field" and "obtaining recognition from my colleagues for contributions to my field" than did those major-ing in other environments. We do not share their expectations, howev-er, that these two items are primarily reflective of Investigative academic environments, and thus we would not have expected Investigative envi-ronments to have a positive effect on either item. Rather, both of the items have a decided status-attainment orientation and, in essence, are more reflective of Enterprising academic environments. In fact, these two items are included in our 1986 and 1990 scales of Enterprising abil-ities and interest, both of which have strong reliability estimates (see Table 3.3, pp. 66-67).

More recently Smart and Feldman (1998) examined patterns of change and stability in the abilities and interests of college students over a four-year period. Their findings provided mixed results in that the changes in abilities and interests of students majoring in Artistic and Enterprising environments generally conformed to expectations of Holland's theory, whereas changes for those majoring in Investigative and Social environments did not. These researchers found an accentuation or sharpening of initial differences among major-field groups on both Artistic and Enterprising abilities and interests. Their findings for Artistic abilities and interests show a clear and strong pattern of accentuation for the combined and separate samples of men and women in that the initial major-field differences were "sharpened" or accentuated over the four-year period; as part of this general accentuation students in Artistic envi-ronments not only had the highest score to begin with but made the greatest gain over the four-year period. Their findings also revealed a somewhat similar, but weaker, pattern of accentuation for the combined sample of males and females for Enterprising abilities and interests. The somewhat weaker support on this measure for the combined sample of male and female students was explained by the pattern of accentuation for Enterprising abilities and interests being clearer and stronger for males than for females. Contrary to expectations derived from Holland's theory, their findings provided no evidence of accentuation for either Investi-gative or Social abilities and interests.

The set of findings just discussed provides only partial support for the validity of the socialization assumption of Holland's theory. In general, the findings show a consistent pattern of support for the socialization effects of Artistic academic environments, a moderately strong pattern of support for the socialization effects of Investigative academic environments, and a mixed pattern for the socialization effects of Social and Enterprising aca-demic environments.

To give specifics, with a single exception (for female students in the study by Walsh, Vaudrin, and Hummel, 1972) each of the seven illustrative studies reviewed above found that students majoring in fields associated with Artistic academic environments reported stronger Artistic abilities and interests than did those majoring in fields associated with other academic environments. Thus, there is a clear and consistent pattern of evidence supporting the socialization assumption for Artistic academic environments. The collective findings of these studies suggest a somewhat similar, but weaker, pattern of support for the socialization effects of Investigative academic environments. In four instances the findings provide clear support for the socialization effects of Investigative environments (Walsh & Lacey, 1969, 1970; Walsh, Vaudrin, & Hummel, 1972; Smart, 1985); in two instances they provide partial support (Huang & Healy, 1997; Smart, 1997); and in one instance they provide no support (Smart & Feldman, 1998). In the two instances where the findings provide partial support, students who majored in Investigative environments did not score higher than those in other environments on items or scales intended to reflect the distinctive abilities and interests reinforced and rewarded by Investigative environments, although they did score lower than students in other academic environments on items or scales intended to represent the distinctive abilities and interests reinforced and rewarded by those other environments. One reason for these results may be that neither of the two studies (Huang & Healy, 1997; Smart, 1997) contained items or scales that were clearly reflective of the prevailing abilities and interests that Investigative environments seek to reinforce and reward. Overall, however, these collective findings provide moderately strong evidence in support of the socialization assumption in Investigative academic environments.

As a whole, the seven studies provide only mixed support for the validity of the socialization assumption for Social and Enterprising academic environments. In approximately half of the instances the socialization assumption was supported in these two environments. Thus, Huang and Healy (1997) and Smart (1997) found that students majoring in Social environments perceived greater growth in Social abilities and interests than did those majoring in other environments; this was not the case in any of the three studies conducted by Walsh and his associates (Walsh & Lacey, 1969, 1970; Walsh, Vaudrin, & Hummel, 1972) or in Smart and Feldman (1998). (Social environments were not considered by Smart, 1985.) A somewhat similar pattern emerged in the collective findings for Enterprising academic environments: three studies provided positive support (Huang & Healy,

1997; Smart, 1997; Smart & Feldman, 1998), and four studies did not (the three studies by Walsh and associates and the one by Smart, 1985).

The degree to which academic environments are "successful" in their efforts to socialize students to their respective patterns of abilities and interests thus appears to differ considerably, with Artistic and Investigative environments being the most "successful" and Social and Enterprising environments being less "successful." Building on the work in this area, the following section presents the findings obtained from our own analyses of patterns of longitudinal change and stability in students' abilities and interests based on their involvement in four of the six academic environments contained in Holland's theory.

Empirical Findings on Socialization

Our investigation of differential change and stability in college students focuses on self-perceptions of their abilities and interests as college freshmen in 1986 and four years later, as well as on their estimates of their own growth over that four-year period. We begin with students' self-reports of their abilities and interests as freshmen and four years later. Recall that the abilities and interests represented in the scales do not reflect the content or subject matter of a specific discipline but are more reflective of broad traits that multiple disciplines value and emphasize to a greater or lesser degree.

Change and Stability in Abilities and Interests

The analysis to follow is of the change and stability in the abilities and interests of students who majored in four of the six academic environments included in Holland's theory. We are interested here in the socialization of *academic environments* irrespective of the students' dominant personality types, given Holland's assumption that these environments reinforce and reward different groups of abilities and interests (as shown in Table 2.2). We examine similarities and differences among students at two points in time (1986 and 1990) to assess the assumption that students' changes in their self-reports of abilities and interests vary on the basis of their academic environments (Investigative, Artistic, Social, and Enterprising). Thus we have an interaction hypothesis: the change in students' self-reports of particular abilities and interests between 1986 and 1990 depends on the Holland academic environment.

In our analyses, described fully in chapter 3, we were interested in changes in students' perceived abilities and interests over time based on their academic majors (environments) and the extent to which these changes over the four-year period were similar for men and women as well as for primary and secondary recruits (indicated by similarity or dissimilarity of the students' majors in 1986 and 1990). Separate analyses were conducted for the Investigative, Artistic, Social, and Enterprising ability and interest scales described in Table 3.3. In each analysis the 1986 scale was adjusted for regression-to-the-mean effects (as described in chapter 3) since we were concerned with changes across time. The within-subjects independent variable in the repeated-measures analysis of variance design was students' assessment of abilities and interests in 1986 and 1990. Three between-subjects factors were included in the analysis to test for the possibility of interactions between the overall change and (1) the final academic major/environment of the student, (2) gender of the student, and (3) type of recruit to the major. A significant interaction between final academic environment and year would indicate that growth in abilities and interests between 1986 and 1990 was different for students in the two focal environments.

Each analysis had two levels for each of the three between-subjects factors as described in chapter 3. Thus, for instance, the two levels of students' academic environments in the analysis of students' change and stability in Social abilities and interests distinguished between students who were in Social academic environments and those who were in other environments, while in the assessment of change and stability in Investigative abilities and interests the two levels of students' academic environments distinguished between those who were and those who were not in Investigative academic environments.

Full results of the four analyses are presented in Appendix 6.A at the end of this chapter. In each analysis the interaction between students' final academic environment and year was statistically significant, indicating that the patterns of change varied in terms of the academic environment. There were also significant interactive effects between students' academic environments and either gender or type of recruit in three of the analyses. The patterns of change and stability in both Investigative and Artistic abilities and interests differed for primary and secondary recruits in the respective academic environments, while the pattern for Social abilities and interests differed for males and females. Results for students who majored in Enterprising and other environments on the Enterprising ability and interest scale were similar for men and women and for primary and secondary recruits.

Table 6.1 presents the means and standard deviations of the four 1986 and 1990 ability and interest scales for students classified according to their respective academic environments (and gender or type of recruit in those instances when significant interactive effects occurred). These means

Table 6.1
Means and Standard Deviations for 1986 and 1990
Ability and Interest Scales [a]

Investigative scale	1986		1990	
	Investigative	Non-Investigative	Investigative	Non-Investigative
Primary	54.956	48.034	56.752	47.717
	(5.999)	(5.670)	(9.402)	(9.461)
Secondary	50.858	49.364	52.725	48.292
	(6.202)	(6.219)	(9.843)	(9.328)

Artistic scale	1986		1990	
	Artistic	Non-Artistic	Artistic	Non-Artistic
Primary	57.770	49.085	62.555	48.338
	(6.579)	(6.383)	(10.001)	(8.843)
Secondary	54.086	49.057	57.930	48.429
	(6.536)	(6.566)	(9.969)	(9.100)

Social scale	1986		1990	
	Social	Non-Social	Social	Non-Social
Males	50.666	49.576	51.966	48.433
	(5.005)	(4.547)	(10.575)	(9.842)
Females	50.414	49.931	51.485	50.160
	(4.498)	(4.563)	(9.804)	(9.825)

Enterprising scale [b]	1986		1990	
	Enterprising	Non-Enterprising	Enterprising	Non-Enterprising
	51.074	49.692	43.391	49.048
	(5.986)	(5.876)	(9.911)	(9.770)

[a] Standard deviations are in parentheses.
[b] Results are similar for males and females, primary and secondary recruits.

Figure 6.1
Patterns of Change in Investigative Abilities and Interests

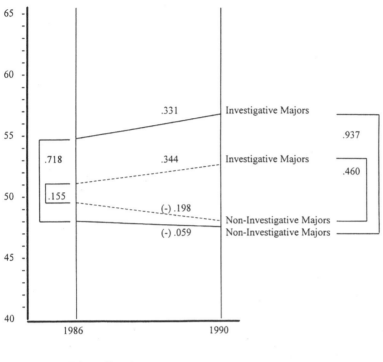

Primary Recruits
Secondary Recruits

are also plotted in Figures 6.1 through 6.4. The magnitude and direction of change for students in each type of academic environment are also shown on the graphs in terms of effect sizes. These effect sizes, which were calculated using the error mean squares from the within-subjects analyses, convert the difference between the 1986 and 1990 means for each group to standard-deviation units. A second set of effect sizes, calculated using the error mean squares from the between-subjects analyses, indicates the differences between students in the two types of academic environments in both 1986 and 1990. Comparison of these 1986 and 1990 effect sizes indicates the extent to which the two groups of students grow further apart in the strength of their abilities and interests as a function of being in an environment associated with those particular abilities and interests or not being in such an environment. We have organized the following discussion of results by the four ability and interest scales (the dependent variables in the analyses).

Investigative abilities and interests. As noted, Table 6.1 presents the means on the 1986 and 1990 Investigative ability and interest scales for students who were in Investigative and non-Investigative academic environments. Further, given the significant interaction between Holland environment and type of recruit, a distinction is made in the table as to whether students were primary or secondary recruits in Investigative and other environments. Because the results are more clearly depicted in the graphical representation of the interactions found, we focus on Figure 6.1.[1] The results presented in

---

[1] Figure 6.1 and all subsequent figures in this chapter as well as in chapters 7 and 8 represent the graphical plotting of the interactive effects of Holland environment and year. In conjunction with the depiction of the interaction, effect sizes have been added to the graphs in order to give more substantive meanings to the differences between the Holland groups and the differences between 1986 and 1990. To assist in the interpretation of these various graphs, we give a detailed description of the information presented in Figure 6.1.

The two solid lines in the figure represent the direction of change in Investigative abilities and interests between 1986 and 1990 for primary recruits. The upward slope for primary Investigative majors indicates that, on average, there was an increase in abilities and interests between 1986 and 1990, and the effect size of .331 denotes an increase of approximately one-third standard deviation. That is, the difference between their 1986 mean of 54.956 and their 1990 mean of 56.752 is approximately one-third standard deviation (see means given in Table 6.1). Equivalently, for the non-Investigative primary recruits, the slight downward slope indicates an average slight decline in Investigative abilities and interests of a magnitude of .059 standard deviations (the standardized difference between their 1986 mean of 48.034 and their 1990 mean of 47.717 given in Table 6.1).

The dashed lines shown in Figure 6.1 indicate the direction of change for secondary recruits. The upward slope for secondary Investigative majors indicates that, on average, these students increased in Investigative abilities and interests between 1986 and 1990, and the effect size of .344 shows that the increase was approximately one-third standard deviation (the standardized difference between their 1986 mean of 50.858 and their 1990 mean of 52.725 given in Table 6.1). The downward slope for secondary non-Investigative majors shows an average decline in Investigative abilities and interests of a magnitude of .198 standard deviation (the standardized difference between their 1986 mean of 49.364 and their 1990 mean of 48.292 given in Table 6.1).

The two effect sizes given in brackets for 1986 (.718 and .155) indicate the magnitude of initial differences in Investigative abilities and interests between Investigative and non-Investigative majors in 1986, for primary and secondary recruits, respectively. Primary Investigative and non-Investigative majors differ in 1986 by .718 standard deviation (the standardized difference between the primary Investigative majors' mean of 54.956 and the primary non-Investigative majors' mean of 48.034 given in Table 6.1) while secondary Investigative and non-Investigative majors differ by only .155 standard deviation (the standardized difference between the secondary Investigative majors' mean of 50.858 and the secondary non-Investigative majors' mean of 49.364 given in Table 6.1).

The comparable effect sizes given for 1990 (.937 and .460 for primary and secondary recruits, respectively) can be used to see how the initial 1986 differences between the focal groups have changed over the four-year period. In this case both differences are larger than they were in 1986. Primary Investigative and non-Investigative majors differ by .937 standard deviation in 1990 (the standardized difference between the primary Investigative majors' 1990 mean of 56.752 and the primary non-Investigative majors' mean of 47.717) while the secondary groups differ by .460 standard deviation (the standardized difference between the secondary Investigative majors' mean of 52.725 and the secondary non-Investigative majors' mean of 48.292).

Figure 6.1 clearly demonstrate not only that students majoring in Investigative environments began with higher self-ratings on the 1986 Investigative ability and interest scale than did students in non-Investigative environments but that they have still higher scores on these abilities and interests four years later, which makes them even more dissimilar (from students in other fields) at the end of college than at the beginning. Consider, for example, the results for primary recruits in Figure 6.1 (see solid lines) comparing the 1986 and 1990 effect sizes for those who began and completed their undergraduate programs in Investigative rather than non-Investigative environments: the effect size of the difference between these two groups increases from .718 in 1986 to .937 in 1990. The equivalent effect sizes for secondary recruits who changed to Investigative environments compared with non-Investigative environments are .155 in 1986 and .460 in 1990 (see dashed lines in Figure 6.1). Changes in the differences between these groups are the results of both groups of Investigative majors moderately *increasing* in their self-rated Investigative abilities and interests (.331 and .344 standard deviations for primary and secondary recruits, respectively) while primary recruits in non-Investigative majors do not really change (a negligible decline of .059 standard deviations) and secondary recruits decline somewhat on these abilities and interests (by .198 standard deviations).

It is reasonable to conclude from the pattern of findings illustrated in Figure 6.1 that Investigative environments do socialize students in a manner consistent with expectations from Holland's theory. These findings provide understanding of the significant interactions shown in Appendix 6.A. The significant interaction between Holland environment and year is manifested by greater differences between students in the two Holland environments in 1990 than in 1986: the magnitude and direction of change in abilities and interests of students are functions of the particular environment. The significant interaction between Holland environment and type of recruit is manifested by the magnitude of the differences between students in the two environments. There are much greater differences between Investigative majors and non-Investigative majors in both 1986 and 1990 for primary recruits than there are for secondary recruits. Nonetheless, the direction of change for Investigative majors is positive and that for non-Investigative majors is negative for both primary and secondary recruits. It is evident that students who began and completed their programs in Investigative environments (primary recruits) had stronger self-rated Investigative abilities and interests at the time they entered college *and* four years later than those who subsequently selected Investigative environments (secondary recruits). Both groups of Investigative majors show a moderate growth in the strength of their self-rated Investigative abilities and interests in absolute and relative terms, unlike their peers whose programs were in non-Investigative environments.

Artistic abilities and interests. The means on the Artistic abilities and interests scales in Table 6.1 are given separately for students who were primary and secondary recruits into Artistic and non-Artistic academic environments because of the significant interaction between environment and type of recruit. These same means together with the two types of effect sizes mentioned previously are presented in Figure 6.2. The interactive effects between environment and year for both primary and secondary recruits are clearly evident in Figure 6.2. Moreover, of the four kinds of interests and abilities under study, these results provide the clearest evidence supporting the socialization assumption of Holland's theory in that students in Artistic academic environments show a decidedly stronger pattern of growth in their self-rated Artistic abilities and interests over the four-year period compared to those in non-Artistic environments. This pattern is consistent for both primary and secondary recruits, and the interaction

Figure 6.2
Patterns of Change in Artistic Abilities and Interests

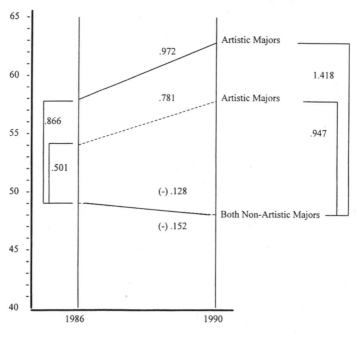

between environment and type of recruit is manifested by the magnitude of differences between Artistic and non-Artistic majors in both 1986 and 1990.

The magnitude of differences between students in Artistic and non-Artistic environments both at time of college entry and four years later is more pronounced than it is for the three other ability and interest scales. The large differences in 1986 indicates the strong selection effects discussed in chapter 5, while the even greater differences in 1990 indicate strong socialization patterns. This is evident in the results for primary recruits in Figure 6.2 (see solid lines) comparing the 1986 and 1990 effect sizes for those who began and completed their undergraduate programs in Artistic versus non-Artistic academic environments: the effect size of the difference between these two groups increases from .866 in 1986 to 1.418 in 1990, an increase of more than half a standard deviation. The equivalent pattern for secondary recruits shown in Figure 6.2 reveals an increase from .501 in 1986 to .947 in 1990, again, approximately half a standard deviation change. These changes in the magnitude of group differences are a result of the strong *increase* in self-rated Artistic abilities and interests for both the primary and secondary Artistic majors (.972 and .781 standard deviations for primary and secondary recruits, respectively) and the slight *decline* in these abilities for both groups of non-Artistic majors (.152 and .128 standard deviations for primary and secondary recruits, respectively).

These findings clearly show that Artistic academic environments not only attract students with stronger Artistic abilities and interests but also contribute significantly to substantial increases in these abilities and interests over the four-year period. Moreover, while there are substantial differences between students who major in Artistic compared with those who major in non-Artistic academic environments initially, these differences become more pronounced over time. Once again the significant interaction term in this analysis (between whether or not students were in Artistic environments and whether they were primary or secondary recruits to the environment) results from the magnitude of differences between the two environments for primary and secondary recruits rather than in the direction of change in this pattern. Students who began and completed their programs in Artistic environments (primary Artistic recruits) had stronger self-rated Artistic abilities and interests at the time they entered college *and* four years later than did those who subsequently selected Artistic environments (secondary Artistic recruits). But both groups of recruits to Artistic environments show a substantial pattern of growth in the strength of their self-rated Artistic abilities and interests in absolute and relative terms, unlike their peers whose programs were in non-Artistic environments

Social abilities and interests. Both the clarity of findings and the attendant support for the socialization assumption of academic environments in Holland's theory clearly evident in the first two analyses are decidedly less so for students' self-rated Social abilities and interests. The means on the Social scales are presented in Table 6.1 separately for male and female students whose undergraduate programs were in Social and non-Social academic environments (given the significant interaction between environment and gender). We focus our discussion on the graphical representation of the results presented in Figure 6.3.

Inspection of the 1986 effect sizes for men and women in Figure 6.3 reveals only small initial differences in the Social abilities and interests between those who majored in Social environments and those with majors in non-Social academic environments. Four years later, however, the magnitude of the differences between males with Social majors and those with majors in non-Social academic environments has more than tripled from .122 to .394, while the equivalent effect size for women in Social and non-Social

Figure 6.3
Patterns of Change in Social Abilities and Interests

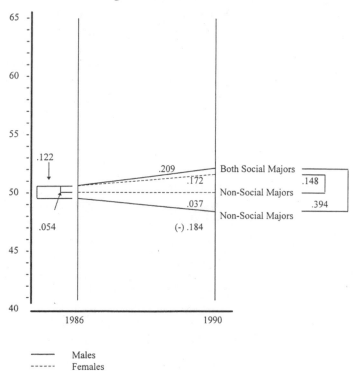

environments has increased from an initial .054 to .148. This change for males is due to both the *increase* in self-rated Social abilities and interests for those in Social majors (.209 standard deviations) and the *decline* (.184 standard deviations) for those in non-Social majors. The change in the magnitude of the group differences for females is due to the *increase* in scores for those in Social majors (.172 standard deviations) and the general *stability* in scores for those in non-Social majors (a change of only .037 standard deviations). While these initial and subsequent group differences are the smallest of any of the scales, the results nevertheless show a pattern of modest growth—for men in particular—in self-rated Social abilities and interests over the four-year period for students who majored in Social academic environments, unlike those who majored in non-Social environments.

Enterprising abilities and interests. The means on the Enterprising abilities and interests scales are given only for students in Enterprising and non-Enterprising environments since there were no interactions by gender or type of recruit. The patterns of change for the two groups of students are shown in Figure 6.4 along with the two types of effect sizes. The overall pattern of findings in Figure 6.4 provides general support for the socialization assumption of Holland's theory similar to those obtained in the analyses of Investigative and Artistic abilities and interests in that the mean differences between those who do and those who do not major in an Enterprising academic environment show increasing differentiation between 1986 and 1990. This pattern is the same for both males and females and for primary and secondary recruits. For the total group of students, the effect-size difference between those who majored in Enterprising and those with majors in non-Enterprising academic environments (on the Enterprising ability and interest scales) has virtually tripled from .141 in 1986 to .444 in 1990. The increase in the difference between the two groups of students is due to students in Enterprising majors *increasing* in their self-rated Enterprising abilities and interests (.413 standard deviations) while students in non-Enterprising majors *decreased* slightly (.115 standard deviations).

While the pattern of findings for Enterprising abilities and interest is generally similar to that obtained for both Investigative and Artistic abilities and interests, there are some subtle differences—mainly in the magnitude of differences between student groups at the time students entered college as well as four years later. In general, the initial and subsequent differences between student groups on the Enterprising ability and interest scales are not as great as those on either the Artistic or Investigative scale (especially the Artistic). Nonetheless, there is a clear and consistent pattern showing that students who majored in Enterprising academic environments developed

Figure 6.4
Patterns of Change in Enterprising Abilities and Interests

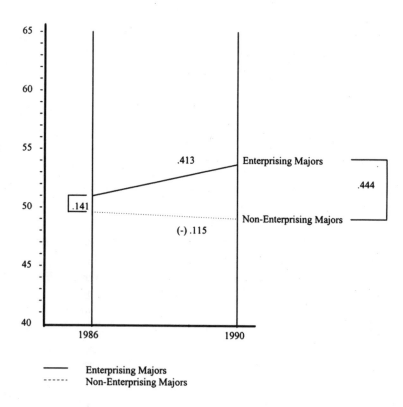

decidedly stronger Enterprising abilities and interests than did their peers in non-Enterprising environments, and this pattern is the same for men and women and for primary and secondary recruits.

Patterns of Self-Reported Growth

We also examined the socialization assumption of Holland's theory using a set of seventeen items (see Table 3.4, p. 69) assessing students' perceptions of their own growth over the four-year period. Based on Holland's assumption that academic environments reinforce and reward different groups of educational values and behaviors, we anticipated that the pattern of student growth and development would vary by chosen academic environment and that this variability would be consistent with the theoretical postulates of Holland's theory. Students majoring in Investigative environments, for example, theoretically should report more growth in areas consistent with descriptions of Investigative environments, those majoring in Social environments should report more growth in areas consistent with the descriptions of Social environments, and so forth.

Table 6.2 shows the assumed relationship between each of the seventeen areas of growth and the four academic environments from Holland's theory. Although the four environments are conceptually distinct, they do share some common emphases in terms of the abilities and interests they

Table 6.2
Relationship between Self-Reported Growth Items and Holland Environments [a]

Self-Reported Growth Items	Holland Environments			
	Investigative	Artistic	Social	Enterprising
Problem-solving skills	Unique			
Critical thinking ability	Shared	Shared		
Interest in graduate school	Shared		Shared	
Preparation for graduate school	Shared		Shared	
Ability to work independently	Shared	Shared		
Confidence in academic abilities	Shared		Shared	
Foreign language ability		Unique		
Cultural awareness		Unique		
Writing skills		Unique		
Public speaking ability		Shared		Shared
Tolerance of people with different beliefs			Unique	
Acceptance of different races and cultures			Unique	
Job-related skills				Unique
Leadership abilities				Unique
Interpersonal skills			Shared	Shared
Competitiveness				Unique
Ability to work cooperatively			Shared	Shared

[a] See Table 3.4 in chapter 3, p. 69, for full wording of items.

seek to reinforce and reward in students. For each of the academic environments in Table 6.2 we have indicated whether each of the seventeen areas of growth is uniquely related to that environment or shared with another environment. A blank space indicates that the area is not reflective of that environment. To give an example, job-related skills, leadership abilities, and competitiveness are attributes that are unique to Enterprising environments, but Enterprising academic environments also share emphases on the development of interpersonal skills and the ability to work cooperatively with Social environments and the development of public speaking ability with Artistic environments. Eleven areas of growth in Table 6.2 are neither uniquely characteristic of Enterprising environments nor shared by Enterprising and other environments.

A full description of the analytical procedures we used is presented in chapter 3. In brief, we used multivariate analysis of variance (MANOVA) to determine whether or not perceptions of growth differed across academic environments and if these differences were the same for male and female students and for primary and secondary recruits. Discriminant analysis was used to determine which patterns of growth on the seventeen self-reported growth items differentiated between the environments when the multivariate test was significant.

Four MANOVAs were conducted, with each analysis comparing a particular environment to the other three environments combined. For example, to assess whether or not the patterns of growth of students in Investigative academic environments were different from those in other environments, students' academic environments were classified as Investigative or non-Investigative. The same dichotomous classification scheme was used for the three other academic environments. Thus, in each analysis the measure of environment was a dichotomous classification of the students' academic environments and the seventeen self-reported growth measures were used to differentiate between the two environments. In addition, the post hoc discriminant analyses were conducted separately for males and females and for primary and secondary recruits when significant interactions emerged in the MANOVA results. Technical results for both the MANOVAs and discriminant analyses are given in Appendix 6.B at the end of the chapter. The findings obtained for each of the four academic environments are presented as follows: first, the correlations between the seventeen individual items and the discriminant function are discussed to identify the dimension of growth that differentiates the two groups of students; second, the centroids, which represent the means for the groups on the discriminant function, are noted; third, the discriminant coefficients, which identify the areas of growth that are the most important in differentiating between the two groups, are analyzed.

Investigative academic environments. Although there are significant overall differences in the perceptions of growth by students in Investigative and those in non-Investigative academic environments, the MANOVA results also indicate that the differences between students in Investigative and those in non-Investigative academic environments are not the same for primary and secondary recruits. Thus, two separate discriminant analyses were performed—one for each type of recruit. For both primary and secondary recruits the discriminant function was significant, and the multivariate effect size indicating the magnitude of the difference in growth between students in Investigative and students in non-Investigative environments is .519 for primary recruits and .382 for secondary recruits. Table 6.3 presents a summary of the results of these two analyses.

Table 6.3

Discriminant Analysis Differentiating between Investigative Majors and Non-Investigative Majors on Self-Reported Growth Items [a]

Self-Reported Growth Items	Primary Recruits	Secondary Recruits
[b] Problem-solving skills	.278 (.477)	.321 (.644)
[c] Critical thinking ability	.056 (.079)	- .181 (- .287)
[c] Interest in graduate school	- .040 (- .380)	.121 (- .040)
[c] Preparation for graduate school	.503 (.833)	.311 (.527)
[c] Ability to work independently	- .154 (.022)	- .233 (- .285)
[c] Confidence in academic abilities	- .255 (- .253)	- .141 (- .146)
Foreign language ability	.032 (.010)	- .317 (- .295)
Cultural awareness	- .023 (.104)	- .263 (- .120)
Writing skills	- .261 (- .357)	- .380 (- .261)
Public speaking ability	- .267 (- .069)	- .378 (- .412)
Tolerance of people with different beliefs	- .241 (- .263)	- .284 (- .118)
Acceptance of different races and cultures	- .159 (.031)	- .245 (- .116)
Job-related skills	- .403 (- .427)	.011 (- .073)
Leadership abilities	- .165 (- .086)	- .054 (.072)
Interpersonal skills	- .137 (- .028)	- .129 (.020)
Competitiveness	- .235 (- .070)	.046 (.067)
Ability to work cooperatively	- .218 (.032)	.131 (.432)
Centroids Investigative	.491	.458
Centroids Non-Investigative	- .235	- .164
Multivariate effect size	.519	.382

[a] Discriminant coefficients are in parentheses; see Table 3.4 in chapter 3, p. 69, for full wording of items.
[b] Trait unique to Investigative environments.
[c] Trait shared with another environment.

Inspection of the correlations between the seventeen items and the discriminant function for both primary and secondary recruits in Table 6.3 shows that the positive end of the dimension is defined primarily by items that are characteristic of Investigative environments (e.g., problem-solving skills and preparation for graduate school), while the negative end of the dimension is defined primarily by items that are neither unique to Investigative environments nor shared by them with other environments (e.g., job-related skills, writing skills, and public speaking ability). This pattern indicates that for both primary and secondary recruits the dimension differentiating students in Investigative environments from those in non-Investigative environments is a bipolar continuum of growth, with the positive end reflecting growth in Investigative areas and the negative end reflecting growth in non-Investigative areas.

The centroids for students in Investigative and non-Investigative academic environments are .491 and -.235, respectively, for primary recruits and .458 and -.164, respectively, for secondary recruits. The signs of the centroids indicate that both groups of students in Investigative academic environments perceive greater growth in Investigative areas and less growth in non-Investigative areas, while both groups of students in non-Investigative environments perceive greater growth in non-Investigative areas and less growth in Investigative areas. This overall pattern of findings provides clear evidence that both primary and secondary recruits in Investigative environments generally report more growth over the four-year period on Investigative traits than do their peers in non-Investigative environments.

The discriminant coefficients indicate that the primary areas of growth that differentiate between students in Investigative and those in non-Investigative environments are a combination of Investigative and non-Investigative traits with the patterns of differentiation consistent with expectations. For both types of students growth in preparation for graduate school (.833 and .527 for primary and secondary recruits, respectively), a trait shared by Investigative and Social environments, and growth in problem-solving skills (.477 and .644 for primary and secondary recruits, respectively), a trait that is unique to Investigative environments, contribute to group differentiation—with students in Investigative environments higher in these areas. For primary recruits growth in job-related skills (-.427), a non-Investigative characteristic, also differentiates students in Investigative environments from those in non-Investigative environments, with the first group of students perceiving less growth than did the second group of students. For secondary recruits perceived growth in public speaking ability

(-.412), a non-Investigative trait, is less for students in Investigative environments than for their counterparts in other environments.

The information in Table 6.3 also assists understanding of the significant interaction between Holland environment and type of recruit in our analysis of Investigative environments. This may be seen by comparing the relative importance of the two variables that define the positive end of the discriminant function in our analysis of differences between primary and secondary recruits in Investigative and other environments (as shown by the discriminant function coefficients in Table 6.3). Whereas perceived growth in problem-solving skills and preparation for graduate school have generally equivalent importance (.644 and .527, respectively) in differentiating between secondary recruits in Investigative and other environments, preparation for graduate school (.833) is decidedly more influential than problem-solving skills (.477) in differentiating between primary recruits in Investigative and those in other environments.

Artistic academic environments. There are significant overall differences in the perceptions of growth by students in Artistic and those in non-Artistic academic environments, with a multivariate effect size of .356. These differences are similar for men and women and for primary and secondary recruits, for no significant interactions were found. The results of the discriminant analyses examining the nature of the differences in the patterns of self-growth reported by students in Artistic environments and those reported by students in non-Artistic environments are presented in Table 6.4.

Inspection of the correlations in Table 6.4 indicates a bipolar continuum of growth, with the positive end of the dimension defined primarily by items that are uniquely characteristic of Artistic environments (foreign language ability, cultural awareness, writing skills), while the negative end of the dimension is defined by items that are neither unique to Artistic environments nor shared by them with other environments (e.g., leadership abilities, competitiveness, ability to work cooperatively). This dimension is similar to that seen with Investigative environments, with the dimension representing a continuum of growth from non-Artistic areas to Artistic areas. The positive group centroid for students majoring in Artistic environments (.572) locates them on the positive end of the function and indicates that they perceive greater growth in Artistic traits, while the negative centroid for students in non-Artistic environments (-.095) indicates that they perceive greater growth in non-Artistic traits. This overall pattern of findings provides clear evidence that students in Artistic environments report more growth over the four-year period on Artistic traits than did their counterparts in non-Artistic environments. The discriminant coefficients

Table 6.4

Discriminant Analysis Differentiating between Artistic Majors and Non-Artistic Majors on Self-Reported Growth Items [a]

Self-Reported Growth Items	All Students [b]
Problem-solving skills	- .117 (- .293)
[d] Critical thinking ability	.274 (.339)
Interest in graduate school	- .178 (- .135)
Preparation for graduate school	- .134 (- .183)
[d] Ability to work independently	- .030 (.120)
Confidence in academic abilities	- .079 (- .113)
[c] Foreign language ability	.486 (.415)
[c] Cultural awareness	.414 (.426)
[c] Writing skills	.468 (.486)
[d] Public speaking ability	- .002 (.055)
Tolerance of people with different beliefs	.111 (- .113)
Acceptance of different races and cultures	.170 (.107)
Job-related skills	- .200 (- .095)
Leadership abilities	- .301 (- .264)
Interpersonal skills	- .101 (- .182)
Competitiveness	- .252 (- .117)
Ability to work cooperatively	- .256 (- .242)
Centroids Artistic	.572
Non-Artistic	- .095
Multivariate effect size	.356

[a] Discriminant coefficients are in parentheses; see Table 3.4 in chapter 3, p. 69, for full wording of items.
[b] Results are similar for males and females, primary and secondary recruits.
[c] Trait unique to Artistic environments.
[d] Trait shared with another environment.

indicate that the primary areas of growth differentiating between the two groups of students are all uniquely Artistic characteristics: foreign language ability (.415), cultural awareness (.426), and writing skills (.486). In sum, the results provide clear and consistent evidence for the successful socialization effects of Artistic academic environments based on their distinctive pattern of reinforcement and reward as defined by Holland's theory.

Social academic environments. Although there are significant overall differences in the perceptions of growth by students in Social and students in non-Social academic environments on the seventeen items, the MANOVA results also indicate that the differences between students in Social and those in non-Social academic environments are not the same for males and females. Thus, separate discriminant analyses were performed for males and females. The discriminant function was significant in each analysis; the multivariate effect sizes are .410 and .235 for males and females, respectively. Table 6.5 presents the overall pattern of results for these two analyses.

For female students the pattern of correlations suggests a dimension similar to that seen for the Investigative and Artistic environments. The strongest positive correlations are associated with Social traits (although they are shared with Investigative environments, e.g., interest in graduate school, preparation for graduate school, confidence in academic abilities), while the strongest negative correlations are associated with non-Social traits (e.g., foreign language ability, problem-solving skills). Thus, the dimension differentiating female students in Social environments from those in non-Social environments is a bipolar continuum of growth, with the negative end reflecting growth in non-Social areas and the positive end reflecting growth in Social areas. The positive centroid for Social females (.219) indicates that they perceive greater growth in Social areas, while the negative centroid for non-Social females (-.163) indicates that they perceive greatest growth in non-Social areas. The discriminant coefficients indicate that the primary contributors to group differentiation are the following: growth in confidence in academic abilities (.513) and interest in graduate school (.303), traits shared by Social and Investigative environments; foreign language ability (-.503), an Artistic trait; and problem-solving skills (-.450), an Investigative trait. The pattern of differentiation is consistent with expectations—with the females in Social environments perceiving greater growth in confidence in academic abilities and interest in graduate school and less growth in foreign language abilities and problem-solving skills than the females in non-Social environments.

For male students the dimension differentiating those in Social and those in non-Social environments is more complex than what we have seen

Table 6.5

Discriminant Analysis Differentiating between Social Majors and Non-Social Majors on Self-Reported Growth Items [a]

Self-Reported Growth Items	Males	Females
Problem-solving skills	- .201 (- .421)	- .360 (- .450)
Critical thinking ability	.262 (.320)	- .167 (.012)
[c] Interest in graduate school	.382 (.454)	.404 (.303)
[c] Preparation for graduate school	.173 (- .152)	.277 (.190)
Ability to work independently	.022 (- .059)	.028 (.067)
[c] Confidence in academic abilities	.197 (.102)	.302 (.513)
Foreign language ability	.335 (.220)	- .545 (- .503)
Cultural awareness	.176 (- .006)	- .058 (- .099)
Writing skills	.343 (.217)	- .253 (- .228)
Public speaking ability	.064 (.100)	- .138 (.009)
[b] Tolerance of people with different beliefs	.305 (.396)	.081 (.018)
[b] Acceptance of different races and cultures	.136 (- .113)	.184 (.243)
Job-related skills	- .518 (- .594)	.136 (.090)
Leadership abilities	- .029 (- .031)	.068 (.100)
[c] Interpersonal skills	.113 (.127)	- .167 (- .217)
Competitiveness	- .034 (.109)	- .192 (- .358)
[c] Ability to work cooperatively	- .235 (- .372)	.023 (.021)
Centroids Social	.458	.219
Non-Social	- .151	- .163
Multivariate effect size	.410	.235

[a] Discriminant coefficients are in parentheses; see Table 3.4 in chapter 3, p. 69, for full wording of items.
[b] Trait unique to Social environments.
[c] Trait shared with another environment.

for students in Investigative and Artistic environments and for females in Social environments. This is because in these latter cases the continuum was clearly bipolar, as anchored by growth in areas not associated with the environment and growth in areas consistent with the environment. By contrast, for male students the strongest positive correlations between the items and the discriminant function are those for growth in interest in graduate school (a trait shared by Social and Investigative environments), foreign language ability (an Artistic trait), writing skills (an Artistic trait), and tolerance of people with different beliefs (a unique Social trait). The strongest negative correlations are those for growth in job-related skills (an Enterprising trait), ability to work cooperatively (a trait shared by Social and Enterprising environments), and problem-solving skills (an Investigative trait). We interpret this pattern as reflecting a more programmatic focus characterizing different majors, with the positive end appearing to be more associated with growth in social science and humanities areas and the negative end associated with growth in areas associated with jobs or careers.

The positive centroid for male students in Social environments (.458) indicates that they perceive greater growth in the social sciences and humanities than do their peers in non-Social environments, while the negative centroid for students in this latter group (-.151) indicates that they perceive less growth in these areas and greater growth in areas associated with jobs or careers. The discriminant coefficients indicate that the primary areas of growth differentiating the two groups are a combination of Social and non-Social characteristics and are generally consistent with expectations. Students in Social environments perceive greater growth in interest in graduate school (.454) and tolerance of people with different beliefs (.396) and less growth in problem-solving skills (-.421), job-related skills (-.594), and ability to work cooperatively (-.372) than do their peers in non-Social environments. The lesser growth seen in the ability to work cooperatively was unanticipated since this trait is shared by Social and Enterprising environments. In all, although the pattern of results for women in Social environments has a more simple structure and is more clearly supportive of Holland's theory, the results for men are also somewhat supportive.

Enterprising academic environments. The results comparing students in Enterprising and students in non-Enterprising environments are similar to those seen in the comparison of students in Artistic and non-Artistic environments. The MANOVA indicates there are significant overall differences in the perceptions of growth by students in Enterprising and those in non-Enterprising academic environments, and these differences are similar for men and women and for primary and secondary recruits (there being no significant interactions). The multivariate effect size indicating the magnitude of difference between the two groups is .551. The results of the discriminant analyses examining the nature of the differences in the patterns of self-growth reported by the two groups of students are presented in Table 6.6.

The pattern of correlations between the items and the function again indicates a rather simple structure, with the strongest positive correlations associated with characteristics of Enterprising environments (e.g., job-related skills, competitiveness, public speaking ability) and the strongest negative ones associated with non-Enterprising environments (e.g., preparation for graduate school). Thus, the dimension is similar to that seen for Investigative, Artistic, and female Social environments, with a bipolar continuum representing growth in non-Enterprising areas on the negative end and growth in Enterprising areas on the positive end. The positive group centroid for students majoring in Enterprising environments (.581) indicates that they perceive the greatest growth in Enterprising areas, while the negative centroid for students in non-Enterprising environments (-.166) indicates that their greatest perceived growth is in non-Enterprising areas. The discriminant coefficients indicate two primary areas of growth that differentiate between the two groups: greater growth in job-related skills (.435), an Enterprising characteristic; and lesser growth in preparation for graduate school (-.634), a non-Enterprising characteristic. This overall pattern of findings provides clear evidence that students in Enterprising environments report more growth over the four-year period on Enterprising traits than do their counterparts in non-Enterprising environments.

Socialization Effects of Academic Environments: Summary Observations

In all cases the findings from students in the four academic environments under study show a consistent pattern of their increasing differentiation (from other students) in the respective sets of abilities and interests that each environment is theoretically presumed to reinforce and reward. In general this pattern is produced by students in the specified academic majors increasing in their scores over four years on the corresponding abilities and interests scales, with students not in these majors decreasing in their scores. Moreover, except for male students in Social environments (where results were less straightforward), the analysis of students' self-reported estimates of their own growth over the four-year period shows a clear pattern of student-perceived growth on various abilities and interests that are characteristics of their respective environments.

Table 6.6

Discriminant Analysis Differentiating between Enterprising Majors and Non-Enterprising Majors on Self-Reported Growth Items [a]

Self-Reported Growth Items	All Students [b]	
Problem-solving skills	- .010	(- .001)
Critical thinking ability	- .174	(- .255)
Interest in graduate school	- .267	(- .037)
Preparation for graduate school	- .566	(- .634)
Ability to work independently	.176	(.033)
Confidence in academic abilities	.064	(- .003)
Foreign language ability	- .169	(- .087)
Cultural awareness	- .214	(- .248)
Writing skills	- .010	(.042)
[d] Public speaking ability	.397	(.259)
Tolerance of people with different beliefs	- .010	(.063)
Acceptance of different races and cultures	- .078	(- .093)
[c] Job-related skills	.454	(.435)
[c] Leadership abilities	.317	(.173)
[d] Interpersonal skills	.201	(.138)
[c] Competitiveness	.407	(.267)
[d] Ability to work cooperatively	.283	(.055)

Centroids	Enterprising	.581
	Non-Enterprising	- .166

Multivariate effect size	.551

[a] Discriminant coefficients are in parentheses; see Table 3.4 in chapter 3, p. 69, for full wording of items.

[b] Results are similar for males and females, primary and secondary recruits.

[c] Trait unique to Enterprising environments.

[d] Trait shared with another environment.

Our findings, then, provide clear evidence of the differential socialization effects of the four academic environments in a manner consistent with the assumptions of Holland's theory. Whether examining actual changes in students' ratings of their abilities and interests or their perceptions of their own growth over a four-year period, the evidence is compelling that students in the four distinctive academic environments change in ways that are consistent with the prevailing norms and values of the respective environments. Moreover, even when statistically significant interactive effects emerged between environment and gender and type of recruit, they generally reflected differences in the magnitude of change reported by male and female students or by primary and secondary recruits rather than differences in the substance of their patterns of change.

Our synthesis of extant research evidence suggested some variability in the extent to which academic environments have been found to be "successful" in their efforts to socialize students to the respective patterns of abilities and interests that each environment is assumed to require, reinforce, and reward. Past research suggests that the socialization efforts of faculty in Artistic and Investigative environments appear to have been more "successful" than those of their colleagues in Social and Enterprising environments. Our empirical findings, however, provide rather consistent evidence that all four academic environments are relatively successful in socializing students in a manner consistent with the assumptions of Holland's theory.

Our findings clearly parallel the strong, consistent, supportive evidence from earlier studies regarding the successful socialization efforts of faculty in Artistic and Investigative environments. At the same time our findings provide stronger supportive evidence for the success of the socialization efforts of faculty in Enterprising and Social environments than typically has been found in prior studies. This is especially the case for Enterprising environments in our analyses, where there is a clear and consistent pattern of increasing differentiation in self-rated Enterprising abilities and interests, as well as areas of perceived growth, between students majoring in Enterprising and those majoring in non-Enterprising academic environments.

To a lesser extent our findings also provide stronger evidence than have past studies for the success of the socialization effects of faculty in Social academic environments. While the initial and subsequent differences between students in Social and those in non-Social environments are not as great as those differences in the three other environments, they are consistent with the socialization assumption of Holland's theory in that, for both males and females, there is nearly a threefold increase in the differentiation between these two student groups' Social abilities and interests over the four-year period (although for female students this increase is from a mere

.054 standard deviation to a .148 standard deviation). Our findings for the Social environment differ from those of the three other environments in that there are substantial gender differences. For example, the pattern of findings for the self-rated abilities and interests of students is more supportive of Holland's theory for men than for women; however, the pattern of findings concerning students' estimates of their own growth is more supportive of Holland's theory for women than for men.

We offer two explanations for the stronger support our findings (compared to those of others) provide for successful socialization efforts of faculty in Enterprising and Social environments. First, the majority of extant studies that failed to support the socialization assumption for these two particular academic environments (Walsh & Lacey, 1969, 1970; Walsh, Vaudrin, & Hummel, 1972) focused solely on college freshmen in introductory psychology courses and examined patterns of change and stability for only one semester or year. It is questionable whether college freshmen have sufficient exposure to academic environments for their socialization efforts to have an effect, and the short time frame of these studies makes detection of any effect problematic. Second, our findings concerning student patterns of change and stability over a four-year period corrected for the regression-to-the-mean effect present in longitudinal research (see chapter 3), and this correction may have contributed to our more clear and consistent findings for students in Enterprising and Social environments.

Our findings are also consistent with the vignettes of the four academic environments presented in chapter 4 that were developed from our synthesis of extant research on faculty and our own empirical findings of differences among faculty in the four academic environments. What seems abundantly clear from these vignettes and from our findings in this chapter are that faculty do create academic environments in a manner consistent with postulates of Holland's theory and that these environments—through the efforts of their respective faculties—are primary contributors to differential patterns of change and stability in their students, irrespective of students' personality types.

The extent to which the socialization effects of the academic environments are comparable for different kinds of students in those environments, however, has not been considered in this chapter. In the next two chapters we use the congruence assumption of Holland's theory, explained in chapter 2, to explore the possibility that student acquisition of the distinctive patterns of abilities and interests that characterize each environment is conditioned by whether students' personality types are congruent or incongruent with their academic environments.

Appendix 6.A

Analysis of Variance Results: 1986 and 1990 Abilities and Interests Scales

Source	df	Investigative		Artistic		Social		Enterprising	
		MS	F	MS	F	MS	F	MS	F
Between-Subjects Effects									
Holland Environment	1	22863.00	245.74***	4618.48	458.61***	2721.66	33.79***	972.45	62.44***
Type of Recruit	1	2272.15	24.42***	2044.76	20.32***	237.04	2.94	241.39	2.52
Gender	1	5653.09	60.76***	510.43	5.07	37.54	.47	2838.02	29.67***
Holland by Type of Recruit	1	4891.58	52.58***	2077.29	20.65***	172.25	2.14	593.86	6.21
Holland by Gender	1	46.34	.50	18.86	.19	676.70	8.40**	399.46	4.18
Type of Recruit by Gender	1	89.84	.97	200.10	1.99	16.92	.21	176.41	1.84
Holland by Type of Recruit by Gender	1	97.16	1.04	27.59	.27	454.96	5.65	6.11	.06
Within plus Residual	2301	93.04		100.60		80.54		9.64	
Within-Subject Effects									
Year	1	255.72	8.69**	1793.32	74.02***	95.45	2.46	552.69	17.53***
Holland by Year	1	1055.17	35.88***	3306.00	136.45***	533.66	13.77***	1645.58	52.20***
Type of Recruit by Year	1	22.01	.75	22.78	.94	112.10	2.89	59.65	1.89
Gender by Year	1	739.04	25.13***	122.44	5.05	140.88	3.64	457.78	14.52***
Holland by Type of Recruit by Year	1	90.07	3.06	31.96	1.32	227.79	5.88	.01	.00
Holland by Gender by Year	1	12.81	.44	3.55	.15	86.94	2.24	7.00	.22
Type of Recruit by Gender by Year	1	12.78	.43	6.11	.25	14.11	.36	5.51	.17
Holland by Type of Recruit by Gender by Year	1	.25	.01	1.13	.05	1.43	.04	43.54	1.38
Within plus Residual	2301	29.41		24.23		38.74		31.53	

** $p < .01$; *** $p < .001$

Appendix 6.B

Multivariate Analyses of Variance and Discriminant Analyses Results: Self-Reported Growth

MANOVA	Investigative (df = 17,2246)		Artistic (df = 17,2246)		Social (df = 17,2246)		Enterprising (df = 17,2246)	
Source	Wilks Λ	F	Wilks Λ	F	Wilks Λ	F	Wilks Λ	F
Holland Environment	.934	9.363***	.958	5.815***	.974	3.561***	.912	12.708***
Type of Recruit	.992	1.084	.988	1.552	.994	.800	.993	.892
Gender	.963	5.014***	.980	2.640***	.959	5.650***	.958	5.852***
Holland by Type of Recruit	.982	2.468**	.992	1.081	.996	.554	.993	.940
Holland by Gender	.991	1.206	.986	1.848	.976	3.270***	.987	1.685
Type of Recruit by Gender	.990	1.365	.991	1.202	.989	1.470	.991	1.142
Holland by Type of Recruit by Gender	.994	.782	.986	1.859	.994	.836	.994	.757

Discriminant Analyses (df = 17):	Wilks Λ	X^2
Investigative—Primary Recruits	.896	120.206***
Investigative—Secondary Recruits	.930	83.520***
Artistic	.948	120.114***
Social—Males	.935	71.370***
Social—Females	.966	41.526***
Enterprising	.912	208.002***

$**p < .01; *** p < .001$

7

Person-Environment Congruence
and College Student Outcomes

I N T H I S chapter we look closely at the assumption of Holland's theory
that each personality type is most likely to flourish in a congruent environment (in Holland's scheme, the environment having the same label)
because each such environment provides opportunities, activities, tasks,
and roles corresponding to the competencies, interests, and self-perceptions of its parallel personality type. Specifically, it is assumed—other
things being equal—that congruence of person and environment is related to higher levels of educational stability, satisfaction, and achievement.

The personal and situational characteristics associated with person-
environment congruence become more explicit with an illustrative example of the formulations for both the personality type and the environment
involved. Consider, for instance, students classified as Artistic types who
are in Artistic academic environments, a clear case of perfect congruence.
Such Artistic students are provided the opportunities to engage in artistic
activities; to use their artistic competencies; to perform creative works
they value; to see themselves as expressive, original, and nonconforming;
and to exhibit personality traits of intuition, creativity, and idealism. In
turn, Artistic environments reinforce the self-images Artistic types bring
to the environment and reward them for the display of artistic values and
artistic personality traits such as expressiveness, creativity, and nonconfor-
mity. Perhaps as important is the other side of this coin: Artistic students

in Artistic academic environments are able to avoid more completely the activities they dislike, the demands for competencies they lack, the tasks and self-images they do not value, and the situations in which their personality traits are not encouraged.

Our findings in the preceding chapter clearly demonstrated the distinctive socialization effects of the respective academic environments. However, the analyses on which those findings were based did not distinguish between students who selected environments that were congruent with their dominant personality types and those who selected environments that were not congruent. This particular distinction is central to this chapter. The congruence assumption of Holland's theory proposes that the likelihood of students further strengthening their dominant patterns of interests and abilities at the time they enter college is contingent upon their subsequent selection of congruent academic environments in college. Although our findings in chapter 5 generally supported the self-selection assumption of Holland's theory—that people search for and select congruent environments—we also found that a substantial portion of college students did *not* initially (or subsequently) select academic environments congruent with their dominant personality types.

We begin this chapter with a review of existing research findings on the validity of the congruence assumption. This review is followed by the findings of our own analyses of the patterns of actual longitudinal change and stability in (self-rated) interests and abilities of students over a four-year period, as well as their perceived growth in these characteristics, for those whose dominant personality types were either congruent or incongruent with their academic environments.

Extant Evidence Concerning the Congruence Assumption

Of interest here is the assumption in Holland's theory that person-environment congruence tends to be positively associated with vocational and educational stability, satisfaction, and success. The most common research strategy used to examine the validity of this assumption has been to determine differences between students and employed adults classified as congruent or incongruent with their environments on a variety of important educational and vocational outcomes (for example, stability or persistence, satisfaction, performance). In general, individuals are classified as being congruent or incongruent based on a comparison of the similarity of their personality profiles (using the VPI, SDS, or SCII, for example) with the Holland code definitions of their environments (using the EAT, *The College*

Majors Finder, Dictionary of Holland Occupational Codes, for example). "The majority of studies have employed primarily the first letter agreement (of person and of environment) as the measure of congruence" (Walsh & Holland, 1992, p. 56). For instance, a student whose dominant personality type is Enterprising and whose choice of a college major (environment) is business administration (also Enterprising) is classified as congruent (first letter agreement index). A more complete description of the measurement of person-environment congruence is given in chapter 2.

In addition to the reviews by Holland (1985, 1997) of the research evidence regarding the validity of the congruence assumption, there have been at least five other comprehensive reviews of the literature (Assouline & Meir, 1987; Spokane, 1985, 1996; Tranberg, Slane, & Ekeberg, 1993; Walsh & Holland, 1992). In general these reviews provide many positive but weak findings suggesting that congruence is associated with educational and vocational stability, satisfaction, and adjustment. Representative of these summaries are those by Assouline and Meir (1987), who conducted a meta-analysis of forty-one congruence studies. Their findings showed a rather small but consistent pattern of correlations indicating a positive relationship between congruence and a variety of important vocational and educational outcomes. Spokane (1985) reported a pattern of consistent but moderate positive relationships between congruence and satisfaction in his meta-analytic study; the correlations ranged from .15 to .54.

As in the two preceding chapters, we present here only some illustrative examples of research findings because of the availability of the comprehensive reviews just noted. We pay primary attention to studies of college students and employed college graduates because of our focus on the applicability of Holland's theory in higher education settings. Since the congruence assumption proposes that person-environment fit will be positively associated with higher levels of educational stability, satisfaction, and success, the following discussion is ordered according to these three important outcomes.

Congruence and Stability

Research in this area generally examines the extent to which person-environment fit is positively associated with persistence (stability) in academic environments by asking whether students whose personality types are congruent with their academic environments (majors) are more likely to persist than those who are incongruent. The findings in general show a weak positive relationship between congruence and stability. For example, Spokane, Malett, and Vance (1978) studied the curricular changes of liberal arts students and found that those whose dominant personality types were congruent rather than incongruent with their initial academic majors (environments) had fewer curricular changes over a five-semester period. Similar findings were reported by Bruch and Krieshok (1981) in their study of engineering students over a two-year period. Those students having a dominant Realistic or Investigative personality type, either of which is congruent with most engineering fields, persisted with significantly greater frequency than those students with Artistic, Social, Enterprising, or Conventional personality types.

The majority of studies in this domain have been based on the career patterns of employed adults, and Holland (1997) concludes that the collective findings in this area suggest that "congruence of person and job leads to stability and continuity over long periods of time" (p. 131). For example, Wiener and Vaitenas (1977) compared the personality profiles of 45 adults employed in management and sales (Enterprising) occupations who intended to make career changes and 66 adults in comparable occupations who intended to remain in the same occupation. Their findings support the positive relationship between congruence and job stability in that those who intended to change career fields had lower scores on such Enterprising personality traits as ascendance, dominance, and endurance. More recently Richards (1993) found that persistence of 2,710 individuals in forty different scientific (Investigative) occupations or specialties was positively associated with their Investigative personality scores and negatively associated with their Social scores—as predicted by the theory. Similar support for the positive relationship between congruence and job stability has been reported by Gade, Fuqua, and Hurlburt (1988); Hesketh and Gardner (1993); and Meir, Melamed, and Abu-Freha (1990). Although such studies have consistently found a positive relationship between person-environment congruence and educational and vocational stability, the magnitude of the relationship tends to be modest in size, as seen in the results of meta-analyses by Assouline and Meir (1987); Spokane (1985, 1996); Tranberg, Slane, and Ekeberg (1993); and Walsh and Holland (1992).

Congruence and Satisfaction

Of the three kinds of relationships being considered here (each for a different outcome), the one between congruence and educational or vocational satisfaction has been the most studied and has produced the strongest and most positive findings. Smart (1987) examined the relationship between person-environment fit and satisfaction with graduate school for a sample of 3,929 students who had completed their baccalaureate degrees and were enrolled in a graduate program. His measure of person-environment fit was based on the congruence between students' undergraduate and graduate majors. Compared with incongruent students, congruent students were significantly more satisfied with faculty-student relations and peer relations in their graduate programs. In addition Smart, Elton, and McLaughlin (1986), who examined the job satisfaction of college students five years after completion of their baccalaureate programs, found that the level of congruence between the undergraduate majors (environments) of these persons and their current occupations was positively related to their current satisfaction with their jobs. Separate analyses conducted for men and women yielded slightly different findings: for males congruence was positively related to their satisfaction with both intrinsic and extrinsic job satisfaction, whereas for females congruence was positively related to intrinsic and overall job satisfaction but not to extrinsic job satisfaction. Elton and Smart (1988) explored the satisfaction of 1,869 college graduates with the incomes, fringe benefits, opportunities for promotion, and security of their jobs five years after completion of their baccalaureate programs. The measure of person-environment fit in this study, like that in Smart, Elton, and McLaughlin, was the congruence between students' undergraduate majors and current occupations. Their findings, in general, showed that congruence was positively related to satisfaction with income, fringe benefits, and opportunity for promotion within present job. Congruence, however, was not related to satisfaction with job security.

The three studies by Smart and his colleagues just reviewed are but more recent examples of literally dozens of studies that have consistently found at least some positive relationships between person-environment congruence and educational or vocational satisfaction. For instance, Holland (1958), who studied 2,347 students at twenty-seven colleges and universities, obtained mixed results for male and female students in terms of the extent to which their congruence with the college environment was related to their overall satisfaction with college: congruence was positively related to satisfaction for females and negatively related for males. Mixed results were also obtained by Morrow (1971) in his study of 323 students majoring in mathematics and sociology. Satisfaction with students' academic majors was significantly related to congruence for mathematics students but not for sociology students.

Walsh and colleagues have conducted a number of studies that specifically tested the congruence-satisfaction assumption. Walsh and Russell (1969) and Walsh and Lewis (1972) found that students who selected congruent major fields of study (environments) had fewer adjustment problems during college than those who made incongruent choices. Specifically, Walsh and Russell found that congruent students reported fewer personal adjustment problems, and Walsh and Lewis found that congruent students had higher levels of personal integration and lower anxiety levels than students who had made incongruent choices of academic environments. Frantz and Walsh (1972), similar to Smart (1987), found that graduate students whose personality types were congruent rather than incongruent with their academic major were more satisfied with their graduate studies. Finally, Walsh, Spokane, and Mitchell (1976) found that male and female undergraduate students who made congruent choices of college majors were more satisfied with their academic choices than were those who had made incongruent choices.

There have been numerous studies of the congruence-satisfaction assumption with samples of employed adults in disparate occupations, and the findings from such studies also tend to support the premise that higher levels of person-environment congruence are positively related to job satisfaction. For example, higher levels of congruence have been found to be significantly related to higher levels of job satisfaction for elementary and secondary teachers (Wiggins, 1976; Wiggins, Lederer, Salkowe, & Rys, 1983), engineers (Meir & Erez, 1981), nurses (Hener & Meir, 1981), accountants (Aranya, Barak, & Amernic, 1981), and bank tellers (Gottfredson & Holland, 1990; Meir & Navon, 1992).

The collective evidence from such studies suggests a consistent pattern of findings that support the premise that person-environment congruence is positively related to individuals' satisfaction with their educational and vocational careers. Although consistent and positive, the findings are far from perfect and occasionally yield contradictory or mixed results. For example, estimates from meta-analytic studies indicate that the strength of the relationship ranges from .15 to .54 (Spokane, 1985, 1996) with a mean correlation of .21 (Assouline & Meir, 1987). In addition, the findings occasionally report discrepant findings for males and females (e.g., Holland, 1958) and for individuals in different academic or work environments (e.g., Morrow, 1971). Nonetheless, the collective weight of the evidence supports the conclusion that person-environment congruence is positively related to educational and vocational satisfaction, albeit to a small-to-moderate extent.

Congruence and Success

Substantially less research has been done on whether or not person-environment congruence is positively related to educational and vocational success (performance, achievement)—as differentiated from stability and satisfaction. Moreover, the extant findings in this area are perhaps the weakest. The relative infrequency of such studies may be due to the sheer conceptual and logistical difficulty of obtaining measures of success, performance, and achievement in either educational or vocational settings. The weak relationship commonly found between congruence and success may be due to conceptual fuzziness and difficulties with measurement associated with assessing educational and occupational success (achievement, performance).

Some supporting evidence has been found for person-environment congruence and success. For example, Posthuma and Navran (1970) used the VPI to assess the congruence between 110 students and 44 faculty members. Their findings were generally positive in that students whose personality profiles were congruent with those of faculty members had higher academic performance levels than did incongruent students. Additional supportive findings were also obtained in other studies. Reutefors, Schneider, and Overtone (1979) examined the relationship between congruence and academic achievement for 392 male and 424 female college freshmen. Their findings showed not only that congruent students achieved higher grade-point averages than incongruent students but that this tendency was true for both males and females. Bruch and Krieshok (1981), in their study of students in an engineering program that emphasized mathematical and scientific (Investigative) course work, found that congruent students (those with high-point VPI code on the Investigative scale) achieved a higher mean grade-point average than incongruent students. Richards's (1993) ten-year longitudinal study of 2,710 population scientists found that those with congruent personality profiles had higher productivity levels than those with incongruent profiles. Smart and Feldman (1998) present data supportive of predictions based on congruence for students in Artistic and Enterprising (but not Investigative or Social) academic majors. Reflective of the weak and even contradictory findings in this area, however, were those obtained by Frantz and Walsh (1972), showing no relationship between congruence and students' academic achievements.

Empirical Analyses of Person-Environment Congruence Assumption

Although our data do not permit a direct test of the explicit propositions in Holland's theory that students' stability in, satisfaction with, and performance in their academic environments are a function of their fit or congruence with those environments, they do enable us to test some of these propositions in an indirect manner. We know from the findings of our preceding analyses that students generally tend to select academic environments that are consistent with their strongest pattern of abilities and interests and their dominant personality types (shown in chapter 5). The findings also show that the academic environments tend to socialize students, irrespective of their personality types, to develop further their abilities and interests that are distinctly consistent with the prevailing norms and values of the respective academic environments (shown in chapter 6). The person-environment congruence assumption would lead us to expect students' patterns of change or growth to be greater for those whose dominant personality types are congruent with their academic environments than for those whose dominant personality types are incongruent with their environments.

The likelihood of change or growth in students' dominant patterns of interests and abilities as college freshmen, then, is predicted to be conditional upon their subsequent entry and persistence in academic environments congruent with their dominant personality types. For example, students with a dominant Artistic personality type enter college with stronger Artistic abilities and interests than their peers with dominant Investigative, Social, and Enterprising personality types. The congruence assumption of Holland's theory postulates that growth in these distinguishing abilities and interests of Artistic students will be a function of whether or not they subsequently enter an Artistic academic environment. Those who major in academic environments classified as Artistic (congruent) should exhibit greater growth in Artistic abilities and interests than do their peers who have in common a dominant Artistic personality type as freshmen but who major in academic environments classified as Investigative, Social, and Enterprising (which are incongruent).

To examine this assumption we focus on the dominant personality types of students at college entrance, their subsequent academic environments, and the change and stability in the patterns of their abilities and interests between 1986 and 1990. The series of analyses to follow differ from those reported in the preceding chapter (on the socialization assumption) in that the present analyses consider both the dominant personality types of students *and* the congruence with their chosen academic environments. (The analyses pertaining to the socialization assumption focused only on students' academic environments and did not consider either the dominant personality types of students or the congruence of those personality types with their academic environments.) We anticipate differential change and stability in students' abilities and interests depending on the congruence or incongruence between their dominant personality types and their academic environments.

Our strategy was as follows. First, we selected students of a given personality type (e.g., Enterprising) according to the procedures described previously in chapter 3. Second, we identified the actual academic majors/environments of these students and determined whether their dominant personality type was congruent or incongruent with those environments. We thus distinguished between students who had been in congruent environments and those who had been in incongruent environments: for example, students with a dominant Enterprising personality type who had been in an Enterprising academic environment were classified as congruent, while those who had been in any of the three other environments were classified as incongruent. Based on Holland's theory, we expected that students with a dominant Enterprising personality type who had been in a congruent academic environment (i.e., Enterprising) would show more growth on Enterprising abilities and interests over the four-year period than would those who had been in other academic environments (i.e., Investigative, Artistic, Social). We followed this strategy of analysis for each of the four personality types.

Our analyses used the same two sets of measures employed in the assessment of the socialization assumption reported in chapter 6. The first set of items included the self-ratings of their abilities and interests by students in 1986 and 1990. These items were used to form the ability and interest scales described in chapter 3 and shown in Table 3.3. The second set of items consisted of student responses on the 1990 follow-up survey to a question about their growth in seventeen areas over the four-year period. These items were also discussed in chapter 3 and are shown in Table 3.4. Given the congruence assumption of Holland's theory, we anticipated that students who had been in academic environments congruent with their dominant personality types would show more growth on items or scales characteristic of those academic environments than would students of similar personality types who were in incongruent environments. Again we want to emphasize that the items and scales used do not reflect content specific to disciplines but rather broad abilities and interests that the disparate disciplines within Holland groups similarly emphasize and value.

Change and Stability in Abilities and Interests

For our analysis we have defined "higher levels of achievement" in Holland's theory as students' growth in abilities and interests reflective of their dominant personality types. Similarities and differences among students are examined at two points in time (1986 and 1990) to assess the assumption that congruence between students' dominant personality types and their academic environments fosters higher levels of achievement of the distinctive abilities and interests that characterize the four personality types and academic environments. We again used analysis of variance with repeated measures to examine this assumption. Separate analyses were conducted for each of the four ability and interest scales shown in Table 3.3. In each analysis the 1986 scale was adjusted for regression-to-the-mean effects since we were concerned with changes across time. This adjustment is also described in chapter 3. The within-subjects independent variable in the repeated-measures analysis of variance was the student's self-rated assessment of abilities and interests in 1986 and 1990. Three between-subjects factors were included in the analysis to test for the possibility of interactions between the overall change and (1) congruence between the student's personality type and his or her academic environment, (2) gender of the student, and (3) similarity or dissimilarity of the student's major in 1986 and 1990 (as an indicator of whether the student was a primary or secondary recruit to the major). The focal interest in these analyses was the pattern of change and stability in self-rated interests and abilities of students over time based on the congruence between their personality types and academic environments and the extent to which these changes were similar for men and women and for primary and secondary recruits. A significant interaction between year and congruence between personality type and academic environment would indicate that growth in abilities and interests between 1986 and 1990 depended on the fit of personality and environment.

Each of the four analyses had two levels for each of the three between-subjects factors. The two gender levels were males and females. The two levels in the similarity of students' 1986 and 1990 academic majors were those who had similar majors (primary recruits) and those who had dissimilar majors (secondary recruits) at these two points in time. The two levels of congruence distinguished between those who majored in academic environments that were congruent and those with majors incongruent with their dominant personality types.

The full results of the four analyses are presented in Appendix 7.A at the end of this chapter. In interpreting our statistical results we used α = .05 for all analyses because of the smaller sample sizes resulting from the selection of students of a single personality type for each analysis. For Investigative, Artistic, and Enterprising students there was a significant interaction between year and the congruence of personality type and academic environment, indicating that the patterns of change varied as a function of academic environment and thus supporting the congruence assumption for three of the four groups of students. There was also a significant interaction for Investigative students involving type of recruit, indicating that the pattern of change differed for primary and secondary recruits. No significant effects were found for Social students.

Table 7.1 presents the means of the four 1986 and 1990 ability and interest scales for students classified according to the congruence between their personality types and academic environments. These means are also plotted in Figures 7.1 through 7.5; the magnitude and direction of change for students in each type of academic environment are also shown on the graphs in terms of effect sizes. These effect sizes, which were calculated using the error mean squares from the within-subjects analyses, convert the difference between the 1986 and 1990 means for each group to standard-deviation units. A second set of effect sizes, calculated using the error mean squares from the between-subjects analyses, indicates the differences between students in congruent and incongruent environments in both 1986 and 1990. Comparison of these 1986 and 1990 effect sizes indicates the extent to which the two groups of students grow further apart in the strength of their abilities and interests as a function of being in congruent and incongruent environments. We have organized the following discussion of results by the four personality types and whether or not they were in congruent or incongruent academic environments.

Investigative personality types. As noted, Table 7.1 presents the means on the 1986 and 1990 Investigative ability and interest scales for students who have a dominant Investigative personality type and who were in congruent (i.e., Investigative) and incongruent academic environments. Separate results are presented for primary and secondary recruits who had a dominant Investigative personality type, for this personality type—alone among the four types—showed a statistically significant interaction term involving type of recruit. The results given in Table 7.1 are more clearly

Table 7.1

Means and Standard Deviations for 1986 and 1990 Ability and Interest Scales [a]

Investigative scale	1986		1990	
	Congruent	Incongruent	Congruent	Incongruent
Primary	57.209	52.576	58.737	53.079
	(5.228)	(4.736)	(9.065)	(9.001)
Secondary	55.109	54.155	57.201	52.286
	(4.945)	(5.354)	(8.705)	(8.863)

Artistic scale [b]	1986		1990	
	Congruent	Incongruent	Congruent	Incongruent
	58.580	56.293	62.369	54.872
	(5.429)	(6.591)	(9.782)	(10.208)

Social scale [b]	1986		1990	
	Congruent	Incongruent	Congruent	Incongruent
	53.798	54.275	54.609	53.730
	(4.106)	(4.243)	(9.824)	(9.880)

Enterprising scale [b]	1986		1990	
	Congruent	Incongruent	Congruent	Incongruent
	55.187	55.241	57.394	55.312
	(4.860)	(4.887)	(9.057)	(9.480)

[a] Standard deviations are in parentheses.
[b] Results are similar for males and females, primary and secondary recruits.

depicted in the graphical representation of the interactions found in Figures 7.1 and 7.2 (see footnote 1 in chapter 6, p. 150, for a detailed description of interpretation of the graphs of the interactions).

The overall pattern of findings for students with a dominant Investigative personality type shown in Table 7.1 and Figures 7.1 and 7.2 provides results consistently supportive of the assumption that those who enter congruent (i.e., Investigative) academic environments generally develop stronger self-rated Investigative abilities and interests over the four-

Figure 7.1

Patterns of Change in Investigative Abilities and Interests—Primary Recruits

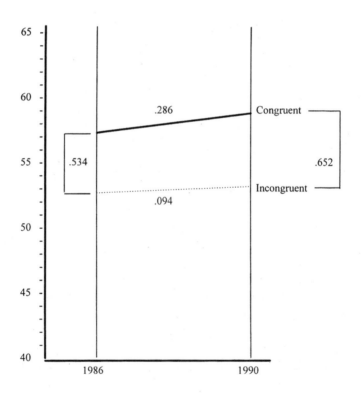

———— Congruent (Investigative Person in Investigative Major)
------ Incongruent (Investigative Person in Non-Investigative Major)

Figure 7.2

Patterns of Change in Investigative Abilities and
Interests—Secondary Recruits

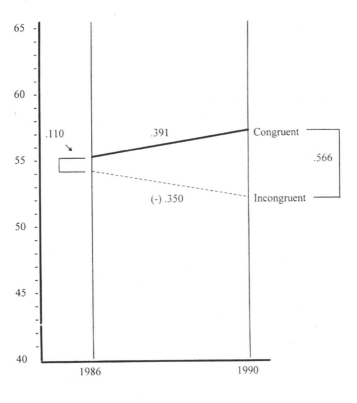

───── Congruent (Investigative Person in Investigative Major)
----- Incongruent (Investigative Person in Non-Investigative Major)

year period than do those who enter incongruent environments. For both
primary and secondary recruits, those who majored in congruent
(Investigative) academic environments showed a decidedly stronger pat-
tern of growth in Investigative abilities and interests than their
Investigative peers who entered incongruent environments (Artistic,
Social, and Enterprising). This is evidenced by the increases in

Investigative interests and abilities over the four-year period of .286 and
.391 standard deviations for primary and secondary recruits, respectively.
By contrast, as shown by the broken lines in Figures 7.1 and 7.2, primary
recruits in incongruent environments were more or less *stable* in their interests and abilities (a change of only .094 standard deviations), whereas
secondary recruits in incongruent environments actually showed a *decrease*
of .350 standard deviations.

The effect sizes comparing Investigative students in congruent environments with those in incongruent environments in 1986 indicate that
the two groups of students differed in the strength of their Investigative
abilities, with students in congruent environments having stronger initial
traits than those in incongruent environments. This tendency was much
greater for primary recruits where the two groups differed by .534 standard deviations than for secondary recruits who differed by only .110 standard deviations. This differentiation between students in congruent and
students in incongruent environments became more pronounced in 1990
(differences of .652 and .566 standard deviations for primary and secondary recruits, respectively). This increase in differentiation between
students in congruent and those in incongruent environments (in
Investigative abilities and interests) during the college years is four times
greater for secondary recruits than for primary recruits. For secondary recruits the difference in effect size between 1986 and 1990 is +.456 (.566 -
.110), whereas the change in effect size for primary recruits is only +.118
(.652 - .534).

Thus, the findings from the separate analyses for primary and secondary recruits show a common pattern of increasing Investigative abilities and interests over the four-year period for those who are congruent.
The greater magnitude of change in differentiation between congruent
and incongruent groups in the findings for secondary recruits results from
the actual decline in Investigative abilities and interests for those who were
in non-Investigative (incongruent) academic environments; for primary
recruits who were in incongruent academic environments the pattern reveals a more or less consistent level of Investigative abilities and interests
over the four-year period. The somewhat different findings obtained for
primary and secondary recruits in these analyses may be a function of the
fact that primary recruits who entered congruent environments and those
who entered incongruent academic environments were considerably more
different from each other in 1986 than were secondary recruits who entered the two types of environments (compare 1986 effect sizes in Figures
7.1 and 7.2). Our confidence in this explanation is not great, however,

since we did not find a similar interaction for the three other personality types.

Artistic personality types. The findings for Artistic personality types provide the strongest support among the four personality types for the congruence assumption in Holland's theory. The means on the 1986 and 1990 Artistic ability and interest scales for students who have a dominant Artistic personality type and who were in congruent (i.e., Artistic) and incongruent academic environments are shown in Table 7.1; these same means together with the two types of effect sizes are presented in Figure 7.3.

Figure 7.3

Patterns of Change in Artistic Abilities and Interests

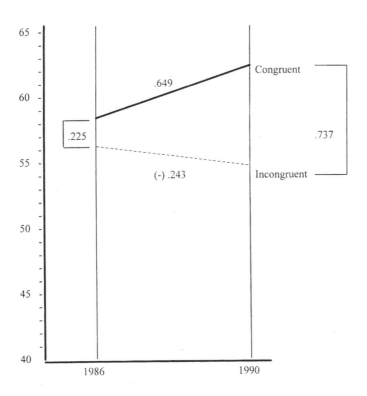

	Congruent (Artistic Person in Artistic Major)
	Incongruent (Artistic Person in Non-Artistic Major)

Inspection of Table 7.1 and Figure 7.3 shows a decided increase in self-rated Artistic abilities and interests over the four-year period for students with a dominant Artistic personality type who majored in congruent academic environments (i.e., Artistic environments) in contrast to their Artistic peers who majored in the three other sorts of environments. Students in congruent environments *increased* their artistic abilities and interests by .649 standard deviations while students in incongruent environments *decreased* in those same areas by .243 standard deviations. In 1986 Artistic students selecting academic majors congruent with their personality were .225 standard deviations stronger in their Artistic abilities and interests than students who selected non-Artistic majors. The differing patterns of change for the two groups of students resulted in much greater differentiation between the two groups in 1990. The effect size reflecting the magnitude of their mean difference in 1990 between students in congruent and those in incongruent fields (.737) is more than a half a standard deviation greater than the equivalent effect size four years earlier (.225). Moreover, the clear and strong pattern of growth in Artistic abilities and interests of Artistic types in Artistic fields and decrease in these abilities and interests in non-Artistic fields is similar for men and women and for primary and secondary recruits

Social personality types. Whereas the findings for students with Artistic personality types provide the clearest and strongest support for the congruence assumption, the corresponding findings for students with a dominant Social personality type provide no support for this assumption. The means on the 1986 and 1990 Social ability and interest scales for students who have a dominant Social personality type and who were in congruent (i.e., Social) and incongruent academic environments are shown in Table 7.1, while Figure 7.4 presents a plotting of these same means along with data on effect sizes. Although the self-rated Social abilities and interests of students who entered congruent academic environments (Social) slightly increased and those of students who entered incongruent environments slightly decreased, the changes were very small. As shown in appendix 7.A, there were no statistically significant effects pertaining to premises from Holland's theory for students whose dominant personality type was Social. These results are also evident in the effect sizes reported in Figure 7.4; there is little difference in Social abilities and interests between students (with a dominant Social personality type) who entered congruent and those who entered incongruent academic environments—either at the beginning or end of the four-year period. Both groups remained rather stable in those traits, with those in congruent environments increasing by

only .127 standard deviations and those in incongruent environments decreasing by only .085 standard deviations. In addition, these findings are
similar for males and females and for primary and secondary recruits. We
conclude that the results for students with a dominant Social personality

Figure 7.4

Patterns of Change in Social Abilities and Interests

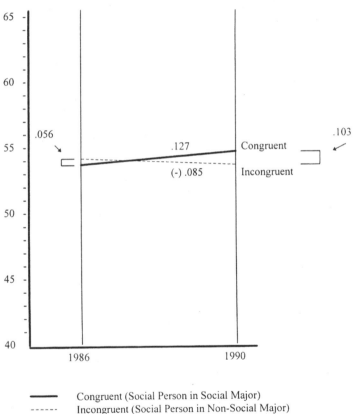

| ------- | Congruent (Social Person in Social Major) |
| ------- | Incongruent (Social Person in Non-Social Major) |

type do not support the congruence assumption of Holland's theory: the
pattern and direction of results meet the expectations of the theory, but
their strength is minimal and not statistically significant.

Enterprising personality types. The means on the 1986 and 1990 Enterprising ability and interest scales for students who have a dominant Enterprising personality type and who were in congruent (i.e., Enterprising) and incongruent academic environments are shown in Table 7.1 (with a plotting of these means and data on effect sizes given in Figure 7.5). The findings for students with a dominant Enterprising personality type show clear support (in direction and pattern of results) for the congruence assumption of Holland's theory. The graphical profile for

Figure 7.5

Patterns of Change in Enterprising Abilities and Interests

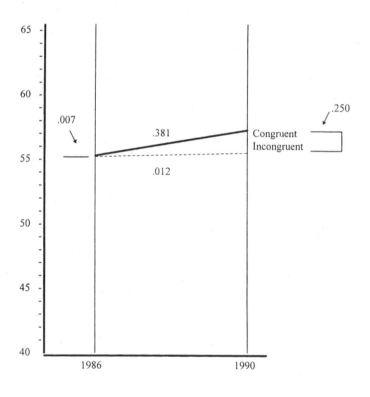

Congruent (Enterprising Person in Enterprising Major)
Incongruent (Enterprising Person in Non-Enterprising Major)

Enterprising students who entered congruent academic environments and those who entered incongruent environments clearly shows a decidedly stronger pattern of growth in self-rated Enterprising abilities and interests for the first group. Students in congruent environments increased with respect to their Enterprising abilities and interests by .381 standard deviations, whereas those in incongruent environments essentially did not change (the difference between their 1986 and 1990 scores being only .012 standard deviations). Although there is essentially no difference in the strength of the Enterprising personality trait for students selecting congruent and those choosing incongruent majors in 1986 (a difference of only .007 standard deviations), in 1990 the two groups differed by one-fourth of a standard deviation. This increased group differentiation is primarily the result of the increase in Enterprising abilities and interests of students in congruent (Enterprising) environments. These findings are the same for male and female students and for primary and secondary recruits.

Although the findings for Enterprising students clearly conform to expectations derived from the congruence assumption of Holland's theory, they are not as strong as those reported earlier for Artistic students in general or for Investigative students who were secondary recruits. They are, however, more supportive of the congruence assumption than those obtained for either Social students in general or for Investigative students who were primary recruits.

Patterns of Self-Reported Growth

We also examined the congruence assumption of Holland's theory using a set of seventeen items (see Table 6.2) assessing students' perceptions of growth over the four-year period. (Because this is the same set of items used in the preceding chapter to assess the socialization assumption and because there is much commonality with the preceding chapter in terms of the procedures employed for handling these items, the interested reader may want to review the more thorough description of the seventeen self-reported growth items and the analytical procedures given in the earlier chapter.) We anticipated that the pattern of student responses to these items would vary as a function of their congruence with their academic environments and that this variability would be consistent with the theoretical postulates of Holland's theory. Thus, students with a dominant Investigative personality type who entered congruent (Investigative) academic environments should report more growth on items consistent with descriptions of Investigative personality types and environments (see Tables 2.1 and 2.2, pp. 37-38 and 45-46) than do their peers in incongruent academic environments (Artistic, Social, Enterprising); students with a dominant Enterprising personality type who entered congruent (Enterprising) academic environments should report more growth on items consistent with descriptions of Enterprising personality types and environments than do their peers in incongruent academic environments (Investigative, Artistic, Social); and so forth.

Multivariate analysis of variance (MANOVA), similar to that described in chapter 6, was used to determine whether or not perceptions of growth differed for students whose personality types and academic environments were congruent rather than incongruent. Separate analyses were conducted for each of the four personality types based on the congruence or incongruence between students' dominant personality types and their academic environments. For example, students with a dominant Investigative personality type who were in Investigative environments were classified as congruent, while students with a dominant Investigative personality type who were in Artistic, Social, and Enterprising environments were classified as incongruent. Parallel dichotomies were used for the three other personality types.

Discriminant analysis, similar to that described in chapter 6, was used to examine which patterns of growth for the seventeen self-reported growth items differentiated between the environments when the multivariate test in the MANOVA was found to be significant. The post hoc discriminant analyses were conducted separately for males and females and for primary and secondary recruits when significant interactions emerged in the MANOVA results. Again, an $\alpha = .05$ was used for all analyses due to the selection of the subgroups of students. Technical results for the MANOVAs and discriminant analyses are given in Appendix 7.B at the end of this chapter. The findings obtained for each of the four personality types are presented in the following order: first, the correlations between the seventeen individual items and the discriminant function are discussed to identify the dimension of growth differentiating between students in congruent and those in incongruent environments; second, the centroids, which represent the means for the groups on the discriminant function, are noted; third, the discriminant coefficients, which identify the areas of growth that are most important in differentiating between the two groups, are analyzed.

Investigative personality types. Although there are significant overall differences in the perceptions of growth between congruent and incongruent students with a dominant Investigative personality type, the MANOVA results also indicated that the differences are not the same for primary and secondary recruits. Separate discriminant analyses were thus performed for each type of recruit. Table 7.2 presents a summary of the overall results of these two analyses. For both primary and secondary recruits the discriminant function was significant, trait the multivariate effect size indicating the magnitude of the difference in growth between students in congruent environments and those in incongruent environments was .748 for primary recruits and .610 for secondary recruits.

The pattern of correlations between the seventeen items and the discriminant function for both primary and secondary recruits indicates that the positive end of the dimension is defined primarily by items characteristic of Investigative environments (e.g., problem-solving skills, interest in graduate school, preparation for graduate school), while the negative end of the dimension is defined by items neither unique to nor shared by Investigative environments (e.g., job-related skills, foreign language ability, writing skills). This pattern suggests that for both primary and secondary recruits the dimension differentiating between Investigative students in congruent and those in incongruent environments is a bipolar continuum of perceived growth, with the negative end reflecting growth in non-Investigative areas and the positive end reflecting growth in Investigative areas.

The centroids for students in congruent and incongruent environments are .397 and -.485, respectively, for primary recruits and .566 and -.234, respectively, for secondary recruits. The signs of the centroids indicate that students in congruent environments perceive greater growth in Investigative areas while students in incongruent environments perceive greater growth in areas not associated with Investigative environments. This pattern of differentiation provides clear evidence that Investigative students in Investigative environments (congruent students) perceive greater growth in Investigative traits than do their peers in non-Investigative environments (incongruent students) whose perceived growth is in non-Investigative traits.

For both primary and secondary recruits the discriminant coefficients indicate that the primary areas of growth differentiating between the two groups of students are a combination of Investigative and non-Investigative traits with the pattern of group differentiation consistent with expectations. Growth in preparation for graduate school (.694 and .406 for primary and secondary recruits, respectively), a trait shared by Investigative and Social environments, and growth in problem-solving skills (.369 and .568 for

Table 7.2

Discriminant Analysis Differentiating between Investigative Personality Types in Congruent and Incongruent Majors on Self-Reported Growth Items [a]

Self-Reported Growth Items	Primary Recruits	Secondary Recruits
[b] Problem-solving skills	.208 (.369)	.230 (.568)
[c] Critical thinking ability	.049 (.058)	- .217 (- .144)
[c] Interest in graduate school	.225 (.013)	.149 (.176)
[c] Preparation for graduate school	.575 (.694)	.187 (.406)
[c] Ability to work independently	- .046(.014)	- .174 (- .057)
[c] Confidence in academic abilities	- .151 (- .193)	- .213 (- .206)
Foreign language ability	.124 (.117)	- .512 (- .491)
Cultural awareness	.039 (.165)	- .328 (- .181)
Writing skills	- .239 (- .424)	- .492 (- .313)
Public speaking ability	- .239 (- .146)	- .396 (- .323)
Tolerance of people with different beliefs	- .143 (- .282)	- .269 (- .106)
Acceptance of different races and cultures	- .085 (.004)	- .187 (- .083)
Job-related skills	- .457 (- .569)	- .064 (- .148)
Leadership abilities	- .107 (.068)	- .165 (.051)
Interpersonal skills	- .061 (.012)	- .245 (- .130)
Competitiveness	- .245 (- .211)	- .049 (.008)
Ability to work cooperatively	- .039 (.165)	.036 (.351)

Centroids	Congruent (Investigative majors)	.397	.566
	Incongruent (Non-Investigative majors)	- .485	- .234

Multivariate effect size	.748	.610

[a] Discriminant coefficients are in parentheses; see Table 3.4 in chapter 3, p. 69, for full wording of items.
[b] Trait unique to Investigative environments.
[c] Trait shared with another environment.

primary and secondary recruits, respectively), a unique trait, contribute to group differentiation—with students in Investigative environments (congruent students) perceiving greater growth in these areas. For primary recruits growth in the non-Investigative areas of job-related skills (-.569) and writing skills (-.424) also differentiates between the two groups of students, with those in non-Investigative environments (incongruent students) perceiving greater growth in these non-Investigative areas. Growth in foreign language ability (-.491) further differentiates between the congruent and incongruent students who were secondary recruits, with the incongruent students perceiving the greater growth on this non-Investigative trait. The significant interaction between congruency of the student's personality and environment and type of recruit is thus manifested by the differences in the primary areas of perceived growth for the incongruent students.

Taken together, these findings clearly support the congruence assumption for students with a dominant Investigative personality type: those who are congruent generally report greater growth than do incongruent students on items reflective of the distinct traits of Investigative people and environments and less growth than incongruent students on items reflective of the three other personality types and environments.

Artistic personality type. The MANOVA results for students whose dominant personality trait is Artistic is similar to that found for students with Investigative personalities. Again, there are significant overall differences in the perceptions of growth by congruent and incongruent students and a significant interaction term indicating that the pattern of differences is not the same for primary and secondary recruits. However, the separate discriminant analyses performed for each type of recruit revealed that the overall difference in the perceptions of growth by congruent and incongruent students with a dominant Artistic personality type held true only for secondary recruits (the multivariate effect size is 1.081). There was no difference on this set of items between congruent and incongruent students who were primary recruits.

Table 7.3 presents a summary of the results from the discriminant analysis for congruent and incongruent Artistic students who were secondary recruits. The general pattern of correlations indicates a bipolar continuum of growth, with the negative end representing growth in non-Artistic areas and the positive end representing growth in Artistic areas. These correlations indicate that the positive end of the dimension is defined primarily by items uniquely associated with Artistic environments (foreign language ability and writing skills), while the negative end of the dimension is defined by items associated with other environments (e.g.,

Table 7.3

Discriminant Analysis Differentiating between Artistic Personality Types in Congruent and Incongruent Majors on Self-Reported Growth Items [a]

Self-Reported Growth Items	Secondary Recruits [b]	
Problem-solving skills	- .207	(- .518)
[d] Critical thinking ability	.179	(.324)
Interest in graduate school	- .032	(- .036)
Preparation for graduate school	.240	(.298)
[d] Ability to work independently	- .042	(.229)
Confidence in academic abilities	- .026	(- .230)
[c] Foreign language ability	.381	(.355)
[c] Cultural awareness	- .004	(.184)
[c] Writing skills	.467	(.562)
[d] Public speaking ability	- .012	(- .010)
Tolerance of people with different beliefs	- .214	(- .141)
Acceptance of different races and cultures	- .171	(- .092)
Job-related skills	- .322	(- .165)
Leadership abilities	- .313	(- .273)
Interpersonal skills	- .355	(- .492)
Competitiveness	- .041	(.127)
Ability to work cooperatively	- .226	(- .065)
Centroids Congruent (Artistic majors)	.738	
Incongruent (Non-Artistic majors)	- .345	
Multivariate effect size	1.081	

[a] Discriminant coefficients are in parentheses; see Table 3.4 in chapter 3, p. 69, for full wording of items.
[b] Results for primary recruits were nonsignificant.
[c] Trait unique to Artistic environments.
[d] Trait shared with another environment

job-related skills, leadership abilities, interpersonal skills). The positive centroid of .738 for the congruent students (Artistic personalities in Artistic majors) locates them on the positive end of the dimension and indicates that they perceive greater growth in Artistic traits than do the incongruent students (Artistic personalities in non-Artistic majors). The negative centroid for the incongruent students (-.345) means these students perceive greater growth in non-Artistic areas.

The discriminant coefficients indicate that the areas of perceived growth that contribute most to differentiating between the congruent and incongruent students are a combination of Artistic and non-Artistic characteristics, and the pattern of differentiation is consistent with Holland's theory. Growth in writing skills (.562), a trait unique to Artistic environments, and growth in problem-solving skills (-.518) and interpersonal skills (-.492), traits associated with other environments, are the dominant areas of differentiation. The signs of the coefficients for these variables indicate that the major differences between the two groups of students are manifested by greater perceived growth in writing skills for congruent students than for incongruent students but less perceived growth for congruent students in problem-solving and interpersonal skills.

These results for students with Artistic personality types provide some (but less than full) support for the congruence assumption in Holland's theory. Because for primary recruits there is no difference in perceptions of growth between students in Artistic majors and students in non-Artistic majors, support for the congruence assumption is not found. However, for the secondary recruits the pattern of differentiation between the congruent and incongruent students supports the congruence assumption: Artistic students in Artistic majors perceive greater growth in Artistic areas and less growth in non-Artistic areas than their peers in non-Artistic majors.

Social personality types. The findings for the patterns of self-reported growth for congruent and incongruent students with a dominant Social personality type have much in common with the general patterns presented in the preceding section on Artistic students, and they provide some (but not full) support for the congruence assumption of Holland's theory. As before, the MANOVA results indicate significant overall differences in the perceptions of growth by congruent and incongruent students as well as a significant interaction. Unlike the findings for Investigative and Artistic students, where the interaction involved primary and secondary recruits, for students with Social personality types the interaction is with gender. Because differences between the congruent and incongruent Social types are therefore not the same for males and females, separate discriminant analyses were performed for the gender groups. These two discriminant analyses revealed that the overall difference in the perceptions of growth by congruent and incongruent students held true only for female students (multivariate effect size is .516). The discriminant results were not significant for male students.

Table 7.4 presents a summary of the discriminant analysis for congruent and incongruent female students with Social personalities. The pattern of correlations between the items and the discriminant function suggests a bipolar continuum of perceived growth in non-Social areas on the negative end of the function and perceived growth in Social areas on the positive end. The strongest positive correlations are associated with growth in preparation for graduate school and confidence in academic abilities, traits shared by Social and Investigative environments. The strongest negative correlations are associated with growth in areas neither unique to Social environments nor shared by Social and other environments (e.g., cultural awareness, problem-solving skills, foreign language ability, critical thinking ability).

The centroids for the two groups of students indicate that congruent female students, whose centroid is .332, perceive greater growth in Social areas and less growth in non-Social areas than do incongruent female students, whose centroid is -.403. Like the results for the previous groups of personality types, the discriminant coefficients indicate that the areas of growth that contribute most to group differentiation reflect areas associated with the environment as well as areas not associated with the environment, with the pattern being consistent with expectations. Growth in confidence in academic abilities is the strongest differentiating variable, and the positive coefficient (.713) indicates that congruent students perceive greater growth in this area than do incongruent students. Congruent students also perceive greater growth in preparation for graduate school (.445). Both these traits are shared by Social and Investigative environments. Conversely, congruent students perceive less growth in cultural awareness (-.467) and problem-solving skills (-.453), both of which are not Social traits.

Our overall conclusion for Social personality types has much in common with that for Artistic personality types: the findings provide some (but not full) support for the congruence assumption of Holland's theory. In this case support for the congruence assumption is not found for male students with Social personalities since there was no difference in perceived growth for congruent and incongruent male students. The findings for female students with Social personalities do provide support for the assumption, but only moderately so. Although the pattern of self-reported growth is

Table 7.4

Discriminant Analysis Differentiating between Social Personality Types in Congruent and Incongruent Majors on Self-Reported Growth Items [a]

Self-Reported Growth Items	Females [b]	
Problem-solving skills	- .331	(- .453)
Critical thinking ability	- .305	(- .122)
[d] Interest in graduate school	.141	(- .171)
[d] Preparation for graduate school	.338	(.445)
Ability to work independently	.054	(.264)
[d] Confidence in academic abilities	.420	(.713)
Foreign language ability	- .317	(- .204)
Cultural awareness	- .366	(- .467)
Writing skills	- .190	(- .245)
Public speaking ability	- .219	(- .175)
[c] Tolerance of people with different beliefs	- .100	(.063)
[c] Acceptance of different races and cultures	- .024	(.195)
Job-related skills	.154	(.039)
Leadership abilities	.058	(.089)
[d] Interpersonal skills	- .167	(- .277)
Competitiveness	.006	(- .082)
[d] Ability to work cooperatively	.085	(.077)

Centroids	Congruent (Social majors)	.332
	Incongruent (Non-Social majors)	- .403

Multivariate effect size		.516

[a] Discriminant coefficients are in parentheses; see Table 3.4 in chapter 3, p. 69, for full wording of items.
[b] Results for males were nonsignificant.
[c] Trait unique to Social environments.
[d] Trait shared with another environment.

consistent with expectations, the two areas of perceived growth that are uniquely associated with Social environments (tolerance of people with different beliefs and acceptance of different races and cultures) fail to correlate with the dimension of growth differentiating between congruent and incongruent students and do not contribute to group differentiation, although the traits that most positively differentiate congruent from incongruent students (confidence in academic abilities and preparation for graduate school) are traits shared by Social and Investigative environments. It appears, then, that the congruence assumption for these students is most true in terms of what does *not* occur; that is, congruence is particularly related to not reporting growth in non-Social areas (cultural awareness and problem-solving skills). This finding, however, does not necessarily contradict the congruence assumption because Holland notes that the selection of congruent environments enables individuals *to avoid* the activities they dislike, the demands for competencies they lack, the tasks and self-images they do not value, and the situations in which their personality traits are not encouraged. We thus conclude that the collective findings provide some support, albeit modest, for the congruence assumption.

Enterprising personality types. The findings for congruent and incongruent students with Enterprising personalities are the strongest of any of the four personality types, standing in rather vivid contrast to those of Artistic and Social students just discussed. The MANOVA results show significant variability in the perceptions of growth over the four-year period for the two groups of students; furthermore, the pattern of differences is similar for male and female Enterprising students and for primary and secondary recruits, for there were no significant interactions. The multivariate effect size for the difference between congruent and incongruent students is .444.

The results of the discriminant analysis are given in Table 7.5 and provide unequivocal support for the congruence assumption. Each area of growth that is either unique to or shared by Enterprising environments is positively correlated with the discriminant function, indicating that the positive dimension of the function represents perceived growth in Enterprising traits. The negative end of the function is defined primarily by the two items representing perceived growth in preparation for and interest in graduate school, distinctly non-Enterprising characteristics. The positive centroid for the congruent students (.458) clearly indicates that Enterprising students in Enterprising majors perceive greater growth in Enterprising areas than do their peers in non-Enterprising majors (whose centroid is -.219).

Table 7.5

Discriminant Analysis Differentiating between Enterprising Personality Types in Congruent and Incongruent Majors on Self-Reported Growth Items [a]

Self-Reported Growth Items	Enterprising Personalities [b]
Problem-solving skills	- .059 (- .077)
Critical thinking ability	- .138 (- .237)
Interest in graduate school	- .293 (.006)
Preparation for graduate school	- .551 (- .633)
Ability to work independently	- .034 (- .289)
Confidence in academic abilities	.037 (- .053)
Foreign language ability	- .073 (- .036)
Cultural awareness	- .136 (- .181)
Writing skills	- .010 (.031)
[d] Public speaking ability	.411 (.263)
Tolerance of people with different beliefs	.053 (.158)
Acceptance of different races and cultures	- .038 (- .150)
[c] Job-related skills	.434 (.395)
[c] Leadership abilities	.277 (.167)
[d] Interpersonal skills	.282 (.349)
[c] Competitiveness	.376 (.329)
[d] Ability to work cooperatively	.298 (.063)

Centroids	Congruent (Enterprising majors)	.458
	Incongruent (Non-Enterprising majors)	- .219

Multivariate effect size	.444

[a] Discriminant coefficients are in parentheses; see Table 3.4 in chapter 3, p. 69, for full wording of items.

[b] Results are similar for males and females, primary and secondary recruits.

[c] Trait unique to Enterprising environments.

[d] Trait shared with another environment.

The discriminant coefficients indicate that the variable contributing most to group differentiation is growth in preparation for graduate school (-.633), with the congruent students perceiving the least growth. With the exception of growth in leadership abilities (.167) and the ability to work co-operatively (.063), the other unique or shared Enterprising items—growth in job-related skills (.395), interpersonal skills (.349), competitiveness (.329), and public speaking ability (.263)—clearly contribute to differentiating between congruent and incongruent students. Although none of the coefficients for these items is as large in absolute value as that for perceived growth in preparation for graduate school, their moderate sizes indicate that each uniquely makes a contribution to group differentiation, with only growth in leadership abilities and ability to work cooperatively contributing redundant information. Thus, congruent Enterprising students perceive decidedly less growth in preparation for graduate school and greater growth in Enterprising traits than do their peers in non-Enterprising majors. These results provide especially strong support for the congruence assumption.

Person-Environment Congruence and College Student Achievement: Summary Observations

Our findings in the preceding chapter on the socialization assumption provided clear evidence that the four focal academic environments (on which we concentrate in this book) contribute to differential patterns of change and stability in students' abilities and interests over the four-year period of college, irrespective of the personalities of students. The socialization assumption, which obviously has a decided sociological orientation with its attention to the collective or overall effects of academic environments, is silent as to the possibility that the effects of the environments might be greater for some students than others. The congruence assumption of Holland's theory, the substance of this chapter, suggests, however, that the effects of the environments will vary for students having different personality types. By emphasizing the differential patterns of change and stability in abilities and interests based on students' congruence or incongruence with environments, the congruence assumption has a psychological element built into it that the socialization assumption does not have. Students in congruent environments should further strengthen their initial dominant abilities and interests because they are in environments that reinforce and reward those abilities and interests, whereas students in incongruent environments should remain stable or decline since their environments do not reinforce and reward those same abilities and interests.

Our findings in this chapter provide strong evidence in support of the congruence assumption in that—with the exceptions to be discussed further—initial differences in the salient abilities and interests between students who enter congruent environments and those who enter incongruent academic environments at the time they enter college become more clear, pronounced, and differentiated four years later. Those who enter academic environments congruent with their primary personality types increase their dominant skills and interests over the four-year period of college, while those entering incongruent environments either increase less or actually decrease their commensurate abilities and interests.

Exceptions to the Rule in Our Overall Findings
Regarding the Congruence Assumption

There are three exceptions to the general pattern of findings just described. Two of them concern students with a dominant Social personality type: (1) we found essentially no difference in average scores on the Social ability and interest scale between Social students in congruent environments and Social students in incongruent environments—either at the beginning of college or four years later; and (2) we found essentially no difference in the pattern of self-perceived growth over the four-year period on a set of traits (including Social traits) for Social males who entered congruent environments and Social males who entered incongruent environments. Those two exceptions lead us to question the validity of the congruence assumption for students with a dominant Social personality type.

Are the decidedly weaker findings for the congruence assumption for students with a dominant Social personality type perhaps reflective of factors relating to a dominant Social personality type or factors relating to Social academic environments? We think the answer lies in our findings in the preceding chapter showing that the socialization effects of Social academic environments, while statistically significant, are decidedly weaker than the comparable effects of the three other environments. Social academic environments in general seem to be less successful than others in reinforcing and rewarding their distinctive set of competencies and interests.

Our belief that the answer lies in the weaker effects of Social academic environments—rather than attributes of the students—becomes more plausible when we examine the initial abilities and interests of students with dominant Social personality types (see Figure 7.4) and students with dominant Enterprising personality types (see Figure 7.5). In both instances the respective abilities and interests of those who were to enter congruent academic environments and those who were to enter incongruent environments were essentially equal. Four years later, however, students with an Enterprising personality type who entered congruent environments had decidedly stronger Enterprising abilities and interests, while the Social abilities and interests of students with a Social personality type who entered congruent environments remained essentially the same as those of students who entered incongruent environments. The answer thus does not appear to be grounded in the students' entering level of abilities and interests but rather in the success—or lack of success—of the academic environments in further developing their distinctive patterns of preferred abilities and interests.

Our findings pertaining to the preferences of faculty in the four academic environments for alternative undergraduate education goals in chapter 4 are likewise instructive in understanding this apparent weakness of Social academic environments to foster students' Social abilities and interests. Faculty in Investigative, Artistic, and Enterprising environments expressed a clear preference for undergraduate education goals commensurate with their norms and values based on Holland's (1997) characterizations of these three environments. Faculty in Social environments were distinctive, however, in that they did not express as clear a preference for the Social undergraduate education goal (provide knowledge of history and the social sciences). In fact, faculty in Social environments expressed a lower preference for this goal than did their colleagues in Artistic environments. Thus, one possible explanation for the apparently weaker "success" of Social environments in the further development of students' Social abilities and interests and for the unexpected lack of support for the congruence assumption pertaining to students with a dominant Social personality type is that Social academic environments, more than others, do not have a focused set of consistent and explicit goals for undergraduate education. The consequence is that students in Social environments are exposed to more conflicting and diverse influences throughout their undergraduate programs—perhaps indicating a lack of environmental identity as conceived by Holland (1997) and described in chapter 2.

The remaining exception to our general findings regarding the congruence assumption is that students with a dominant Artistic personality type who had similar academic majors in 1986 and 1990 (primary recruits) and were in congruent (Artistic) academic environments did not perceive more growth in Artistic traits over the four-year period than did their counterparts in incongruent environments (as indicated in our discriminant analyses of seventeen self-reported growth items). We find this exception more difficult to explain because of the very positive socialization effects of Artistic environments described in chapter 6 and the very strong pattern of differentiation in terms of self-ratings of Artistic abilities and interests both in 1986 and 1990 between students with an Artistic personality type who were in congruent academic environments and those who were in incongruent environments (see Figure 7.3).

We think this exception may be attributable to the interaction of two possible influences. The first is the inherent nature of primary recruits and secondary recruits. The second is the two sets of items used to assess the validity of the congruence assumption (self-ratings of abilities and interests in 1986 and 1990 and self-reports of growth over the four-year period). One interpretation is that primary recruits entered and persisted in their academic majors and thus had a more clear and consistent perception of both themselves and their chosen academic environments than did their counterparts who were secondary recruits. If there is validity to this interpretation, it is reasonable to assume that primary recruits who have an Artistic personality type did not perceive as much growth in Artistic traits as their peers who were secondary recruits, even though their actual self-ratings of abilities and interests in 1986 and 1990 were generally equivalent, because they had a more clear and consistent perception of themselves, their involvement in Artistic environments was anticipated initially, and their collegiate experiences were wholly in these environments. Secondary recruits, on the other hand, who were "migrants" into their academic environments, possibly found their experiences there more fresh and novel, which thus may have contributed to their perceptions of greater growth over the four-year period. Our confidence in this interpretation is limited because clear and substantial differences between primary and secondary recruits were not present for the three other personality types and because all of our other findings concerning the socialization effects of Artistic environments (see chapter 6) as well as the increased differentiation between Artistic students in congruent environments and those in incongruent academic environments (shown in this chapter) strongly support the congruence assumption of Holland's theory.

The Rule: Person-Environment Congruence Is Related to Student Achievement

Our analyses of the differential patterns of change and stability (over a four-year period) in the self-rated abilities and interests of congruent and incongruent students, as well as their self-perceived growth, constitute an indirect assessment of the relationship between person-environment congruence and student achievement in four-year college settings. Within the context of Holland's theory, we expected that growth or achievement of students would be a function of the congruence or fit between individuals' personality types and their academic environments.

Our extended consideration of the three exceptions should not detract from our principal overall finding that congruence or fit between students' personality types and their academic environments is clearly related to growth in students' dominant pattern of abilities and interests. Our collective findings provide strong evidence in support of the congruence assumption in that initial differences in the salient abilities and interests between students who were to enter congruent academic environments and those who were to enter incongruent academic environments became more clear, pronounced, and differentiated during the college years. With the exceptions noted, those who entered academic environments congruent with their primary personality types as freshmen increased their dominant skills and interests over the four-year period, while those entering incongruent environments either increased less or actually decreased in the commensurate abilities and interests.

The strength of positive support for the congruence assumption that our findings provide is noteworthy in the context of findings obtained in prior research (see, for example, Assouline & Meir, 1987; Spokane, 1985, 1996; Tranberg, Slane, & Ekeberg, 1993; Walsh & Holland, 1992). We found changes in the effect-size differences on self-rated interests and abilities between congruent and incongruent students over a four-year period of approximately one-half a standard deviation for both Artistic students (both primary and secondary recruits) and Investigative students (secondary recruits only), and of approximately one-fourth a standard deviation for Enterprising students (see 1986 and 1990 effect sizes in Figures 7.1 through 7.5). These differential patterns of change in student abilities and interests appear to be very strong relative to prior research evidence.

We offer two possible reasons for the stronger support our findings provide for the congruence assumption. First, our study examined patterns of change and stability in student abilities and interests over a longer period of time than is commonly the case. Most prior research examined such change over a semester or academic year, whereas ours extended over a four-year period. Second, unlike prior research on Holland's theory and the vast majority of longitudinal research on how college affects students, we made adjustments in students' initial abilities and interests to deal with the basic problem of regression to the mean, which is a common threat to the internal validity of longitudinal research designs.

All Other Things Are Not Equal: Let the Researcher Beware

We found a number of instances of variability in our overall findings for males and females and for primary and secondary recruits. The distinction between primary and secondary recruits was important in both of our two types of analyses for Investigative students and for the analysis of the items of self-reported growth for Artistic students; the distinction between males and females was important for the analysis of the items of self-reported growth for Social students. Analyses of the data for Enterprising students constitute the only instance in which significant interactive effects did not emerge. Holland (1997) prefaces the assumptions in his theory with the important phrase "other things being equal" (p. 13) and discusses a number of personal and environmental characteristics that should be considered in tests of those assumptions. Our findings suggest the need for future studies of the congruence assumption to consider gender and students' initial proclivity for, or initial choice of, academic environments.

Appendix 7.A

Analysis of Variance Results: 1986 and 1990 Abilities and Interests Scales

Source	Investigative (df = 1, 781)		Artistic (df = 1, 369)		Social (df = 1, 545)		Enterprising (df = 1, 582)	
	MS	F	MS	F	MS	F	MS	F
Between-Subjects Effects								
Holland Environment	4653.80	61.75***	3932.83	38.04***	35.69	.49	334.38	4.81*
Type of Recruit	238.47	3.16	33.84	.33	46.35	.64	11.10	.16
Gender	1776.48	23.57***	1034.11	10.00**	3.67	.05	3030.52	43.60***
Holland by Type of Recruit	363.12	4.82*	18.76	.18	148.28	2.04	90.87	1.31
Holland by Gender	99.71	1.32	.93	.01	172.38	2.37	238.50	3.43
Type of Recruit by Gender	92.58	1.23	230.52	2.23	12.95	.18	91.81	1.32
Holland by Type of Recruit by Gender	232.87	3.09	85.30	.83	215.84	2.97	72.29	1.04
Within plus Residual	5863.68		38146.07		39651.61		40452.77	
Within-Subject Effects								
Year	74.74	2.62	260.52	7.63**	6.19	.15	255.52	7.62**
Holland by Year	401.36	14.05***	956.14	28.02***	85.25	2.08	317.96	9.49**
Type of Recruit by Year	68.64	2.40	5.17	.15	1.59	.04	3.26	.10
Gender by Year	245.68	8.60**	92.11	2.70	204.23	4.98*	913.26	27.25***
Holland by Type of Recruit by Year	215.48	7.54**	11.95	.35	144.78	3.53	.10	.00
Holland by Gender by Year	65.31	2.29	74.91	2.20	16.89	.41	.28	.01
Type of Recruit by Gender by Year	1.16	.04	.03	.00	27.20	.66	50.60	1.51
Holland by Type of Recruit by Gender by Year	15.53	.54	1.77	.05	47.11	1.15	6.36	.19
Within plus Residual	22314.63		12591.21		22331.76		19508.54	

* p < .05; ** p < .01; *** p < .001

Appendix 7.B

Multivariate Analyses of Variance and Discriminant Analyses Results: Self-Reported Growth

MANOVA	Investigative (df = 17, 754)		Artistic (df = 17, 346)		Social (df = 17, 520)		Enterprising (df = 17, 554)	
Source	Wilks Λ	F	Wilks Λ	F	Wilks Λ	F	Wilks Λ	F
Holland Environment	.897	5.094***	.914	1.920*	.956	1.761*	.908	3.301***
Type of Recruit	.982	.803	.919	1.798*	.977	.714	.966	1.161
Gender	.948	2.448**	.924	1.666*	.928	2.366**	.930	2.464**
Holland by Type of Recruit	.963	1.686*	.991	1.748*	.982	.560	.980	.666
Holland by Gender	.980	.924	.950	1.075	.945	1.767*	.969	1.050
Type of Recruit by Gender	.984	.714	.946	1.168	.978	.673	.972	.944
Holland by Type of Recruit by Gender	.983	.780	.955	.959	.973	.855	.967	1.129

Discriminant Analyses (df = 17):	Wilks Λ	X^2
Investigative—Primary Recruits	.838	73.963***
Investigative—Secondary Recruits	.883	42.288***
Artistic—Primary Recruits	.915	13.876
Artistic—Secondary Recruits	.795	44.313***
Social—Males	.887	22.862
Social—Females	.881	42.054***
Enterprising	.909	54.450***

* p < .05; ** p < .01; *** p < .001

Extension and Overview

The Importance of Academic Environments

THE PRECEDING three chapters presented the findings from our analyses based on the basic assumptions of Holland's theory: (a) students search for and select academic environments that match their distinctive patterns of abilities, interests, and personality profiles (chapter 5); (b) academic environments differentially socialize students toward the acquisition of distinctive patterns of abilities, interests, and values that reflect the abilities, interests, and values presumably reinforced and rewarded by the respective environments (chapter 6); and (c) student achievement is a function of the congruence or fit between the dominant personality type and the academic environment (chapter 7). The findings as a whole support the validity of all three basic assumptions, although specific findings do so with varying degrees of strength: some conform fully to the assumptions while others provide only modest support (if that). One purpose of this chapter, then, is to assess briefly the relative level of support for each of the three basic assumptions of Holland's theory.

The variability in support for the three assumptions led us to explore (and to report in this chapter) what we call a "second type of incongruence" (evidenced by students in a particular Holland-defined academic field whose dominant personality does not fit the field). Such exploration helps us to understand more fully the presumed socialization effect and the presumed congruence effect of having a fit between the dominant personality type of the student and his or her academic environment. Thus, a second purpose of this chapter is to present findings concerning this second type of incongruence and to discuss the implications of these findings in terms of the relative merits of the socialization and congruence assumptions that flow from Holland's theory. In doing so, we will gauge the importance of the academic environment to the change and stability of different types of students.

Relative Support for the Assumptions of Holland's Theory

As noted, our findings generally support the validity of each of the three basic assumptions of Holland's theory, but they do so with varying degrees of strength. Here we briefly compare and contrast the findings pertaining to each assumption in order to make an overall determination of their relative merits.

Self-Selection Assumption

To examine the validity of the assumption that students search for and select academic environments that parallel their personality types, we explored differences in the self-rated abilities and interests of those who initially selected Investigative, Artistic, Social, and Enterprising academic environments and also sought information about the proportions of students who initially selected academic environments analogous with their dominant personality types. Both sets of analyses provide solid support for the self-selection assumption, although differences are evident in the relative strength of support provided by each. The findings concerning the patterns of abilities and interests of students initially selecting the four academic environments are decidedly more supportive of the validity of the self-selection assumption than are the findings concerning the proportions of students who initially select academic environments analogous with their dominant personality types.

We found that, in all instances, students who entered a particular academic environment have higher mean scores on the analogous ability and interest scale than do their peers who entered other environments (although the magnitude of differences varied across the four academic environments). So, for example, students initially selecting Investigative academic environments have stronger Investigative abilities and interests than those initially selecting other environments. Such findings, then, provide unequivocal support for the validity of the self-selection assumption of Holland's theory.

In further examining the validity of the self-selection assumption—by classifying students based on their dominant personality types and looking at their intended academic environments as freshmen—we again found support for the validity of this assumption, but with less consistency and more exceptions. Clearly, students with dominant Investigative and Enterprising personality types evidence a decided inclination to select majors in Investigative and Enterprising academic environments, respectively. This, however, is not the case for freshmen who have a dominant Artistic personality type; they were not inclined to select majors in Artistic academic environments. Moreover, our findings for students with a dominant Social personality type reveal gender differences in that females show an inclination to enter Social academic environments whereas males are as inclined to enter Investigative as they are to enter Social environments.

There is also a consistent pattern of gender differences in the choices of academic environments—both initially and four years later—of students with dominant Investigative, Artistic, and Enterprising personalities who did *not* choose to major in their analogous academic environments. In each instance female students were decidedly more inclined to major in a field associated with Social academic environments whereas male students were somewhat more inclined to major in fields associated with either Enterprising or Investigative academic environments. We interpret this general pattern of findings as suggesting that female college students continue to select in disproportionately large numbers academic majors in traditionally female-dominated Social fields (e.g., elementary education and social work), whereas their male counterparts continue to select in disproportionately large numbers academic majors in traditionally male-dominated Investigative (e.g., mathematics) and Enterprising (e.g., business administration) fields.

Socialization Assumption

We examined the validity of the assumption that academic environments reinforce and reward differential patterns of abilities, interests, and values in students—irrespective of their personality types—by exploring longitudinal patterns of actual change and stability in the (self-rated) abilities and interests of students in the four academic environments and by their estimates of self-growth over a four-year period. Although the strength of results across the four academic environments varies, the findings from both sets of analyses provide very strong support for the validity of the socialization assumption of Holland's theory. This conclusion is clearly evident for Investigative, Artistic, and Enterprising academic environments, though decidedly less so for Social environments (where significant gender differences emerged).

The findings for students in Investigative, Artistic, and Enterprising academic environments show, over a four-year period, a clear and consistent pattern of increasing differentiation (of these students from other students) in the respective sets of abilities and interests that each environment is hypothesized to reinforce and reward in Holland's theory. Moreover the *increase* in effect sizes (comparing students in a particular academic field with students in other fields) of the respective ability and interest scales was fairly large—ranging from one-third to one-half a standard deviation. In all cases this pattern was produced by students in the specified academic majors increasing their scores over four years on the corresponding abilities and interests scales, with students not in these majors decreasing in their scores. Furthermore, the pattern of increasing differentiation (from other students) for Investigative, Artistic, and Enterprising students is also evident in the analysis of students' self-reported estimates of their own growth over the four-year period: students in each of these three academic environments show a clear pattern of perceived growth on items that are characteristic of their respective environments.

The weakest support for the validity of the socialization assumption was for the Social academic environment, where a significant and substantive gender interactive effect exists. The evidence in support of the validity of the socialization assumption differs for male and female students in Social environments on both sets of analyses. Consistent with expectations from Holland's theory, over the four-year period the males in Social academic environments show an increasing pattern of differentiation (from their peers in other academic environments) in Social abilities and interests—again resulting from students in these environments increasing their scores and students not in these environments decreasing their scores. This pattern, however, was much weaker for females in Social environments, who are nearly undifferentiated from their peers in other academic environments both at the time they began college (1986) and four years later. The absolute pattern for females does conform to expectations from Holland's theory, but only weakly. The initial effect-size difference between females in the Social environment compared to those in other academic environments is extremely small to begin with, although it increases (slightly) four years later. As for self-reported growth items, the results are clearer and more supportive for females than for males.

Congruence Assumption

Our analyses to assess the validity of the congruence hypothesis, like those pertaining to the socialization assumption, were of longitudinal patterns of change and stability in the self-rated abilities and interests of students and their estimates of self-growth over a four-year period. Here, however, we focused on the congruence or fit based on the dominant personality type of students *and* their academic environments.

Our findings concerning change in student abilities and interests basically support the congruence assumption in terms of student change on Investigative, Artistic, and Enterprising abilities and interests. That is to say, for example, that the likelihood of students with a dominant Artistic personality type further developing their Artistic abilities and interests is contingent upon their entry into an Artistic academic environment: those who enter a congruent, Artistic academic environment show decidedly greater growth in these attributes than those who enter an incongruent, non-Artistic academic environment (whose Artistic abilities and interests actually decline). This clear pattern of increasing differentiation is not true, however, for the Social abilities and interests of students with a dominant Social personality type. Achievement in the acquisition of Social abilities and interests for these students is essentially unrelated to whether they select congruent or incongruent academic environments.

As for estimates of self-growth over the four-year period, for students with dominant Enterprising and Investigative personalities the estimates for Enterprising and Investigative interests are contingent upon entry into Enterprising and Investigative academic environments, respectively, in accord with the congruence assumption. This is less true, however, for students with dominant Artistic and Social personalities where significant interactive effects occurred. The findings conform to expectations for Artistic personality types for secondary recruits (but not primary recruits) and somewhat for female (but not male) Social personality types.

A Second Type of Incongruence

The central objective of our multiple analyses has been to develop greater understanding of differential patterns of change and stability in college students. The socialization and congruence assumptions of Holland's theory provide different, if not alternative, explanations for these differential patterns.

Placing importance on congruence is intended to help individual students select educational settings in which they have a greater likelihood of long-term stability, satisfaction, and success. This emphasis on individual student behavior reflects a type of psychological (or even social psychological) orientation underlying the congruence assumption, which blends considerations of the personality type of students with the reinforcement efforts of faculty in the respective academic environments. According to the congruence assumption, the likelihood of a student developing any specific repertoire of competencies and values is *jointly dependent* on the student's own personality type and the congruence or fit between it and the student's entry into an academic environment that requires, reinforces, and rewards that particular repertoire. Our findings in the preceding chapter provide generally strong support for the validity of this assumption (with some exceptions). Thus, both the student's personality type *and* the substantive nature of academic environments are essential components in assisting individual students' selection of educational settings in which they presumably have the greatest potential to persist, to be satisfied, and to be successful. Consideration of both the individual and the environment is presumably essential to understanding the potential consequences of individual behavior in academic settings. We might call this the psychological (or perhaps the social psychological) component of Holland's theory.

By contrast, the socialization assumption postulates that the key element in promoting student acquisition of one rather than another set of competencies and talents is the academic environment. Here the roles of faculty members and their collective efforts to socialize students to the prevailing norms and values of their respective academic environments is the primary component, and the personality types and associated initial abilities and interests of students are of less importance and perhaps even irrelevant. That is to say, for example, that the likelihood of students collectively developing any specific repertoire of competencies and values is *singularly dependent* upon their entry into an academic environment that requires, reinforces, and rewards that particular repertoire. In this respect the socialization assumption has a decided sociological orientation because of its focus on the collective group effects of academic environments. Our findings in chapter 6 provide generally strong support for the validity of this assumption (again, with certain exceptions).

The effects of academic environments in Holland's theory are not assumed to be inherently dependent on the attributes of individual students who enter them. In other words, the respective academic environments are assumed to have similar effects on all students in them—irrespective of the students' personality types. Thus we expected to find, and did find, strong socialization effects for the academic environments (in chapter 6), but we did not explore at the time whether these effects were comparable for students with similar and dissimilar personality types in each of the four academic environments. It is the possibility that these effects might be similar (or dissimilar) that we now consider.

We explore the patterns of change and stability of students' abilities and interests for those personality types that are congruent and for those that are incongruent with given environments to determine if the effects of a particular environment are comparable for the two different kinds of students. If students with a congruent personality type in a particular environment consistently make greater gains than do students whose personality types are incongruent with that particular environment, then one might say a "personality dynamic" is at work in that the "right personality type" enhances gain over and above the influence of the environment. On the other hand, if the pattern of change is comparable for the two groups of students, then we might say that a "socialization dynamic" is at work since even a "wrong personality type" in a particular environment shows a pattern of change comparable to that of the "right personality type."

Holland's theory provides essentially no guidance in terms of the relative merits of these alternative perspectives since it does not seek to disentangle potential group and individual effects. From the *group* perspective, the socialization assumption implicitly hypothesizes a uniform pattern of reinforcement and reward by faculty members in the respective academic environments, or at the very least it does not consider potentially different patterns of longitudinal change and stability in student abilities and interests depending on students' congruence with the environment (or lack thereof). This is so because the concern of the socialization assumption is on the collective actions and effects of academic environments. From the *individual* perspective, the congruence assumption hypothesizes a differential pattern of longitudinal change and stability in abilities and interests for comparable individuals (i.e., two students with similar personality profiles): those entering congruent environments will grow or gain more than those entering incongruent environments. But the congruence assumption is silent as to the collective effects of the respective academic environments on students with different personality profiles in them. This is so because the concern of the congruence assumption is the pattern of change and stability of individual students in different environments.

Thus, we are unable to make formal predictions about the possibility of uniform versus differential patterns of change in student abilities and interests *within* the different academic environments. Nonetheless, we were eager to explore this issue for we believe the results from such an inquiry have the potential to shed some insights upon the relative merits of the congruence and socialization assumptions. Thus, in our effort to understand the influences of academic environments, we set out to explore the extent to which a personality dynamic or a socialization dynamic is at work. To repeat: if, on the one hand, students having a personality type congruent rather than incongruent with a particular environment consistently make greater gains on traits associated with that environment, then one might say that a personality dynamic is at work in that being the "right personality type" enhances gain over and above the effect of the environment; if, on the other hand, the pattern of change is comparable for the two groups of students, then we can say that a socialization dynamic is at work because even a "wrong personality type" in a particular environment shows a pattern of change comparable to that of the "right personality type."

As background for understanding the one table and five figures to be presented in this section, recall that chapter 6 reported results of longitudinal change and stability of students' abilities and interests based solely on their academic environments. It did not explore whether or not the effects of this environment were comparable for students with congruent personality types and those with incongruent types. Recall, further, that chapter 7 explored students' change and stability based on personality traits congruent with that environment but not the change and stability of students whose personality types were not congruent with that particular environment. Rather, the comparison group for a particular type (say an Enterprising personality type) in a congruent environment (Enterprising environment) was that particular personality type (Enterprising) in a noncongruent environment (in this case, Investigative, Artistic, or Social). We now conceive of this latter group of students (already studied in chapter 7) as evidencing *one kind of incongruence*.

Not considered in chapter 7 (or shown in the pertinent tables and figures within that chapter) is the change and stability of students in a *particular* academic field (say the Enterprising field) who are not congruent with that particular field (that is, students who are Investigative, Artistic, and Social personality types in the Enterprising field). Data for this *second type of incongruence* are given in Table 8.1 and Figures 8.1 through 8.5 in the present chapter by adding information to data already presented in chapter 7 (in Table 7.1 and Figures 7.1 through 7.5). Thus, the one table and five figures of this chapter are exactly the same as the parallel tables presented in chapter 7 with the important exception that the third and sixth columns of Table 8.1 are new, as is the third graph line (nonbold, nonbroken) in Figures 8.1 through 8.5. The additional data (from comparison sets of students not heretofore considered) will help us distinguish between the effects of a socialization dynamic and a personality dynamic (see footnote 1 in chapter 6 for a detailed description of the interpretation of figures).

There are certain similarities in results across the four academic environments, as found in Table 8.1 and Figures 8.1 through 8.5; these data reveal a socialization dynamic rather than a personality dynamic at work. Notice, first, that in each of the five figures the pattern for the second type of incongruent student (nonbold, nonbroken lines) and the congruent students (bold, nonbroken lines) are, for all intents and purposes, *parallel*. That is, the pattern of gain or growth on the analogous cluster of abilities and interests for each academic environment is essentially the same for all students in that environment, whether the student's dominant personality type is congruent or incongruent with that environment. While students whose personality types are incongruent with the environment began with a lower score in 1986, they experienced essentially the same amount of gain (or growth) as those whose personality type is congruent with the environment. This pattern of longitudinal change clearly suggests that an essentially uniform socialization dynamic is at work within each of the four academic environments rather than a personality dynamic. Of interest here is that the presumed socialization effect on the incongruent students (second type) was not so strong as to close (or significantly reduce) the initial gap between them and the congruent students (thus the parallel lines rather than converging lines).

Second, notice for each environment that the second type of incongruent student (nonbold, nonbroken lines in the figures) made absolute positive gains on average between 1986 and 1990 in the abilities and interests being considered, whereas the first type of incongruent student (nonbold, broken lines in the figures) either remained about the same (Investigative primary recruits in Figure 8.1, all Social recruits in Figure 8.4, and all Enterprising recruits in Figure 8.5) or decreased (Investigative secondary recruits in Figure 8.2 and all Artistic recruits in Figure 8.3) in these abilities and interests. The largest gain (in terms of effect sizes) on a given cluster of abilities and interests by the second type of incongruent student was made by students in the Artistic environment (.747), followed by primary recruits in Investigative environments (.430) and students in the Enterprising

Table 8.1

Means and Standard Deviations for 1986 and 1990 Ability and Interest Scales [a]

Investigative scale	1986			1990		
	Congruent	Incongruent I	Incongruent II	Congruent	Incongruent I	Incongruent II
Primary	57.209	52.576	50.732	58.737	53.079	53.032
	(5.228)	(4.736)	(4.999)	(9.065)	(9.001)	(8.911)
Secondary	55.109	54.155	48.712	57.201	52.286	50.465
	(4.945)	(5.354)	(5.648)	(8.705)	(8.863)	(9.626)

Artistic scale [b]	1986			1990		
	Congruent	Incongruent I	Incongruent II	Congruent	Incongruent I	Incongruent II
	58.580	56.293	53.743	62.369	54.872	58.107
	(5.429)	(6.591)	(6.814)	(9.782)	(10.208)	(10.138)

Social scale [b]	1986			1990		
	Congruent	Incongruent I	Incongruent II	Congruent	Incongruent I	Incongruent II
	53.798	54.275	48.810	54.609	53.730	50.133
	(4.106)	(4.243)	(4.003)	(9.824)	(9.880)	(9.865)

Enterprising scale [b]	1986			1990		
	Congruent	Incongruent I	Incongruent II	Congruent	Incongruent I	Incongruent II
	55.187	55.241	48.629	57.394	55.312	51.011
	(4.860)	(4.887)	(5.206)	(9.057)	(9.480)	(9.638)

[a] Standard deviations are in parentheses; see text and figures for definitions of incongruence.
[b] Results are similar for males and females, primary and secondary recruits.

Figure 8.1

Patterns of Change in Investigative Abilities
and Interests—Primary Recruits

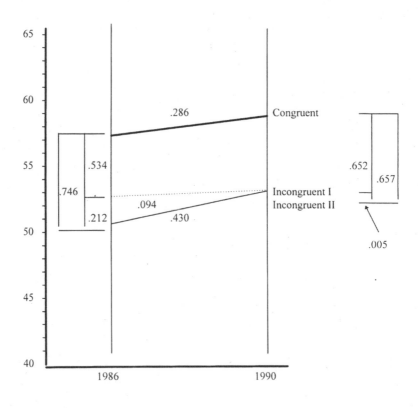

Congruent (Investigative Person in Investigative Major)
Incongruent I (Investigative Person in Non-Investigative Major)
Incongruent II (Non-Investigative Person in Investigative Major)

Figure 8.2

Patterns of Change in Investigative Abilities and Interests—Secondary Recruits

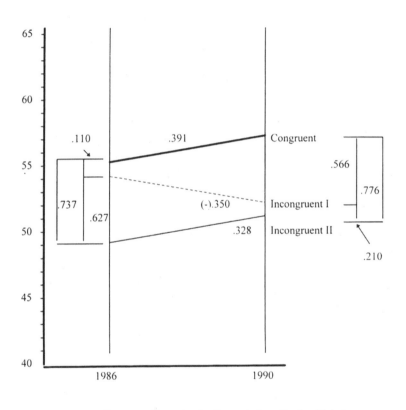

Congruent (Investigative Person in Investigative Major)
Incongruent I (Investigative Person in Non-Investigative Major)
Incongruent II (Non-Investigative Person in Investigative Major)

Figure 8.3

Patterns of Change in Artistic Abilities and Interests

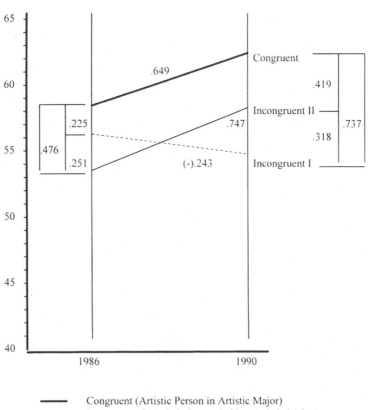

        Congruent (Artistic Person in Artistic Major)
- - - - - Incongruent I (Artistic Person in Non-Artistic Major)
        Incongruent II (Non-Artistic Person in Artistic Major)

Figure 8.4

Patterns of Change in Social Abilities and Interests

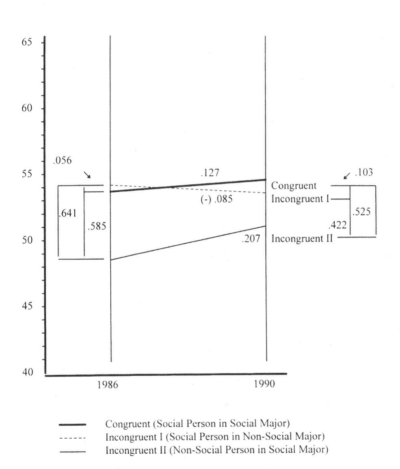

————— Congruent (Social Person in Social Major)
- - - - - Incongruent I (Social Person in Non-Social Major)
————— Incongruent II (Non-Social Person in Social Major)

Figure 8.5

Patterns of Change in Enterprising Abilities and Interests

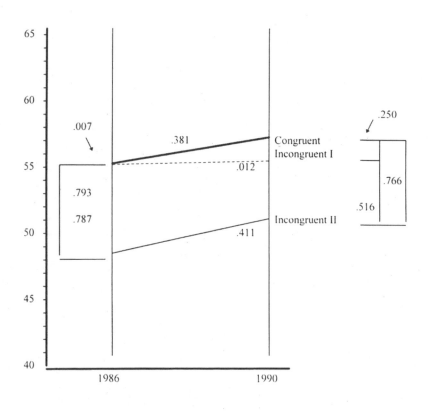

Congruent (Enterprising Person in Enterprising Major)
Incongruent I (Enterprising Person in Non-Enterprising Major)
Incongruent II (Non-Enterprising Person in Enterprising Major)

environment (.411), and finally by secondary recruits in Investigative environments (.328) and students in Social environments (.207). In short, students who do *not* enter a "fitting" environment (first type of incongruence) either maintain or decrease in the interests and abilities promoted by the environment that they did not enter, whereas students who enter a "nonfitting" environment (second type of incongruence) actually increase in the interests and abilities of the environment that they did enter.

It is also instructive to note that in all cases the second type of incongruent student started with a lower mean score in 1986 than did the first type of incongruent student. For instance, the mean score on Artistic abilities and interests for the second type of incongruent student (53.743 in Table 8.1) is lower than the mean score for the first type of incongruent student (56.293 in Table 8.1). But in all instances—due, we speculate, to the greater prevalence of a socialization dynamic than a personality dynamic—the initial gap between these two groups shrank by 1990 (compare the nonbold, nonbroken lines in Figures 8.1 through 8.5 with the nonbold, broken lines in those figures). This is most evident for the findings concerning the longitudinal pattern of scores for Artistic abilities and interests presented in Figure 8.3, where the second type of incongruent students actually ended up with a higher mean score than did the first type of incongruent students.

How might we explain the present set of findings in the context of the set of findings pertaining to the congruence assumption in chapter 7—the earlier set showing that gain or growth on any given cluster of abilities and interests for students with an analogous personality type (e.g., growth in Investigative abilities and interests by students with an Investigative personality type) was greater for those who entered congruent academic environments than for those who entered incongruent environments? Are the two sets of findings contradictory? We think not given the following explanation. The examination of the validity of the congruence assumption in chapter 7 focused specifically on four particular subsets of students, based upon their dominant personality types, and examined their longitudinal patterns of change and stability on a specific cluster of abilities and interests that paralleled (or fit) their personality types. Those findings (repeated in the tables and figures of this chapter) did in fact support the congruence assumption in that, for instance, students with a dominant Enterprising personality type tended to grow or gain in Enterprising abilities if they entered Enterprising, but not other, academic environments. In this sense, a congruent academic environment reinforced the dominant pattern of abilities and interests of this particular subset of students. If the question is whether or not academic environments are tools to perpetuate the distinctive abilities and interests of students at the time they enter college, then the answer is yes, they are: those distinctive patterns of abilities and interests will be enhanced if, and only if, students enter academic environments that reinforce and reward those specific abilities and interests. Indeed, as seen in the tables and figures within this chapter, such students ended up higher on these particular abilities and interests than did the other two groups of students under consideration.

But now a different question in terms of the potential impacts of academic environments can be raised: to what extent are academic environments successful in their efforts to socialize a disparate collection of students to the distinctive pattern of preferred abilities and interests of the environments? Are these environments as "effective" with students who begin with lower levels of commensurate abilities and interests as those with higher levels of commensurate abilities and interests? The various profiles of patterns of students evidencing the second type of incongruence reported in this chapter provide the basis for an affirmative response: that is, yes, the impacts of academic environments appear to be comparable for students whose personality types are congruent or incongruent with the respective environments (although the initial gap between the two groups of students does not lessen). Thus, we do not find the two sets of findings to be in conflict but rather directed toward two distinct but related questions.

Holland's Theory and Academic Environments: Summary Observations

The Importance of Academic Environments: Overview

What we take to be particularly noteworthy in the preceding analysis are the existence, strength, and uniformity of the impacts of academic environments on students who enter them—whether or not the students are initially congruent in personality with those environments. That is, for each of the four kinds of academic environments, students whose (self-rated) abilities and interests were particularly congruent with that environment, as well as students whose abilities and interests were not congruent, made roughly the same degree of positive gains in these abilities and interests. It makes sense, then, to present a brief overview of the major findings of the analyses presented in various chapters of this book, now organized by the four academic environments under study rather than (as we did at the beginning of this chapter) by the three basic Holland assumptions (self-selection, socialization, congruence). These environments, as we have seen, have distinctive norms and values as manifested in the typical professional attitudes and values of their respective faculties (chapter 4). Moreover, it is from these environments that students ultimately select specific academic majors (chapter 5); and it is these environments that affect which abilities and interests of students are strengthened, maintained, or diminished during their college years (chapters 6, 7, and 8). We begin with the Investigative and Enterprising academic environments, whose associations with students' choices, interests, and abilities have been found to be the most straightforward of those in our analyses.

Investigative academic environments. Investigative academic environments, which emphasize a basic understanding of mathematics and science, have faculties with a strong general orientation toward scholarship, intellectualism, and conventional notions of academic rigor. We found that faculty members in Investigative environments place primary attention on the development of students' analytical, mathematical, and scientific competencies and relatively little attention on students' character and career development. They rely more heavily than faculty in other academic fields on more formal and structured teaching-learning strategies (e.g., lecture-discussion) that are strongly subject-matter centered, believing that students learn best by meeting specific, clear-cut a priori course requirements. They also place a high value on examinations and grades and seek to develop specific skills and competencies in their students that are consistent with their general orientation to scholarship, intellectualism, mathematics, and science. Although faculty in Investigative environments are satisfied with the current level of curricular specialization, they do not express a decided preference for teaching either specialized or general courses or for interacting with students who have either clear or indefinite career plans.

When we analyzed students' abilities and interests in connection with Investigative academic environments, we found consistent (and usually strong) associations. Thus, students who intended to major in Investigative academic fields had much higher (self-rated) Investigative abilities than did those not intending to major in such fields. Moreover, students (especially males) with a dominant Investigative personality type entered college with a greater likelihood of wanting to major in Investigative academic environments than in any other environments. Also of some interest here is the fact that of the four kinds of academic environments under study, Investigative environments had the highest percentage (54.3 percent) of primary recruits.

Students who majored in Investigative fields, either as primary or secondary recruits, increased moderately in their (self-rated) Investigative abilities and interests, whereas primary recruits in the other three kinds of academic environments typically did not change in Investigative abilities and interests and secondary recruits in these other environments typically decreased somewhat in Investigative abilities and interests. As for students who majored in Investigative fields but did not have dominant Investigative personalities, they increased as much on these abilities and interests as did students with dominant Investigative personalities in these fields. This was the case for both primary and secondary recruits. Dominant investigative personalities who did not major in Investigative academic fields either remained the same on these abilities and interests (if they were primary recruits to the other fields) or decreased in them (if they were secondary recruits to these fields). Finally, we found that students' perceptions of their own growth on a variety of abilities and interests were consistent with these environmental effects.

Enterprising academic environments. The defining orientation of Enterprising academic environments is a strong emphasis on the career preparation of students and status acquisition. This orientation is clearly evident in the uncommonly high emphasis faculty place on the vocational and career development of their students as well as their efforts to develop students' leadership competencies, to motivate them to strive to be successful in terms of common indicators of career and organizational status, and to acquire and use power to attain organizational and career goals. This distinctive orientation is also evident in the preferences of faculty to teach students who have definite career plans and to teach specialized undergraduate courses. Like their colleagues in Investigative environments, faculty members in Enterprising environments are satisfied with the current level of curricular specialization in their institutions. The nature of student-faculty interaction and the specific teaching-learning strategies used by faculty in Enterprising environments are the most balanced or undifferentiated of any of the four kinds of academic environments. Faculty use both formal, structured, subject-matter-centered instructional strategies (e.g., lecture-discussion) and informal, unstructured, and student-centered teaching (e.g., small-group discussion) approaches. In addition, they place equivalent emphasis on student-faculty interactions characterized by a faculty-centered orientation (in which there is a strong emphasis on grades, examinations, and students meeting specific clear-cut requirements) and by a student-centered orientation (which places a high value on student freedom and independence in the learning process, a collegial mode of interaction with students, and a belief that students do their best work when they are on their own).

Students who initially intended to major in Enterprising academic fields showed higher (self-rated) Enterprising abilities and interests than did those intending to major in the other academic fields under study, with students having dominant Enterprising personalities entering college with a somewhat greater likelihood of wanting to major in Enterprising academic environments than in any of these other environments. Students who majored in Enterprising fields increased in their Enterprising abilities and interests (as much so for those students whose dominant personalities were congruent with this environment as for those students whose dominant personalities were not), whereas students who majored in the three other kinds of academic fields (if anything) typically decreased slightly. Enterprising personalities who did not enter majors associated with Enterprising academic environments remained the same in Enterprising abilities and interests. Students' perceptions of their own growth in various abilities and interests were consistent with these environmental effects.

Artistic academic environments. Artistic academic environments are characterized by a strong commitment to aesthetics and an emphasis on emotions and sensations (as well as the mind). This broad orientation and emphasis are reflected in curricula which stress acquisition of an appreciation of literature and the arts and enhancing students' creative thinking. Faculty members in Artistic environments not only place primary attention on the development of students' literary abilities and competencies associated with innovation and creativity, but they also emphasize the values and character development of their students. Like their colleagues in Enterprising environments, they use a blending of both formal, structured, subject-matter-centered instructional strategies and informal, unstructured, and student-centered teaching approaches. They also place a high value on student freedom and independence in the learning process, prefer a collegial mode of interaction with students, and believe that students do their best work when they are on their own. They are concerned that the current level of curricular specialization is too strong. Yet their orientation here is not one-sided, for they (like their counterparts in Investigative environments) do not express a decided preference for teaching either specialized or general courses or for interacting with students who have either clear or indefinite career plans.

Of particular interest when turning to data collected from students is that only about one-third of the students who actually majored in Artistic fields (compared to roughly one-half in each of the other three kinds of environments) were primary recruits to the field. This is to say that about two-thirds of the students in this academic environment did not anticipate being majors in Artistic fields when they entered college. Moreover, contrary to the findings for the other kinds of academic environments, students with dominant Artistic personalities were not more likely initially to intend to major in Artistic academic environments. (Male students were twice as likely to intend to major in Enterprising academic environments, and female students were a little more likely to select fields associated with Enterprising or Social environments.) However, despite these circumstances, students who initially intended to major in an Artistic academic environment nevertheless had decidedly stronger (self-rated) Artistic abilities and interests than did students not intending to major in this kind of environment.

Students who majored in Artistic fields, either as primary or secondary recruits, showed large increases in their (self-rated) Artistic abilities and interests, whereas the Artistic abilities and interests of students in the three other academic environments decreased somewhat. Moreover, the increase was about the same for students who initially had Artistic dominant personalities and those who did not. Students with dominant Artistic personalities who did not major in Artistic fields decreased in Artistic abilities and interests. Students' perceptions of their own growth on a variety of interests and abilities were consistent with these environmental effects with one exception (for self-perceived growth of primary recruits with dominant Artistic personalities who majored in Artistic fields compared to their counterparts who majored in the other three kinds of academic fields).

Social academic environments. Social academic environments have a strong community orientation with a particular emphasis on creating a workplace climate for faculty characterized by warmth and friendliness. We found that Social and Artistic academic environments share certain similar characteristics but not others. Like the curricular offerings in Artistic academic environments, those in Social academic environments stress student acquisition of knowledge of history and the social sciences, and the faculties of both environments place an emphasis on values and the character development of students. The faculty in Social environments, however, place a distinctly greater emphasis on the development of humanitarian, teaching, and interpersonal competencies in their students. The general nature of student-faculty interaction in Social environments is also similar to that of Artistic environments in that their respective faculties place a high value on student freedom and independence in the learning process, prefer a collegial mode of interaction with students, believe that students do their best work when they are on their own, and are concerned that the current level of curricular specialization is too strong. Unlike the more balanced approach of their counterparts in Artistic environments, however, faculty in Social environments place strong reliance on informal, student-centered teaching strategies (e.g., small-group discussions) and prefer to teach less specialized undergraduate courses and to teach undergraduate students who do not have clear career plans.

The findings of our analyses of data collected from students interested in or actually majoring in Social fields tended to be weak or inconsistent. Male students who initially intended to major in Social academic environments showed higher (self-rated) Social abilities and interests than did those initially intending to major in the other academic fields under study. This association, however, was only very weakly evident for female students. Yet female students with a dominant Social personality type were much more likely (initially or subsequently) to select Social academic fields than other fields, whereas this same tendency was only slightly evident for males with dominant Social personalities.

Male and female students who majored in Social fields were not much different in their (self-rated) Social abilities and interests from students who majored in other academic fields. Students in Social academic environments did make small increases in their Social abilities and interests—which was the case for students with and without dominant Social personalities—whereas students in the other academic environments either remained the same on Social abilities and interests (male students) or decreased slightly in them (female students). This environmental (socialization) effect was the smallest we found for the four kinds of academic fields. Students' perceptions of their own growth in Social abilities and interests provided support for this environmental effect (particularly for female students). Considering only students who had dominant Social personalities, we found that it did not matter whether or not they entered congruent (Social) academic fields in terms of the degree of change in their Social abilities and interests (although to some extent it did for female students regarding their self-perceptions of growth on various Social abilities and interests).

Holland's Theory and the Centrality of Academic Environments:
Concluding Comments

We began this chapter with a review of our findings and the extent to which they support (or refute) the three basic assumptions of Holland's theory. We concluded from this review that our collective findings do support the validity of all three assumptions, albeit with varying degrees of strength. Our findings with regard to the socialization assumption (presented in chapter 6) and the congruence assumption (presented in chapter 7) led us to consider what we call a second type of incongruence in an effort to explore the extent to which a personality dynamic or a socialization dynamic is more highly related to understanding differential patterns of change and stability in the abilities and interests of students over a four-year period. Those findings, presented in this chapter, clearly show the primacy of the socialization dynamic that reflects the essentially uniform effects of academic environments on disparate groups of students in the four academic environments. That is to say, the effect of any one of the four academic environments is essentially equivalent irrespective of whether the student has the "right personality type" or the "wrong personality type."

The generally clear and consistent pattern of increasing differentiation in the abilities and interests of students majoring in each of the four academic environments shown in chapter 6 and the primacy of the socialization dynamic (relative to the personality dynamic) that emerged in the findings presented in this chapter lead us to conclude that our collective findings provide especially strong support for the validity of the socialization assumption of Holland's theory. Academic environments and their respective faculties have clear and powerful influences on what students do and do not learn over the course of their undergraduate education.

The centrality of academic environments in understanding differential patterns of change and stability in students' abilities and interests discerned from our analyses parallels the findings of Pace (1990) that academic majors are an important influence "on the extent and direction of students' progress in college" (p. 76) and his conclusion that "students learn what they study" (p. 76). Some might interpret this conclusion narrowly as implying that academic majors and environments are simply "knowledge factories" dispensing only subject matter knowledge and content. Such an interpretation would be consistent with Pascarella and Terenzini's (1991) conclusion that "students tend to demonstrate the highest levels of learning on subject-matter tests most congruent with their academic major . . . [whereas] the impact of major field of student on noncognitive outcomes is substantially less apparent or consistent" (p. 614).

Are academic environments indeed simply "knowledge factories" dispensing straightforward subject-matter knowledge and content? We think not and offer the following interpretation based on the premises of Holland's theory and our collective findings. Holland's (1997) theory postulates that environments require, reinforce, and reward a wide range of abilities, interests, attitudes, and values. His descriptions of the six environments repeatedly note that they foster the development of different competencies and achievements, encourage people to see themselves and the world in different ways, stimulate people to engage in different kinds of activities, and reward people for their display of alternative values and attitudes (see pp. 43–48, in Holland, 1997). Theoretically, then, academic environments do not merely dispense subject-matter knowledge and content. Rather, they seek to influence a full spectrum of personal and professional self-perceptions, competencies, attitudes, interests, and values. Our findings similarly show that academic environments contributed to growth or development in a wide range of student abilities, interests, and attitudes reflected in the diversity of items and scales used to assess change and stability of students (see Tables 3.3 and 3.4, chapter 3, this volume, pp. 66-67 and 69). Thus we conclude here with a reaffirmation of the fundamental thesis of this book stated in chapter 1 that thorough knowledge of academic disciplines and environments is a prerequisite to understanding variations in the professional attitudes and behaviors of college faculty and differences in the patterns of student change and stability resulting from the college experience.

Given this reaffirmation and the support of our findings for the three basic assumptions of Holland's theory, we turn to a discussion of various research and policy implications of his theory in the following chapter. We believe this theory has much potential to assist us in understanding and promoting student learning and in improving the organizational structure and administrative processes of colleges and universities that affect the quality of student and faculty life in these institutions.

Educational and Organizational
Implications of Holland's Theory
in Higher Education Settings

A S BASED on data from both faculty and students, our findings in the five preceding chapters generally support the three basic assumptions (self-selection, socialization, congruence) of Holland's theory, although, as we have noted, they do so with varying degrees of strength. In this chapter we suggest certain research and policy implications of Holland's theory for various aspects of the lives of college faculty and students, as well as for the organization and management of colleges and universities.

Holland's theory has specific value in understanding the fundamental diversity that has historically defined American colleges and universities. This diversity is reflected in systematic differences in the professional attitudes and behaviors of faculty members associated with distinct clusters of academic disciplines. Diversity is also reflected in the dissimilar patterns of change and stability in the abilities and interests of college students who major in distinctive academic environments, each with its own prevailing set of preferred norms and values. We believe not only that systematic knowledge of the distinctive norms and values of disparate clusters of academic disciplines (environments) *within* institutions of higher learning is central to an understanding of the diversity that characterizes the lives of college faculty and students in these institutions, but also that Holland's theory has the potential to assist in theory-based research that will contribute to the accumulation of such systematic knowledge. Moreover, the premises of Holland's theory have applicability to the manner in which colleges and universities are organized and managed.

The research and policy implications of Holland's theory discussed in this chapter grow from a need to make sense of the fundamental diversity of American higher education and the implications that flow from the knowledge of this diversity. Thus, we begin with a brief overview of organizational diversity in American higher education to provide a context for our subsequent discussion of the implications of Holland's theory for research and policy.

Organizational Diversity in American Higher Education

Finn and Manno (1996), in documenting many of the dramatic changes in American higher education throughout the past five decades, note that "the culture of higher education is expansion oriented" (p. 46). One manifestation of this expansion is the sheer growth in the number of institutions from seventeen hundred before World War II to over thirty-seven hundred today. Numerous scholars contend, however, that the growing number of institutions has not contributed to organizational diversity in American higher education because newer institutions tend to imitate existing institutional forms (Birnbaum, 1983; Fairweather, 1996; Jencks & Riesman, 1968; Newman, 1971; Riesman, 1956).

The orientation of higher education toward expansion has also been manifested within individual colleges and universities in terms of the greater heterogeneity of students enrolled, the proliferation of programs offered, and the services rendered to meet the many distinctive needs of these students (Callan, 1997; Finn & Manno, 1996). As Mitchell (1997) maintains, such dramatic changes "in the kinds of people who attend as students and work as faculty alter the nature of the enterprise in fundamental ways" (p. 268). The trends noted by Finn and Manno seem unlikely to diminish, for the next generation of college students will be "the most diverse in higher education's history" (Callan, 1997, p. 104). These and other developments that have been evolving over the past two decades have led scholars to conclude that organizational diversity in American higher education is more evident within institutions than between them (Carnegie Council, 1980; Stadtman, 1980; Trow, 1988).

Organizational diversity is critical to the long-term vitality of higher education because it affects the system's capacity to respond to pressures of the environment and to maintain its essential character and integrity (Altbach & Berdahl, 1981; Birnbaum, 1983; Bok, 1986; Huisman, 1998; Mitchell, 1997;

Pace, 1974; Trow, 1988). The perceptions of scholars about the relative salience of diversity, both within and between educational institutions, also have important research implications for those who study the organization and management of colleges as well as for those who study the attitudes and performance of college faculty and students, for these perceptions influence what researchers actually study in their investigations. With respect to college students, for example, those persuaded that diversity *between* institutions is paramount will focus their attention on whether or not different kinds of institutions (e.g., control, selectivity, size) have differential influence on student change and stability during college, whereas those who advocate the growing importance of diversity *within* institutions will focus their attention on determining the relative influence of different collegiate environments or experiences within institutions (e.g., residency patterns, academic majors, student-faculty interactions) on student change and stability. As for research on college faculty, the institutional setting and the academic discipline of faculty are commonly regarded as the two major influences on the norms, values, and activities of the American professoriate (Bowen & Schuster, 1986; Clark, 1987a; Finkelstein, 1984; Light, 1974a; Light, Mardsen, & Corl, 1973; Rothblatt, 1997). Researchers who believe that between-institution diversity is paramount will concentrate on differences in the norms, values, and activities of faculty based on the type of institution with which faculty are affiliated, whereas researchers who advocate the growing importance of within-institution diversity will concentrate on differences in the norms, values, and activities of faculty affiliated with different academic disciplines within their institutional settings.

Although diversity has long been noted as the central distinguishing feature of American higher education and the major determinant of faculty life, little sustained, systematic, theory-based research exists on this phenomenon. True, there have been literally hundreds of what Hobbs and Francis (1973) term "analysis and recommendation" descriptive studies, but there have been relatively few systematic, theory-based inquiries. The potential of Holland's theory to ameliorate this neglect is the central consideration of this chapter. We spell out this potential by providing some examples of how Holland's theory can be used to understand and promote student learning and to enhance the organizational structure and managerial processes of colleges and universities.

Understanding and Promoting Student Learning

We first note that scholars who study college effects on students might associate only cognitive outcomes with college majors and not consider the impact of major fields on the development of students' affective traits. We think this is a mistake given the findings reported by Feldman and Newcomb (1969), as well as our own syntheses in chapters 5, 6, and 7 of the research literature concerning Holland's theory. Furthermore, we wish to emphasize that our findings on the differential patterns of longitudinal change in students' abilities and interests are based on a broad repertoire of cognitive and affective attributes of students. This repertoire includes a broad range of measures of students' self-reported abilities (e.g., academic, artistic, leadership, mathematical, writing), self-concepts (e.g., intellectual and social self-confidence, popularity), and interests (e.g., making a theoretical contribution to science, writing original works, helping to promote racial understanding, being very well off financially). Also included are students' perceptions of their gains over the four-year period across a diverse array of common college outcomes (e.g., problem-solving skills, cultural awareness, tolerance of other people with different beliefs, competitiveness). In sum, it is clear that our findings pertaining to the differential patterns of change in students associated with their major field of study are based on a wide array of both cognitive and affective college outcomes.

We now explore how the use of Holland's theory might contribute to a greater understanding and promotion of student learning in its broader sense. We offer some observations regarding the potential of the theory to advance knowledge of patterns of change and stability in college students, and we then discuss the possible use of the theory in curricular design.

Research on Patterns of Change and Stability in College Students

We began this book by providing a rationale for our belief that knowledge of academic disciplines is a prerequisite to understanding academic lives through a comparison of the general perspective(s) of scholars who study college faculty with the general perspective(s) of those who study college students. In comparing these two streams of research, we noted that those who study the professional lives of faculty have largely assumed and accepted the centrality of academic disciplines in their inquiries, whereas this has not been the case—especially in more recent years—for those who study longitudinal change and stability of college students. We suggested that this difference has both conceptual and methodological implications for the research agendas and research methods evident in the two domains of inquiry.

With particular reference to the differential importance of academic disciplines in the respective literatures on patterns of change and stability in college students' abilities and interests reviewed by Feldman and Newcomb (1969) and Pascarella and Terenzini (1991), we wonder whether the stronger influences of academic disciplines discerned by the former authors may have resulted from their greater reliance on certain earlier analysts who had a more sociologically oriented research paradigm, while the weaker influences of academic disciplines discerned by the latter authors may be a consequence of their relying on a more psychologically oriented research paradigm by some contemporary scholars. In the end, we raised the possibility that what scholars find in their inquiries may be influenced by what they look for and that the weaker influence of academic disciplines on patterns of change and stability in students' abilities and interests may be due to the fact that these considerations of the possible impacts of academic disciplines as well as other group influences in colleges and universities are not as important in the psychological-research paradigm as they are in the sociological-research paradigm.

At any rate, we believe that the evidence we have presented in the intervening chapters—based on our review of the extant research literature and our own empirical findings—clearly supports our fundamental premise that academic disciplines are a highly important source of influence on the academic lives of both college faculty and students. The fundamental differences in the professional norms and values of college faculty in the four distinct academic environments and the different change and stability patterns in the abilities and interests of students in these respective environments were summarized in the previous chapter.

The collective evidence we have presented leads us to reaffirm our initial contention that academic disciplines are an essential component in efforts to understand how students change as a result of their collegiate experiences. We have presented consistent evidence from the extant literature and our own empirical findings that faculty members in different clusters of academic disciplines create distinctly different academic environments as a consequence of their preference for alternative goals for undergraduate education, their emphasis on alternative teaching goals and student competencies in their respective classes, and their reliance on different approaches to classroom instruction and ways of interacting with students inside and outside their classes. We have also presented consistent empirical evidence that these distinctive academic environments created by their respective faculties have a strong socializing influence on change and stability in students' abilities and interests—that is, what students do and do not learn or acquire as a consequence of their collegiate experiences. In general, our findings support the conclusion reached by Pace (1990) that academic disciplines (environments) are a primary influence on "the extent and direction of student progress in college" (p. 76).

In essence, students learn what they study, which is to say the distinctive repertoire of professional and personal self-perceptions, competencies, attitudes, interests, and values that their respective academic disciplines/environments distinctly reinforce and reward (in addition to the specific content/factual knowledge associated with the discipline).

Such a conclusion may not appear to be profound on the surface, but we think it has important implications for understanding the apparent conflict in the respective conclusions reached by Feldman and Newcomb (1969) and Pascarella and Terenzini (1991) concerning the relative influence of academic disciplines on change and stability of college students. In addition we feel that this conclusion has implications for future research on this phenomenon. What follows in this section are our observations and concerns about the fundamental nature of contemporary research on how colleges affect change and stability in college students and our suggestions to improve this important line of inquiry through theory-based studies.

Many of the models—reviewed in chapter 1—that have guided research over the past two decades on how colleges affect students incorporate elements of student-faculty interactions within and outside the classroom, and studies grounded in these models often incorporate some indicator of the students' academic major. Why then are the reviews of the findings of this literature by Feldman and Newcomb (1969) and Pascarella and Terenzini (1991) in such seeming contradiction?

We think the answer is twofold and is a consequence of (1) the manner by which scholars classify academic majors/environments and (2) the nature of the measures used in their studies to explain the relative importance of alternative features in overall collegiate experiences contributing to student growth—or lack thereof. The following is a discussion of how these two possible factors may have contributed to the seeming contradiction in the findings of Feldman and Newcomb (1969) and Pascarella and Terenzini (1991), as well as our suggestions of how reliance on Holland's theory might ameliorate such difficulties in future research on understanding and promoting student learning in colleges and universities.

Theory-based classifications of academic environments. As we previously noted in this chapter, as well as in chapter 1, scholars who study change and stability of college students have not been as inclined as their peers who study college faculty to assume and accept the centrality of academic disciplines in their studies. One consequence of this neglect is that substantive conceptual and empirical knowledge about the classification of students' academic majors or environments is not as evident in the literature concerning how colleges affect students as in the literature on differences in faculty attitudes and behaviors. For instance, it is much more common to find classifications of students' academic majors based on such idiosyncratic and crude indicators as science versus nonscience and liberal arts versus professional than on systematic classifications based on empirically (Biglan, 1973a, 1973b) or theoretically (Holland, 1966, 1973, 1985, 1997) derived typologies of academic disciplines. The use of such crude and simplistic classification schemas for students' academic majors/environments may well have contributed to weaker findings regarding the impact of those majors on students' patterns of change and stability.

We encourage scholars to classify students' academic majors or environments in ways that have theoretical merit and are empirically defensible in future efforts to discern those environments' potential influences on student learning. Holland's theory appears to be especially useful in this respect given its strong theoretical grounding and the abundant empirical evidence supporting its premises (see chapter 2 for an overall summary of this evidence).[1] *The College Majors Finder* (Rosen, Holmberg, & Holland, 1989, pp. 4–22) and the *Dictionary of Holland Occupational Codes* (Gottfredson & Holland, 1996a, pp. 675–693) are especially valuable references in that they classify literally hundreds of specific academic majors into the six academic environments. Both references also give three-letter Holland codes for each academic major, thus allowing more fine-grained analyses of differences *within* each of the six academic environments.

We offer this suggestion not to imply that Holland's theory provides the only basis for such classification, but rather to point out that it is a well-established theoretical framework that is germane to such inquiries and one that has been validated in dozens of studies. We believe that reliance on such a theoretically based and empirically defensible classification scheme of academic environments is a more valid way of capturing the inherent diversity of academic disciplines than the more simplistic, unsystematic classifications commonly used; it thus has more potential to contribute to greater understanding of the extent to which academic disciplines influence student learning. In addition, reliance on such a classification scheme would facilitate efforts to synthesize the evolving literature on the extent to which academic disciplines influence student learning, thereby contributing to a more systematic understanding of this important phenomenon than does adherence to idiosyncratic classification schemas prevalent in contemporary research.

---

[1] Also useful are the summaries of research evidence pertaining to specific assumptions of Holland's theory concerning faculty in chapter 4 and college students in chapters 5, 6, and 7.

Measures incorporated in prevalent college-impact models. Many of the models reviewed in chapter 1 that have guided much contemporary research on the effects of colleges on students, in fact, include measures of student-faculty interaction inside and outside formal classroom settings—for example, measures of the teaching behaviors students encounter in class settings and the frequency and nature of student-faculty interactions outside formal classes. The inclusion of such measures is consistent with Pascarella and Terenzini's (1991) statement that "one of the most inescapable and unequivocal conclusions we can make is that the impact of college is largely determined by the individual's quality of effort and level of involvement in both academic and non-academic activities" (p. 610) and their advice to researchers to focus "more on such factors as curricular experiences and course work patterns, the quality of teaching, the frequency and focus of student-faculty nonclassroom interaction, the nature of peer group and extracurricular activities, and the extent to which institutional structures and policies facilitate student academic and social involvement" (p. 596). The difficulty associated with such measures is that they are very global or general in character and lack theoretical grounding; they essentially tap the extent to which students take advantage of people within the general institutional setting and the multitude of services and facilities provided by colleges and universities.

The global character of such measures and the ways they are commonly employed in contemporary research on student learning contribute to three concerns we have that could be ameliorated by reliance on theory-based measures. Our first concern is simply that the commonly used measures lack strong theoretical underpinnings in terms of explaining why students should learn more from their greater frequency of either formal or informal interaction with others (e.g., peers, faculty) or from their greater frequency of use of available services or facilities provided by their institutions. What theoretical premise explains, for example, why students who interact more frequently with other students and faculty and who are more engaged in active learning activities should achieve greater growth in such diverse areas as general education, literature, history, philosophy, arts, writing, synthesizing knowledge, and knowledge of the world in general? The failure to ground inquiries in appropriate theories contributes to an unguided search for the correlates of student learning—correlates that most often lack theoretical origins and acquire legitimacy only by virtue of the fact that others have found these correlates to be important, significant predictors of the specific student outcome being explored.

Although it is true that the current approach has contributed to the accumulation of growing and increasingly consistent evidence showing that some predictors have more influence on student learning than others, such efforts have also contributed to an emerging tendency to search for and endorse uniform "good practices for undergraduate education" (Chickering, Gamson, & Barsi, 1989; Kuh & Vespers, 1997), a tendency that is in direct conflict with the inherent diversity of American higher education noted earlier in this chapter. This leads to our second concern that the relative importance of such measures of "good practice" may differ depending on the specific student competencies (outcomes) that particular academic environments seek to develop in their respective student bodies. Simply put, "good practices" may well vary across different academic environments whose faculties emphasize different teaching and learning goals and use different instructional approaches.

Our portraits in chapter 4 of the academic environments created by faculty and our summary of research findings in the preceding chapter provide a number of examples of how academic environments differ on measures commonly used to understand which particular facets of collegiate experiences are most related to students' patterns of change and stability. To give but a single illustration, faculty in Investigative environments rely predominantly on structured and formal teaching-learning strategies that are decidedly subject-matter centered; they believe that students learn best by meeting specific, clear-cut a priori course requirements; and they place high value on examinations and grades. In comparison, their colleagues in Artistic environments use a blending of both subject-matter and student-centered instructional approaches, place a high value on student freedom and independence in the learning process, prefer a collegial mode of interaction with students, and believe that students do their best work when they are on their own. Thus, although we have shown that both Investigative and Artistic academic environments are comparably successful in promoting their respective patterns of student learning, they do so in different ways.

Why then should one assume or expect that there are generic "good practices" that promote the distinctive patterns of student outcomes that the respective academic environments seek to reward and reinforce in their students? We think it is more plausible to assume that different teaching or instructional approaches are related to different student outcomes. Searching for uniform "good practices for undergraduate education" in the face of this clear diversity of actual practices by faculty in these disparate academic environments has the potential to be misleading and to inject a search for uniformity that runs counter to the inherent diversity of American higher education.

Our third concern is in part related to our second one. The use of global measures—such as measures of frequency of general student-faculty interaction and teaching behaviors students generally encounter—to explain and understand patterns of change and stability in students also runs counter to extant knowledge that it is these very kinds of interaction and behaviors that vary among faculty in the four academic environments. As we have shown, faculty members in Investigative, Artistic, Social, and Enterprising academic environments have decidedly different preferences for how they interact with students, and they use different instructional approaches in their respective classes and interactions with students. The consequence of including global or general measures in studies of student learning leads to our third concern—that much of the potential influence of the particular and specific academic majors/environments (however classified) is lost to these general measures of faculty members' instructional approaches and interactions with students. That is to say, if analysts ignore the manner by which faculty in specific sorts of academic environments teach students in their classrooms and interact with students outside class settings—if analysts, in essence, subsume these specific matters under a more general assessment—then much of the potential influence of the specific academic major/environment on patterns of student change and stability is hidden or masked.

The underlying bases for these three concerns are our convictions (1) that there are theory-based linkages between what students learn and the instructional approaches faculty employ to promote learning and (2) that academic disciplines—which differentially emphasize the relative importance of different student outcomes and which employ alternative instructional approaches to achieve student leaning of these different outcomes—constitute the fundamental element for these theoretical linkages. We encourage scholars to ground their studies of student learning in theoretical frameworks that recognize the centrality of academic environments and their faculties to student learning. Such theoretical grounding would result in the selection of both dependent and independent variables that have theoretical meaning. That is to say, for example, that future research would benefit from focusing on student outcomes (dependent variables) that are an integral component of an appropriate theory and on explanatory/independent variables that have an assumed theoretical relationship with whatever student outcome is of interest to the particular investigator(s). Holland's theory provides such a framework through a theoretical classification of academic disciplines that incorporates theory-based assumptions of the respective student abilities and interests reinforced and rewarded by the distinctive academic environments. Subsequent research, reviewed in chapter 4, has assisted in understanding how the alternative instructional approaches and distinctive patterns of interaction with students used in each environment contribute to student learning of the distinctive abilities and interests that the faculties of those respective environments reinforce and reward.

Detecting disciplinary effects. Being guided by theory for the appropriate selection of measures, however, is a necessary but not sufficient condition for the detection of disciplinary effects. Even if classifications of disciplines are theoretically sound and the selection of measures to include in studies are theoretically based and specifically related to the discipline classifications and outcomes under study, the use of statistical techniques such as multiple regression or analysis of covariance will continue to preclude the appearance of discipline effects. If the purpose of the research is to understand how disciplines contribute to *change* in students, these approaches do not allow the assessment of actual change (see footnote 1 in chapter 1, p. 24); a repeated-measures approach is more appropriate to assess magnitude and direction of change. If the purpose is to assess the influence or impact of disciplines on outcomes, the inclusion in the statistical models of both discipline classifications *and* instructional practices and types of faculty-student interactions specific to the disciplines statistically equates the disciplines on characteristics that differentiate between disciplines. Once these characteristics are controlled for and the faculty "equated" across the respective academic environments, the disciplinary effect has been controlled—that is, it has already been accounted for by other measures in the analysis. There may not be a direct impact of discipline if the discipline effect is completely manifested through the instructional practices and types of faculty-student interactions.

An alternative to the approach based on standard regression/analysis of covariance is the use of path-analytic procedures. The utility of path analysis in studying the influence of disciplines on student outcomes is twofold. First, path analysis calls for a strong theory that links student experiences with student outcomes; second, the influence of disciplines on student outcomes that is manifested indirectly through the differing teaching practices and types of interactions can be measured and tested. We believe the adoption of these suggestions is likely to yield a more "true" estimate of the influence of academic environments and that such estimates will affirm the importance of academic environments to what students do and do not learn as a result of their college experiences.

Path-analytic models are already commonly used to examine the effects of colleges on students, but we think such models have been misdirected because they have not been especially well grounded in theory. That is, theory has not guided either the classification of academic departments or the assumed linkages among students' college experiences and the student outcomes under investigation. In essence, we believe that the "cause-effect" premises of most models have little theoretical grounding and that Holland's theory provides a strong theoretical basis for formulating and testing such models since it provides a theoretical basis for both the classification of academic environments and the linkages among the instructional approaches of faculty and longitudinal patterns of student change and stability.

Reliance on a theory such as Holland's would have at least two major benefits. First, variation in patterns of student learning would be theoretically linked to specific academic environments. Take, for example, two studies that seek, respectively, to examine change and stability of students in terms of their critical thinking and interpersonal skills. According to Holland's theory, the first study would assume that development of critical thinking skills would be greater among students majoring in an Investigative academic environment because that environment reinforces and rewards students for the display of such attributes as being analytical, critical, independent, and rational; alternatively, the second study would assume that development of interpersonal skills would be greater among students majoring in a Social academic environment because that environment reinforces and rewards students for seeing themselves as liking to help others, understanding others, and being cooperative, empathic, and sociable. Thus, in the first study the author(s) might create a dichotomous measure of academic environments distinguishing between students who had majored in Investigative academic environments versus students who had chosen other academic environments, while in the second study the author(s) might create a dichotomous measure of academic environments distinguishing between students who had majored in Social environments versus students who had majored in other academic environments. The point emphasized here is that there is a direct theoretical link between specific academic environments and specific student outcomes.

Second, there would be a theoretical connection between the specific experiences students encounter in their collegiate careers and the particular outcome under investigation. In terms of the two student outcomes just discussed, Holland's theory, together with the accumulated research evidence on the alternative instructional approaches used by faculty in the respective academic environments, would lead to the selection of different college experiences for inclusion in the model. For example, the study of critical thinking skills might incorporate measures of the extent to which the learning experiences of students were predominantly in structured and formal settings that were subject-matter centered (e.g., lecture-discussion); that placed a strong emphasis on their learning specific, clear-cut a priori requirements; and that placed a high value on examinations and grades since these are reflective of the prevailing instructional approaches used by faculty in Investigative environments. Alternatively, the study of interpersonal skills might incorporate measures of the extent to which the learning experiences of students were predominantly in less structured and more informal settings that were more student-centered (e.g., small-group discussions) and that placed a stronger emphasis on student freedom and independence in the learning process and a more collegial mode of student-faculty interaction, since these are reflective of the prevailing instructional approaches used by faculty in Social environments. The point we wish to emphasize here is that there is a clear theoretical link between students' learning experiences and their learning outcomes.

We believe that the use of path-analytic procedures incorporating these features will yield a better estimate of the influence of academic disciplines on student learning than has resulted from the use of less-theory-based inquiries in recent years. The use of Holland's theory to link alternative student outcomes to theory-based categories of academic environments has the potential to yield more accurate, and we believe stronger, estimates of the *direct effects* of academic disciplines on students' learning because the disciplines would not be "expected" to influence student learning on outcomes that they do not reinforce and reward. The use of Holland's theory to establish specific theory-based links between specific student experiences and specific student learning outcomes also has the potential to yield more accurate, and we believe stronger, estimates of the *indirect effects* of academic disciplines on student learning since the studies would be based on analyzing instructional approaches that are at least theoretically related to the specific student learning outcome(s) being investigated.

Curricular Design: Alternative Schemas

Holland's theory has implications for the design of alternative curricular patterns. These implications, however, vary rather dramatically depending on the intended outcomes to be achieved. We provide two illustrations.

The first focuses on efforts to enhance student persistence in the freshman year and thus has a very specific objective and a relatively short-term time frame. The second provides an example of how Holland's theory might be used to promote a more systematic broadening of students' learning experiences and patterns of learning over the duration of the students' undergraduate careers and thus is more general in character with a longer time frame.

Enhancing freshman year persistence. The topic of student attrition is of major importance to both students and their institutions. A college education is a major investment for students and their families, and it has important consequences for students' growth and development as well as students' long-term career and economic success. Student attrition is also a salient issue to institutions, for college tuition is a primary source of their total revenue. Because student attrition is most acute in the freshman year, any effort or intervention that might diminish the likelihood of student attrition would have important positive implications for both students and their institutions.

The typical curricular pattern of most colleges and universities is for freshmen to take a variety of general-education courses in their first (and often second) year of enrollment. One consequence of this pattern is that students are required (or encouraged) to enroll in a wide variety of course work immediately following matriculation, and many of these courses are new and foreign to students' primary interests and abilities. It is quite possible that this requirement could contribute to lower levels of student stability, satisfaction, and success during the critical freshman year given the congruence assumption of Holland's theory, addressed in chapter 7, which suggests that college students are most likely to flourish in congruent academic environments or majors because these environments provide opportunities, activities, tasks, and roles that correspond to the competencies, interests, and self-perceptions of students.

An alternative curricular pattern that appears potentially useful for reducing the current level of student attrition (and for promoting satisfaction and success) in the freshman year is to allow students to take a greater proportion of course work in subject-matter areas that are more congruent with their personality types. Holland's theory offers particular promise in this respect because of the associated measures to determine both students' personality types and the relative congruence of alternative academic environments and their respective courses (see chapter 2 for a more extended description of these procedures). Students' personality types could be discerned from the use of several well-established and validated instruments, such as the Self-Directed Search, the Vocational Preference Inventory, and the Strong-Campbell Interest Inventory. The relative congruence between students' dominant personality types and the alternative academic environments would be discerned from use of the hexagonal model shown in Figure 2.1. For example, students with a dominant Enterprising personality type would be encouraged as freshmen to take a greater proportion of course work in equivalent (Enterprising) or adjacent (Social, Conventional) academic environments, while those freshmen with a dominant Investigative personality type would be encouraged to take a greater proportion of course work in equivalent (Investigative) or adjacent (Realistic, Artistic) academic environments. Such a change in curricular patterns in the freshman year would appear to have the potential for promoting student persistence, satisfaction, and success in this critical year of college enrollment (given the congruence assumption of Holland's theory).

Such a change, which would be a dramatic shift from past and current practices, may appear to promote greater narrowness in student learning. This outcome need not necessarily be the case, however, assuming that "disciplines are not inherently narrow," as Rothblatt (1997, p. 249) contends, and that "all, even the most vocational [disciplines], can effectively stretch the mind . . . [since they have] a capacity for breadth, connecting certain forms of knowing and their methods with others, reaching outward into adjacent disciplines and fields of interest, and encouraging exploration by means of connected and systematic systems of evidence gathering and evaluation" (Rothblatt, 1997, p. 249). What might well be necessary, however, would be to assure that freshman courses in the respective academic disciplines/environments do in fact achieve their inherent "capacity for breadth" suggested by Rothblatt.

Promoting systematic growth of multiple competencies. The preceding comments have focused specifically on the freshman year as critical to the issue of student retention and persistence. Thus a relatively short time frame is involved: the suggestions are designed to achieve specific outcomes—persistence, satisfaction, success—in the freshman year. The hexagonal model shown in Figure 2.1 and the logic of its use described in chapter 2 might also be used over the duration of students' total academic careers to provide a theory-based and systematic curricular design that is intended to broaden students' learning over this longer time interval. The hexagonal model suggests a specific progression for broadening students' abilities and interests during their college years. For example, and as just discussed, a greater proportion of students' course work in the freshman year would be devoted to subjects in either congruent or adjacent academic environments. In subsequent years, however, students would be required or encouraged to take course work in academic environments that are progressively dissimilar to their dominant personality types, perhaps returning in their final year to capstone or culminating courses in their specific academic majors/environments. For example, entering students with a dominant Social personality type would be encouraged or required to take course work in the analogous (Social) or adjacent (Artistic, Enterprising) academic environments during the freshman year; they would take courses in adjacent (Artistic, Enterprising) or once-removed (Investigative, Conventional) environments during the sophomore year; they would study courses in the once-removed (Investigative, Conventional) and distant (Realistic) environments their junior year; and they would return to capstone and culminating course work in their analogous environment (Social) in their senior year. Our aim here is not to provide a mechanistic format for individualized programs of study based on students' dominant personality type, but rather to illustrate the utility of Holland's theory to promote focused and broadening student learning over both short-term and long-term time frames of students' college careers.

Organizational Structure and Administrative Processes

In this section we first provide a series of illustrations depicting the basic utility of Holland's theory to the organization and management of institutions of higher learning and to research on the performance of those institutions. We focus initially on the organizational structure of colleges and universities. This is followed by a discussion of managerial and leadership practices within these institutions. We provide in each section a description of the policy or practice implications of Holland's theory as well as research hypotheses that flow from adoption of the inherent assumptions of the theory.

Organizational Structure: Making Sense of Diversity

Structure is obviously a common feature of all organizations, though the particular nature of that structure may vary substantially according to such attributes as the organization's specific goals, strategies, size, core processes, and workforce nature. Structure is a primary way by which complex organizations seek to balance the inherent tension between internal coordination and adaptation to the external environment. Although organizational structure is often conceived of as machinelike and inflexible, there is a growing tendency to design structures that are more flexible and emphasize the participation of organizations' members. For example, Bolman and Deal (1997), in illustrating their fundamental point that "successful organizations employ a variety of methods to coordinate individual and group efforts and to link them with desired goals" (p. 41), juxtapose the tightly controlled and highly centralized structure of McDonald's (where most major decisions are made at the top) with the decidedly more decentralized structure of Harvard University (where most major decisions are made at the lowest possible level in the organization).

Holland's theory has clear implications for the organizational structure of institutions of higher learning. These institutions traditionally are organized on the basis of schools and colleges, with the assumption that there are more common interests within these organizational units than across them. Yet the assignment of specific academic departments to colleges (or schools) historically has been made without the benefit of theory-based understanding of the similarities and differences among diverse academic environments/departments. The consequence is that we have colleges structured along the lines of external accreditation agencies and general professional associations (e.g., colleges of business, education, engineering, etc.), creating collegiate units that often include academic departments whose orientations are markedly dissimilar in terms of the premises of Holland's theory.

The hexagonal model shown in Figure 2.1, in conjunction with the *Dictionary of Holland Occupational Codes* (Gottfredson & Holland, 1996a) and *The College Majors Finder* (Rosen, Holmberg, & Holland, 1989), provides a theoretically based and empirically supported method for the assignment of specific academic departments to broader collegiate units. Table 9.1 provides an illustrative comparison between the traditional assignment of academic departments (columns) characterizing the typical structure of contemporary colleges and universities and the assignment (rows) suggested by the hexagonal model shown in Figure 2.1 and based on the first-letter code of academic disciplines (that is, their primary type).

It is readily apparent from Table 9.1 that each traditional collegiate unit (columns) is composed of multiple types of academic departments based on the classification of specific academic departments to the six academic environments proposed by Holland (based upon classifications using the *Dictionary of Holland Occupational Codes* and *The College Majors*

Table 9.1
Alternative Collegiate Organizational Structures

| Holland Environments | Traditional Colleges of | | |
	Education	Business	Arts and Sciences
REALISTIC	Agricultural Educ.	(none)	(none)
	Industrial Arts Educ.	(none)	(none)
INVESTIGATIVE	Science Education	Business Economics	Economics
	Mathematics Educ.	Systems Analysis	Mathematics
	Educational Research	Operations Research	Physics
			Statistics
ARTISTIC	Art Education	(none)	Art History
	Music Education	(none)	Music
	Foreign Lang. Educ.	(none)	French
			Theater/ Drama
SOCIAL	Elementary Education	(none)	Philosophy
	Educ. Administration	(none)	Area Studies
	Special Education	(none)	Political Science
	Counselor Education	(none)	History
ENTERPRISING	Business Education	Marketing	Communi- cations
	Higher Ed. Research	Labor Relations	Journalism
		Personnel Mgmt.	
		Advertising	
CONVENTIONAL	(none)	Accounting	(none)

Finder). For example, Colleges of Education often are composed of academic departments or programs that are members of five of Holland's academic environments; the academic departments in Colleges of Arts and Sciences customarily represent at least four of the academic environments; and Colleges of Business typically include academic departments that are members of three environments.

Holland (1997) proposes that organizations with high levels of congruence will be more likely "to interact with mutually satisfying relationships . . . to have members with higher levels of involvement and satisfaction . . . [and] be economically productive" (p. 54). These theory-based premises suggest that the realignment of academic departments into collegiate units consistent with the hexagonal model (reflected in the rows in Table 9.1) would enhance faculty involvement, job satisfaction, and productivity. Thus, Holland's theory provides both (1) a theoretical framework for the organizational structure of academic departments into broader collegiate units and (2) a set of theory-based propositions of the benefits that would be expected to accrue from implementation of this framework.

Similarly, various premises regarding the internal diversity of existing collegiate units are evident from Holland's premise that congruence is positively related to vocational and educational stability, satisfaction, and success. The basic expectation is that faculty members in academic departments that are most congruent with the college's norms and values should be more stable, satisfied, and successful than those in departments that are not congruent with the college's norms and values. Let us illustrate this contention by using the description of Colleges of Education in Table 9.1. These colleges are composed predominantly of Social academic departments (e.g., elementary education, educational administration, special education, counselor education), and secondarily of Realistic (agricultural and industrial arts education), Investigative (science and mathematics education, educational research), Artistic (art, music, and foreign language education), and Enterprising (business education, higher education research) departments. Based on the hexagonal model shown in Figure 2.1 and with all other things being equal (e.g., seniority and pay of faculty, size and prestige of department), it would be expected that Education faculty members in Social departments would be the most stable, satisfied, and successful, followed by their colleagues in Artistic and Enterprising departments; those in Investigative and Realistic departments would be the least stable, satisfied, and successful. Obviously these and other premises from Holland's theory regarding the organizational structure of colleges and universities need to be subjected to empirical study before they can be accepted.

Just as Holland's theory provides a basis for the assignment of specific academic disciplines to theory-based collegiate organizational units, so too it provides a basis for understanding similarities and differences *within* these units (i.e., the rows in Table 9.1). Both the *Dictionary of Holland Occupational Codes* and *The College Majors Finder* provide three-letter codes for each academic discipline. The use of the first-letter code to assign specific disciplines to theory-based collegiate units in Table 9.1 is intended to provide an overall organizational structure in which disciplines within the respective collegiate units share more in common with one another than they do with those in other units. Disciplinary differences within these theory-based collegiate units will still exist, however. The use of the second-letter code of disciplines—their secondary type—provides a basis for understanding similarities and differences among disciplines within these theory-based collegiate units. For example, of the ten Investigative disciplines in Table 9.1 two have an Artistic second-letter code (Business Economics, Economics), one has an Enterprising second-letter code (Systems Analysis), and the remaining seven have a Realistic second-letter code. The premises just discussed concerning faculty stability, satisfaction, and success within the overall collegiate units also would be applicable to understanding diversity within these specific units. For instance, faculty in the discipline within the Investigative collegiate unit in Table 9.1 that has an Enterprising second-letter code (Systems Analysis) should be less stable, satisfied, and successful than those that have either a Realistic or Artistic second-letter code because the latter are adjacent to the Investigative type in the hexagonal model shown in Figure 2.1.

The point here is simply that Holland's theory might guide those responsible for restructuring institutions of higher learning by providing a theory-based framework that, if followed, offers the promise of improving the professional stability, satisfaction, and success of faculty within these institutions. At the same time his theory provides a series of theory-based hypotheses for assessing variations in the current levels of stability, satisfaction, and success of colleges and universities as organizational entities in addition to the variability in the stability, satisfaction, and success of their individual members. We predict, for instance, that the extent to which colleges and universities are structured in ways consistent with the premises of Holland's theory will be positively related to their successful performance as measured by the collective levels of their members' stability (e.g., lower turnover), satisfaction (e.g., higher involvement and participation), and success or achievement (e.g., more effective teaching, higher research productivity, and greater service contributions).

Administrative Processes: The Management of Diversity

The diversity that characterizes American higher education imposes a major challenge to those responsible for the administration of these diverse institutions—namely, establishing administrative policies and procedures that are fair and equitable (uniform), on the one hand, and that reflect the unique (differentiated) norms and values of the diverse academic units that constitute these institutions, on the other hand. To strike a balance between these two seemingly contradictory objectives is made difficult by the conflict and competition for power among individual members and interest groups entrenched by their enduring differences regarding the appropriateness of alternative values, beliefs, information, interests, and perceptions. Although it might be "normal" to conceive of such conflict as abnormal and counterproductive, Bolman and Deal (1997)—and other organizational theorists such as Quinn (1988)—note that "conflict is inevitable" (p. 164) and that "it is naive and romantic to hope that politics can be eliminated in organizations" (pp. 165–166). Hearn and Anderson (1998) have observed, for example, that colleges and universities are certainly not immune from the ubiquity of conflict that characterizes all complex organizations. These analysts have provided an excellent summary of research findings demonstrating conflicts among academic departments in terms of their preferences for alternative governance models, approaches to academic program cuts, peer-review processes for promotion and tenure, research priorities, and roles within the academy (e.g., teacher vs. researcher).

The first step in managing large and complex organizations and in developing strategies and tactics to cope with inevitable conflict is to understand the fundamental diversity of these organizations and the leadership and managerial implications that naturally accrue from this diversity. Here again Holland's theory has much utility. Our review of the research literature on college faculty and our own empirical findings, as presented in chapter 4, show wide differences in the work environments of faculty in academic departments classified according to Holland's academic environments. The collective findings from the extant studies reveal substantial differences in academic departments classified according to Holland's six academic environments in terms of organizational and teaching goals, instructional practices, student competencies emphasized by faculty, the nature of student-faculty interactions within the environments, the duties performed by department heads/chairs and the sources of their overall job satisfaction, and the level of graduate students' satisfaction with the program. In addition, our own findings presented in chapter 4 reveal broad differences among faculty members in the academic environments as to their preferences for alternative goals for undergraduate education, their comfort with the current level of curricular specialization, and the types of undergraduate courses and students they prefer to teach.

These collective findings, which clearly indicate the broad and theoretically consistent differences among faculty in the six academic environments proposed by Holland, demonstrate the usefulness of Holland's theory in understanding the inherent internal diversity of American colleges and universities and in formulating administrative policies and procedures that are equitable and, at the same time, recognize this internal diversity. This balancing between equitability and diversity is perhaps most evident in the formulation of criteria and performance standards used to evaluate the performance of faculty and academic programs. While institutional officials may use common criteria in these evaluations, the standards of their performance should differ given the unique characteristics of the six clusters of academic departments noted earlier. The lesson to be learned from extant findings is twofold. First, the use of universalistic criteria is questionable given the demonstrated internal diversity of institutions. Second, regardless of the criteria employed, the formulation of performance standards for program and personnel evaluations should recognize differences among diverse academic departments—diversity which is generally both systematic and consistent with the premises of Holland's theory.

Suggestions for Future Research Using Holland's Theory

The collective findings presented in chapters 4 through 8 testify to the potential of Holland's theory to guide systematic research on the differential patterns of longitudinal change in the abilities and interests of college students. We hope that these findings, in conjunction with the description in chapter 3 of the methodological procedures we employed, will stimulate scholars to conduct similar theory-based studies in this important area of inquiry. We offer here some suggestions for those who are interested in grounding their research in the context of Holland's theory. Our intent is not to be exhaustive, but rather to select and present a few suggestions that we consider important. We begin with a consideration of Holland's caveat of "other things being equal." This consideration is followed by a discussion of the need to explore the socialization mechanisms of academic environments in an effort to undersand how these environments contribute to the differential patterns of longitudinal change in students' abilities and interests (such as those presented in preceeding chapters). Finally, we offer some suggestions about how Holland's theory might be used to guide research on student persistence in colleges and universities.

Other Things Being Equal: The Importance of Conditional Effects

Holland (1997), in noting that his theory "cannot be applied successfully without the observation of a few boundary conditions" (p. 13), offers the general caveat that the validity of the basic assumptions of the theory is conditional on the premise of "other things being equal" (p. 13). He refers specifically to the need to consider such factors as the "intelligence, social class, gender, and educational level" (p. 40) of the individuals in research on the validity of the assumptions of the theory, and he notes that "the 'other things being equal' clauses in the theory need more attention" (p. 166).

Our response to this caution was to examine the extent to which our findings were equally true for male and female students and for those with similar ("primary recruits") and dissimilar ("secondary recruits") initial and final choice of academic majors in our sample. Our findings presented in chapters 5, 6, 7, and 8 reveal several instances of differences between male and female students and between primary and secondary recruits, though, as we repeatedly noted, these differences were basically in the magnitude of change rather than in the substance of the patterns of change. Nonetheless, we believe that our set of findings affirm the wisdom of Holland's warning that other things may not always be equal; and we suggest that subsequent research on Holland's theory also use research designs that enable scholars to examine possible conditional effects. Given our findings, we specifically encourage those who use Holland's theory to study differential patterns of change and stability in students' abilities and interests to examine the extent to which their findings are applicable for both males and females and for primary and secondary recruits to academic majors. Other attributes of individuals that Holland suggests should be incorporated in research include their age, intelligence, ethnicity, and social class.

Socialization Mechanisms of Academic Environments

While our findings as a whole support the validity of all three basic assumptions in Holland's theory, albeit with varying degrees of strength, we examined the relative merits of the congruence and socialization assumptions (in chapter 8)—referring to the former as the "personality dynamic" in the theory and the latter as the "socialization dynamic." Our findings clearly show the primacy of the socialization dynamic in that the effect of any one of the four academic environments is essentially equivalent irrespective of whether or not the student has the "right personality type" for the environment. We think this is an important finding that has broad implications for subsequent research based on Holland's theory, especially given the paucity of research on environments (noted in chapter 6). We refer specifically to the need to explore more systematically the socialization mechanisms of academic environments that in part produce the differential patterns of longitudinal change in the college students' abilities and interests.

Holland (1997) offers a number of potential explanations for the differential success of environments in reinforcing and rewarding the characteristic patterns of abilities and interests of their associated personality types. In general, he notes that highly differentiated environments and those with strong identity are more successful in reinforcing their preferred pattern of abilities and interests than are those that are undifferentiated and have a diffuse identity. Highly differentiated environments are defined as encouraging a narrow range of behaviors in explicit ways, whereas undifferentiated environments stimulate a broader range of behaviors and offer ambiguous guidance to individuals. Similarly, environments with high identity have a limited set of consistent and explicit goals, whereas those with a diffuse identity are characterized by a large set of conflicting and poorly defined goals. Thus, the constructs of environmental differentiation and identity, described in chapter 2, essentially define the clarity and focus of academic subenvironments.

It seems reasonable to assume that one possible explanation for the differential success of the four academic environments in our study in promoting student change over the four-year period in a manner consistent with the characteristic pattern of abilities and interests of their associated personality types could be differences in the levels of their environmental differentiation and identity. Are, for example, Investigative, Artistic, and Enterprising academic environments more highly differentiated and do they have higher identity levels than Social environments? Do faculty in Investigative, Artistic and Enterprising environments in fact encourage a more narrow range of behaviors in explicit ways, and are the goals of these faculty members more explicit and consistent than those of their colleagues in Social environments? These are important questions in efforts to develop deeper understanding of the differential success of socialization mechanisms used by academic environments in promoting self-defined goals and objectives for student change.

To date, Holland's theory has been especially helpful in providing theory-based explanations of differential patterns of change and stability in the abilities and interests of students based upon their selection of and involvement in disparate groups of academic majors. Little attention, however, has been given to specific organizational features of academic environments (e.g., their clarity and focus) and to specific socialization mechanisms (e.g., classroom practices, out-of-class faculty-student interactions) employed within such environments that might be related to differential success in promoting their own self-defined goals and objectives for student change. The time has clearly arrived for such in-depth analyses in order to advance our understanding of the differential success of these academic subenvironments in promoting student learning.

We suggest specifically focusing on the collective and individual efforts of faculty members in these disparate academic environments. The collective actions of faculty contribute to the overall clarity and focus (i.e., environmental differentiation and identity) of the respective environments. While it is known that there are statistically significant differences in the educational goals of the different subenvironments (Smart & McLaughlin, 1974; Smart, 1982), we are not aware of any research that examines the extent to which the alternative academic environments espouse a narrow range of behavior in explicit ways (environmental differentiation) or embrace a limited set of consistent and explicit goals (environmental identity). Similarly, statistically significant differences in classroom learning climates have been found across the disparate environments (Astin, 1965; Hearn & Moos, 1978) as have differences in the extent to which faculty in these environments emphasize the development of alternative competencies in their students (Thompson & Smart, 1998); yet more research is needed like that of Peters (1974), which examines the extent to which individual faculty members in the respective academic environments actually employ different instructional approaches in classroom settings, or vary in terms of the amount and nature of their interactions with students outside of formal class settings. Such research has the potential to advance our understanding of why some academic environments are more successful than others in promoting their own self-defined goals and objectives for student change.

In addition to the suggestions based on Holland's work, we think the conceptual model of undergraduate socialization proposed by Weidman

(1989) would be useful in efforts to advance systematic knowledge of the socialization mechanisms of academic environments. His model incorporates situational and individual developmental constraints that limit student choices in academic environments as well as a set of socialization processes that influence the normative contexts and the interpersonal relations among faculty and students in academic environments.

Holland's Theory and Research on College Student Persistence

The vast majority of studies of student persistence are grounded in the premises of Tinto's (1970, 1987, 1993) theory of college student departure or extensions of that theory by Bean (1985) and Cabrera, Nora, and Castanda (1993). While occasionally using other terminology, all of these models or theories are essentially theories of person-environment fit, and seek to assess the extent to which students fit or conform to institutional norms. And yet none of these theories has an operational definition of the extent to which students fit with the norms and expectations of their campus environments. The concept of fit is often described in terms of the degree to which students become integrated into or conform to the academic and social norms of their institutions. It is generally assumed that "more is better"—that is, the higher students' scores on measures of academic and social integration, the more likely the students are to persist. But institutions as well as individuals have different norms and values, and the question of how much academic or social integration reflects what level of fit with any institution is not addressed.

Holland's theory too is a theory of person-environment fit. It differs, however, from the theories just noted by providing specific ways for assessing the degree of fit between students and their institutions. This assessment may be accomplished through use of the Environmental Assessment Technique (EAT) described in chapter 2. The EAT is predicated on the assumption of Holland and others "that the attributes of people, not the nature of the external environment, or organizational technology, or organizational structure, are the fundamental determinants of organizational behavior" (Schneider, 1987, p. 437). Holland (1997) similarly notes that "many of the psychologically important features of the environment consist of or are transmitted by the people in it" (p. 48).

This logic led to the formulation of the EAT which, when used in colleges and universities, is a straightforward census of the academic majors of college students and/or academic department affiliation of college faculty, since choice of an academic major or department is an expression of one's personality type. The EAT thus yields a profile or distribution for each institution and there is abundant empirical evidence (reviewed in chapter 4) showing that perceptions of the overall environments of colleges and universities, as measured by the College Characteristics Index (Pace, 1969) and the College and University Environment Scales (Pace & Stern, 1958), vary in accordance with the distribution of students and faculty across the six personality types. The EAT is thus a means of measuring institutional environments, and the profile that it yields is a three-level classification of the distribution or proportion of students and/or faculty members on a given campus across the six personality types. Take, for instance, an institution that has the following distribution of faculty members (and/or students): 25 percent in Realistic departments; 35 percent in Investigative departments; 15 percent in Artistic departments; 10 percent in Social departments; 10 percent in Enterprising departments; and 5 percent in Conventional departments. This campus would have an EAT code of "IRA" since most faculty are in Investigative departments, followed by those in Realistic and Artistic departments, respectively.

The personality types of students can also be measured in a variety of ways, as described in chapter 2, with individuals given a three-level code based upon their primary, secondary, and tertiary scores on measures of their resemblance to each of the six personality types. It thus becomes possible to determine the degree of congruence or fit between individual students and their respective campus environments. Given Holland's assumption that educational stability is dependent on the fit between students and their institutions, and given the underlying assumption of person-environment fit of Tinto's (and other related) theory, it is reasonable, for example, to assume that a student with a dominant Artistic personality type would be more likely to persist in an institution that has an "AIS" EAT code than one that has a "CRE" EAT code. The point we wish to make here is simply that Holland's theory provides an operational definition of the degree of person-environment congruence or fit capable of being integrated with the primary constructs in the person-environment fit theories, which themselves have been so instrumental in increasing our understanding of the factors that contribute to students' persistence in or withdrawal from colleges and universities.[2]

---

[2] More than a dozen different indices of the degree of congruence or fit between individuals and their environments have been developed and their respective strengths and weaknesses have been reviewed by Assouline and Meir (1987), Brown and Gore (1994), Camp and Chartrand (1992), Holland (1997), and Spokane (1985). Most of these indices provide much more complex and precise measurements of the degree of person-environment fit than used in this example.

A Concluding Comment

No doubt the possibility exists of misusing Holland's theory and the associated findings in ways that would be harmful to faculty and students. This potential for misuse is most evident in the context of "social engineering"—using the theory to assess students' personality types and to require students to enter academic majors that are "right for them." We do not think the theory is designed for that purpose, nor do we think the accumulated research evidence is sufficiently strong to warrant such actions. Our intent throughout this book has been to show how Holland's theory might contribute to theory-based research on college students and to greater understanding of the disciplinary work environments of faculty, as well as the educational and organizational implications of the theory in higher education settings. All of these efforts have been to understand the diversity that has historically characterized American higher education for the ultimate purpose of serving individuals better and improving the performances of colleges and universities.

REFERENCES

Altbach, P. G., & R. O. Berdahl, eds. 1981. *Higher education in American society.* Buffalo, N.Y.: Prometheus Books.

Anderson, N. H. 1963. Comparison of different populations: Resistance to extinction and transfer. *Psychological Review* 70:162–179.

Antony, J. S. 1998. Personality-career fit and freshman medical career aspirations: A test of Holland's theory. *Research in Higher Education* 39:679–698.

Apostal, R. A. 1970. Personality type and preferred college subculture. *Journal of College Student Personnel* 11:206–209.

Aranya, N., A. Barak, & J. Amernic. 1981. A test of Holland's theory in a population of accountants. *Journal of Vocational Behavior* 19:15–24.

Assouline, M., & E. I. Meir. 1987. Meta-analysis of the relationship between congruence and well-being measures. *Journal of Vocational Behavior* 31:319–332.

Astin, A. W. 1963. Further validation of the Environmental Assessment Technique. *Journal of Educational Psychology* 54:217–226.

———. 1965a. Effects of different college environments on the vocational choices of high aptitude students. *Journal of Counseling Psychology* 12:28–34.

———. 1965b. *Who goes where to college?* Chicago: Science Research Associates.

———. 1968. *The college environment.* Washington, D.C.: American Council on Education.

———. 1984. Student involvement: A developmental theory for higher education. *Journal of College Student Personnel* 25:297–308.

———. 1985. *Achieving educational excellence: A critical assessment of priorities and practices in higher education.* San Francisco: Jossey-Bass.

Astin, A. W., & J. L. Holland. 1961. The environmental assessment technique: A way to measure college environments. *Journal of Educational Psychology* 52:308–316.

Baird, L. L. 1988. The college environment revisited: A review of research and theory. In *Higher education: Handbook of theory and research*, ed. J. C. Smart, vol. 4, 1–52. New York: Agathon Press.

Baldridge, J. V. 1971. *Power and conflict in the university.* New York: John Wiley.

Barker, R. G. 1968. *Ecological psychology.* Stanford, Calif.: Stanford University Press.

Bayer, A. E. 1987. The 'Biglan model' and the Smart messenger: A case study of eponym diffusion. *Research in Higher Education* 26:212–223.

Bean, J. 1985. Interaction effects based on class level in an explanatory model of college student dropout syndrome. *American Educational Research Journal* 22:35–64.

Bean, J., & B. Metzner. 1985. A conceptual model of nontraditional undergraduate student attrition. *Review of Educational Research* 55:485–540.

Becher, T. 1989. *Academic tribes and territories: Intellectual inquiry and the cultures of disciplines.* Milton Keynes, U.K.: Open University Press.

Biglan, A. 1973a. The characteristics of subject matter in different academic areas. *Journal of Applied Psychology* 57:195–203.

———. 1973b. Relationships between subject matter characteristics and the structure and output of university departments. *Journal of Applied Psychology* 57:204–213.

Birnbaum, R. 1983. *Maintaining diversity in higher education.* San Francisco: Jossey-Bass.

Blackburn, R. T., & J. H. Lawrence. 1995. *Faculty at work: Motivation, expectation, satisfaction.* Baltimore, Md.: Johns Hopkins University Press.

Bok, D. 1986. *Higher learning.* Cambridge, Mass.: Harvard University Press.

Bolman, L. G., & T. E. Deal. 1997. *Reframing organizations: Artistry, choice, and leadership.* 2d ed. San Francisco: Jossey-Bass.

Bowen, H. R., & J. H. Schuster. 1986. *American professors: A national resource imperiled.* New York: Oxford University Press.

Bowers, K. S. 1973. Situationism in psychology: An analysis and critique. *Psychological Review* 80:307–336.

Boyer, E. L., P. C. Altbach, & M. J. Whitelaw. 1994. *The academic profession: An international perspective.* Princeton, N.J.: The Carnegie Foundation for the Advancement of Teaching.

Braxton, J. M., & L. L. Hargens. 1996. Variation among academic disciplines: Analytical frameworks and research. In *Higher education: Handbook of theory and research,* ed. J. C. Smart, vol. 11, 1–46. New York: Agathon Press.

Bray, J., & Maxwell, S. E. 1982. Analyzing and interpreting significant MANOVAs. *Review of Educational Research* 52:340–367.

Brown, S. D., & P. A. Gore, Jr. 1994. An evaluation of interest congruence indices: Distribution characteristics and measurement properties. *Journal of Vocational Behavior* 45:310–327.

Bruch, M. A., & T. S. Krieshok. 1981. Investigative versus realistic types and adjustment in theoretical engineering majors. *Journal of Vocational Behavior* 18:162–173.

Bryk, A. S., & H. I. Weisberg. 1976. Value-added analysis: A dynamic approach to the estimation of treatment effects. *Journal of Educational Statistics* 1:127–155.

Cabrera, A., A. Nora, & M. Castaneda. 1993. College persistence: Structural equation modeling test of an integrated model of student retention. *Journal of Higher Education* 64:123–136.

Callan, P. M. 1997. Stewards of opportunity: America's public community colleges. *Daedalus* 126:95–112.

Camp, C. C., & J. M. Chartrand. 1992. A comparison and evaluation of interest congruence indices. *Journal of Vocational Behavior* 41:162–182.

Campbell, D. P., & J. C. Hansen. 1981. *Manual for the SVIB-SCII.* Stanford, Calif.: Stanford University Press.

Carnegie Council on Policy Studies in Higher Education. 1980. *Three thousand futures: The next twenty years for higher education.* San Francisco: Jossey-Bass.

Carnegie Foundation for the Advancement of Teaching. *Codebook for the 1989 national survey of faculty.* Princeton, N.J.: Author.

Chickering, A. W., Z. F. Gamson, & L. M. Barsi. 1989. *Inventories of good practice in undergraduate education.* Winona, Minn.: Seven Principles Resource Center, Winona State University.

Clark, B. R. 1987a. *The academic life: Small worlds, different worlds.* Princeton, N.J.: The Carnegie Foundation for the Advancement of Teaching.

———. 1987b. Conclusions. In *The academic profession: National, disciplinary, and institutional settings,* ed. B. R. Clark, 371–399. Berkeley: University of California Press.

Cronbach, L. J., & L. Furby. 1970. How should we measure "change"—or should we? *Psychological Bulletin* 74:68–80.

Dannefer, D. 1984a. Adult development and social theory: A paradigmatic reappraisal. *American Sociological Review* 49:100–116.

———. 1984b. The role of the social in life-span developmental psychology, past and future: Rejoinder to Baltes and Nesselroade. *American Sociological Review* 49:847–850.

Eccles, J. S. 1994. Understanding women's educational and occupational choices. *Psychology of Women Quarterly* 18:585–609.

Elton, C. F., & J. C. Smart. 1988. Extrinsic job satisfaction and person-environment congruence. *Journal of Vocational Behavior* 32:226–238.

Ethington, C. A., & T. B. Polizzi. 1996. An assessment of the construct validity of the CCSEQ quality of effort scales. *Research in Higher Education* 37:711–730.

Fairweather, J. S. 1996. *Faculty work and public trust: Restoring the value of teaching and public service in American academic life.* Boston: Allyn and Bacon.

Featherman, D. L., & R. M. Lerner. 1985. Ontogenesis and sociogenesis: Problematics for theory and research about development and socialization across the life span. *American Sociological Review* 50:659–676.

Feldman, K. A. 1972. Some theoretical approaches to the study of change and stability of college students. *Review of Educational Research* 42:1–26.

———. 1991. "How college affects students": What have Pascarella and Terenzini wrought? Keynote address presented at Assessment of College Teaching and Learning: Implications for Research, Policy, and Practice conference. Jointly sponsored by the Public Policy Analysis and Higher Education Ph.D.

programs at the University of Illinois at Chicago and the National Center on Postsecondary Learning, Teaching and Assessment.

————. 1994. Introduction to the Transaction Edition. In *The impact of college on students*, K. A. Feldman and T. M. Newcomb, ix–xxiii. New Brunswick, N.J.: Transaction Publishers.

————, & T. M. Newcomb. 1969. *The impact of college on students.* San Francisco: Jossey-Bass.

————, & J. Weiler. 1976. Change in initial differences among major-field groups: An exploration of the 'accentuation effect.' In *Schooling and achievement in American society*, ed. W. H. Sewell, R. M. Hauser, and D. L. Featherman, 373–407. New York: Academic Press.

Finkelstein, M. J. 1984. *The American academic profession: A synthesis of social scientific inquiry since World War II.* Columbus: Ohio State University Press.

Finn, C. E., & B. V. Manno. 1996. Behind the curtain. *Wilson Quarterly* 20:44–53.

Forer, B. R. 1948. A diagnostic interest blank. *Rorschach Research Exchange and Journal of Projective Techniques* 12:1–11.

Foster, J. F. S. 1968. A political model for the university. *Educational Record* 49:435–443.

Frantz, T. T., & E. P. Walsh. 1972. Exploration of Holland's theory of vocational choice in graduate school environments. *Journal of Vocational Behavior* 2:223–232.

Gade, E., D. Fuqua, & G. Hurlburt. 1988. The relationship of Holland's personality types to educational satisfaction with a Native-American high school population. *Journal of Counseling Psychology* 35:183–186.

Gamson, Z. F. 1991. Why is college so influential? The continuing search for answers. *Change* 23:50–54.

Gellerman, S. W. 1959. The company personality. *Management Review* 48:69–76.

Ginzberg, E., S. W. Ginzberg, S. Axelrad, & J. L. Herma. 1951. *Occupational choice: An approach to a general theory.* New York: Columbia University Press.

Glaser, B. G. 1978. *Theoretical sensitivity: Advances in the methodology of grounded theory.* Mill Valley, Calif.: Sociology Press.

Glaser, B. G., & B. G. Strauss. 1967. *The discovery of grounded theory: Strategies for qualitative research.* Chicago: Aldine.

Goodman, P. 1962. *The community of scholars.* New York: Random House.

Gottfredson, G. D. 1991. Using the Holland occupational-environmental classification in research and practice. Invited address at the annual meeting of the American Educational Research Association, Chicago, Illinois.

Gottfredson, G. D., & J. L. Holland. 1990. A longitudinal test of the influence of congruence: Job satisfaction, competency utilization, and counterproductive behavior. *Journal of Counseling Psychology* 37:389–398.

————. 1991. *The position classification inventory: Professional manual.* Odessa, Fla.: Psychological Assessment Resources.

―――. 1996a. *Dictionary of Holland occupational codes.* 3d ed. Odessa, Fla.: Psychological Assessment Resources.

―――. 1996b. The environmental identity scale. Unpublished manuscript.

Hackett, G., & R. W. Lent. 1992. Theoretical advances and current inquiry in career psychology. In *Handbook of counseling psychology,* ed. S. D. Brown and G. Hackett, 2d ed., 419–451. New York: Wiley.

Hagstrom, W. O. 1964. Traditional and modern forms of scientific teamwork. *Administrative Science Quarterly* 9:241–263.

―――. 1965. *The scientific community.* New York: Basic Books.

Halpern, S. A. 1987. Professional schools in the American university. In *The academic profession: National, disciplinary, and institutional settings,* ed. B. R. Clark, 304–330. Berkeley: University of California Press.

Hargens, L. L., & L. Kelly-Wilson. 1994. Determinants of disciplinary discontent. *Social Forces* 72:1177–1195.

Hearn, J. C., & M. S. Anderson. 1998. Conflict in academic departments: A longitudinal analysis. Paper presented at the annual meeting of the American Educational Research Association, San Diego, California.

Hearn, J. C., & R. H. Moos. 1976. Social climate and major choice: A test of Holland's theory in university student living groups. *Journal of Vocational Behavior* 8:293–305.

Hener, T., & E. I. Meir. 1981. Congruence, consistency, and differentiation as predictors of job satisfaction within the nursing occupation. *Journal of Vocational Behavior* 18:304–309.

Hesketh, B., & D. Gardner. 1993. Person-environment fit models: A reconceptualization and empirical test. *Journal of Vocational Behavior* 42:315–332.

Higher Education Research Institute. 1986. *Cooperative Institutional Research Program codebook for 1980 freshman survey and 1990 followup survey.* Los Angeles: Author.

Hobbs, W. C., & J. B. Francis. 1973. On the scholarly activities of higher educationists. *Journal of Higher Education* 44:51–60.

Hogan, R., R. Hall, & E. Blank. 1972. An extension of the similarity-attraction hypothesis to the study of vocational behavior. *Journal of Counseling Psychology* 19:238–246.

Holland, J. L. 1958. A personality inventory employing occupational titles. *Journal of Applied Psychology* 42:336–342.

―――. 1959. A theory of vocational choice. *Journal of Counseling Psychology* 6:35–45.

―――. 1963. Explorations of a theory of vocational choice and achievement: II. A four-year prediction study. *Psychological Reports* 12:537–594.

―――. 1964. *Explorations of a theory of vocational choice: One year prediction study.* Moravia, N.Y.: Chronicle Guidance Professional Services.

―――. 1966. *The psychology of vocational choice.* Waltham, Mass.: Blaisdell.

———. 1973. *Making vocational choices: A theory of careers.* Englewood Cliffs, N.J.: Prentice-Hall.

———. 1985. *Making vocational choices: A theory of vocational personalities and work environments.* 2d ed. Englewood Cliffs, N.J.: Prentice-Hall.

———. 1997. *Making vocational choices: A theory of vocational personalities and work environments.* 3d ed. Odessa, Fla.: Psychological Assessment Resources.

Holland, J. L., & G. D. Gottfredson. 1976. Using a typology of persons and environments to explain careers: Some extensions and clarifications. *Counseling Psychologist* 6:20–29.

Holland, J. L., & G. D. Gottfredson. 1994. *Career Attitudes and Strategy Inventory.* Odessa, Fla.: Psychological Assessment Resources.

Holland, J. L., & R. C. Nichols. 1964. Explorations of a theory of vocational choice: III. A longitudinal study of change in major field of study. *Personnel and Guidance Journal* 43:235–242.

Holland, J. L., D. C. Daiger, & P. G. Power. 1980. Some diagnostic scales for research in decision-making and personality: Identity, information, and barriers. *Journal of Personality and Social Psychology* 39:1191–1200.

Holland, J. L., B. A. Fritzsche, & A. B. Powell. 1994. *The self-directed search technical manual.* Odessa, Fla.: Psychological Assessment Resources.

Hoppock, R. 1957. *Occupational information.* New York. McGraw-Hill.

Huang, Y., & C. C. Healy. 1997. The relations of Holland-typed majors to students' freshman and senior work values. *Research in Higher Education* 38:455–477.

Huberty, C. J., & J. D. Morris. 1989. Multivariate analysis versus multiple univariate analyses. *Psychological Bulletin* 105:302–308.

Huberty, C. J., & L. L. Lowman. 1998. Discriminant analysis in higher education research. In *Higher education: Handbook of theory and research*, ed. J. C. Smart, vol. 13, 181–234. New York: Agathon Press.

Huisman, J. 1998. Differentiation and diversity in higher education systems. In *Higher education: Handbook of theory and research*, ed. J. C. Smart, vol. 13, 75–110. New York: Agathon Press.

Institute for Scientific Information. 1980. *Current Contents.* Citation classics. Philadelphia: Author.

Jencks, C., & D. Riesman, D. 1968. *The academic revolution.* Garden City, N.Y.: Doubleday.

Kelly, R., & B. D. Hart. 1971. Role preferences of faculty in different age groups and academic disciplines. *Sociology of Education* 44:351–357.

Kerlinger, F. 1986. *Foundations of behavioral research.* 3d ed. New York: Holt, Rinehart & Winston.

Kuh, G. D., & N. Vespers. 1997. A comparison of student experiences with good practices in undergraduate education between 1990 and 1994. *Review of Higher Education* 21:43–61.

Kuhn, T. S. 1962. *The structure of scientific revolutions.* Chicago: University of Chicago Press.

Lattuca, L. R., & J. S. Stark. 1994. Will disciplinary perspectives impede curricular reform? *Journal of Higher Education* 65:401–426.

Light, D., Jr. 1974a. Introduction: The structure of the academic professions. *Sociology of Education* 47:2–28.

———. 1974b. Thinking about faculty. *Daedalus* 103:258–264.

Light, D., Jr., L. R. Mardsen, & T. C. Corl. 1973. *The impact of the academic revolution on faculty careers.* Washington, D.C.: American Association for Higher Education.

Linn, R. L. 1980. Discussion: Regression toward the mean and the interval between test administrations. *New Directions for Testing and Measurement* 8:83–89.

Linton, R. 1945. *The cultural background of personality.* New York: Century.

Lipset, S. M., & E. C. Ladd. 1971. The divided professoriate. *Change* 3:54–60.

Lodahl, J. B., & G. Gordon. 1972. The structure of scientific fields and the functioning of university graduate departments. *American Sociological Review* 37:57–72.

———. 1973. Differences between physical and social sciences in university graduate departments. *Research in Higher Education* 1:191–213.

Meir, E. I., & M. Erez. 1981. Fostering a career in engineering. *Journal of Vocational Behavior* 18:115–120.

Meir, E. I., & M. Navon. 1992. A longitudinal examination of congruence hypotheses. *Journal of Vocational Behavior* 41:35–47.

Meir, E. I., S. Melamed, & A. Abu-Freha. 1990. Vocational, avocational, and skill utilization congruences and their relationships with well-being in two cultures. *Journal of Vocational Behavior* 36:153–165.

Metzger, W. P. 1987. The academic profession in the United States. In *The academic profession: National, disciplinary, and institutional settings,* ed. B. R. Clark, 123–208. Berkeley: University of California Press.

Metzner, B., & J. Bean. 1987. The estimation of a conceptual model on nontraditional undergraduate student attrition. *Research in Higher Education* 27:15–38.

Millett, J. 1962. *The academic community.* New York: McGraw-Hill.

Mischel, W. 1968. *Personality and assessment.* New York: Wiley.

———. 1973. Toward a cognitive social learning reconceptualization of personality. *Psychological Review* 80:252–283.

Mitchell, T. R. 1997. Border crossings: Organizational boundaries and challenges to the American professoriate. *Daedalus* 126:265–292.

Mommsen, W. 1987. The academic profession in the Federal Republic of Germany. In *The academic profession: National, disciplinary, and institutional settings,* ed. B. R. Clark, 60–92. Berkeley: University of California Press.

Morrow, J. M., Jr. 1971. A test of Holland's theory. *Journal of Counseling Psychology* 18:422–425.

Morstain, B. R. 1973. *The faculty orientations survey: Technical notes.* Newark: University of Delaware.

Morstain, B. R., & J. C. Smart. 1976. Educational orientations of faculty: Assessing a personality model of the academic professions. *Psychological Reports* 39:1199–1211.

Newman, F. 1971. *Report on higher education.* Washington, D.C.: U. S. Department of Health, Education, and Welfare.

Nora, A. 1987. Determinants of retention among Chicano college students. *Research in Higher Education* 26:31–59.

O'Brien, K., W. E. Sedlacek, & J. J. Kandell. 1994. Willingness to volunteer among university students. *National Association of Student Personnel Administrators Journal* 32:67–73.

Osipow, S. H., & L. Fitzgerald. 1995. *Theories of career development.* 4th ed. Needham Heights, Mass.: Allyn & Bacon.

Pace, C. R. 1969. *College and University Environment Scales: Technical manual.* 2d ed. Princeton, N.J.: Educational Testing Service.

——. 1974. *The demise of diversity?* Berkeley, Calif.: Carnegie Commission on Higher Education.

——. 1979. *Measuring outcomes of college: Fifty years of findings and recommendations for the future.* San Francisco: Jossey-Bass.

——. 1980. Measuring the quality of student effort. *Current Issues in Higher Education* 2:10–16.

——. 1984. *Measuring the quality of college student experiences.* Los Angeles: University of California, Higher Education Research Institute.

——. 1990. *The undergraduates.* Los Angeles: University of California, Los Angeles, Center for the Study of Evaluation.

Pace, C. R., & G. G. Stern. 1958. An approach to the measurement of psychological characteristics of college environments. *Journal of Educational Psychology* 49:269–277.

Parsons, T., & G. M. Platt. 1973. *The American university.* Cambridge, Mass.: Harvard University Press.

Pascarella, E. T. 1985. College environmental influences on learning and cognitive development: A critical review and synthesis. In *Higher education: Handbook of theory and research,* ed. J. C. Smart, vol.1, 1–61. New York: Agathon Press.

Pascarella, E. T., & P. T. Terenzini. 1980. Predicting voluntary freshman year persistence/withdrawal behavior in a residential university: A path analytic validation of Tinto's model. *Journal of Higher Education* 51:60–75.

——. 1991. *How college affects students: Findings and insights from twenty years of research.* San Francisco: Jossey-Bass.

Pedhazur, E. J. 1982. *Multiple regression in behavioral research.* 2d ed. New York: Holt, Rinehart & Winston.

Perkin, H. 1987. The academic profession in the United Kingdom. In *The academic profession: National, disciplinary, and institutional settings*, ed. B. R. Clark, 13–59. Berkeley: University of California Press.

Peters, D. S. 1974. The link is equitability. *Research in Higher Education* 2:57–64.

Pike, G. R. 1995. The relationship between self reports of college experiences and achievement test scores. *Research in Higher Education* 36:1–21.

———. 1996. Limitations of using students' self-reports of academic development as proxies for traditional achievement measures. *Research in Higher Education* 37:89–114.

Posthuma, A. B., & L. Navran. 1970. Relation of congruence in student-faculty interests to achievement in college. *Journal of Counseling Psychology* 17:352–356.

Quinn, R. E. 1988. *Beyond rational management: Mastering the paradoxes and competing demands of high performance.* San Francisco: Jossey-Bass.

Reisner, E. R., M. C. Alkin, R. F. Boruch, R. L. Linn, & J. Millman. 1982. Assessment of the Title I Evaluation and Reporting System. Washington, D.C.: U. S. Department of Education.

Reutefors, D. L., L. J. Schneider, & T. D. Overtone. 1979. Academic achievement: An examination of Holland's congruence, consistency, and differentiation prediction. *Journal of Vocational Behavior* 14:181–189.

Richards, J. M., Jr. 1993. Career development: A ten-year longitudinal study of population scientists. *Journal of Career Assessment* 1:181–192.

Richards, J. M., Jr., & R. Seligman. 1969. Measurement of graduate school environments. Paper presented at the annual meeting of the American Educational Research Association, Los Angeles.

Richards, J. M., Jr., L. P. Rand, & L. M. Rand. 1966. Description of junior colleges. *Journal of Educational Psychology* 57:207–214.

Richards, J. M., Jr., R. Seligman, & P. K. Jones. 1970. Faculty and curriculum as measures of college environment. *Journal of Educational Psychology* 61:324–332.

Riesman, D. 1956. *Constraint and variety in American education.* Lincoln: University of Nebraska Press.

Riesman, D., & C. Jencks. 1962. The viability of the American college. In *The American college: A psychological and social interpretation of the higher learning*, ed. N. Sanford, 74–192. New York: Wiley.

Roberts, A. O. H. 1980. Regression toward the mean and the regression-effect bias. *New Directions for Testing and Measurement* 8:59–82.

Roe, A. 1956. *The psychology of occupations.* New York: Wiley.

———. 1957. Early determinants of vocational choice. *Journal of Counseling Psychology* 4:212–217.

Rogosa, D. 1988. Myths about longitudinal research. In *Methodological issues in aging research*, ed. K. W. Schale, R. T. Campbell, W. Merideth, and S. C. Rawlings, 171–209. New York: Springer.

Rosen, D., K. Holmberg, & J. L. Holland. 1989. *The college majors finder.* Odessa, Fla.: Psychological Assessment Resources.

Rothblatt, S. 1997. The 'place' of knowledge in the American academic profession. *Daedalus* 126:245–264.

Ruscio, K. P. 1987. The distinctive scholarship of the selective liberal arts college. *Journal of Higher Education* 58:205–222.

Schneider, B. 1987. The people make the place. *Personnel Psychology* 40:437–451.

Sergent, M. T., & W. E. Sedlacek. 1989. *Volunteer motivations across student organizations: A test of person-environment fit theory.* Research Report No. 7. College Park: University of Maryland, Counseling Center.

Smart, J. C. 1975. Environments as reinforcer systems in the study of job satisfaction. *Journal of Vocational Behavior* 6:337–347.

———. 1976a. Distinctive career orientations of Holland personality types. *Journal of Vocational Behavior* 8:313–319.

———. 1976b. Duties performed by department chairmen in Holland's model environments. *Journal of Educational Psychology* 68:194–204.

———. 1982. Faculty teaching goals: A test of Holland's theory. *Journal of Educational Psychology* 74:180–188.

———. 1985. Holland environments as reinforcement systems. *Research in Higher Education* 23:279–292.

———. 1987. Student satisfaction with graduate education. *Journal of College Student Personnel* 28:218–222.

———. 1997. Academic subenvironments and differential patterns of self-perceived growth during college: A test of Holland's theory. *Journal of College Student Development* 38:68–77.

Smart, J. C., & C. F. Elton. 1975. Goal orientations of academic departments: A test of Biglan's model. *Journal of Applied Psychology* 60:580–588.

———. 1976. Administrative roles of department chairmen. *New Directions for Institutional Research* 10:39–60.

———. 1982. Validation of the Biglan model. *Research in Higher Education* 17:213–229.

Smart, J. C., & K. A. Feldman. 1998. 'Accentuation effects' of dissimilar academic departments: An application and exploration of Holland's theory. *Research in Higher Education* 39:385–418.

Smart, J. C., & G. W. McLaughlin. 1974. Variations in goal priorities of academic departments: A test of Holland's theory. *Research in Higher Education* 2:377–390.

———. 1978. Reward structures of academic disciplines. *Research in Higher Education* 8:39–55.

Smart, J. C., C. F. Elton, & G. W. McLaughlin. 1986. Person-environment congruence and job satisfaction. *Journal of Vocational Behavior* 29:216–225.

Smith, H. F. 1957. Interpretation of adjusted treatment means and regression in analysis of covariance. *Biometrics* 13:282–308.

Smith, J. A., R. Harre, & L. Van Langenhove, eds. 1995. *Rethinking methods in psychology.* London, U.K.: Sage.

Spokane, A. R. 1985. A review of research on person-environment congruence in Holland's theory of careers. *Journal of Vocational Behavior* 26:306–343.

———. 1996. Holland's theory. In *Career choice and development,* ed. D. Brown and L. Brooks, 3d ed., 33–74. San Francisco: Jossey-Bass.

Spokane, A. R., S. D. Malett, & F. L. Vance. 1978. Consistent curricular choice and congruence of subsequent choices. *Journal of Vocational Behavior* 13:45–53.

Staats, A. W. 1975. *Social behaviorism.* Homewood, Ill.: Dorsey.

———. 1981. Paradigmatic behaviorism, unified theory, unified theory construction methods, and the zeitgeist of separatism. *American Psychologist* 36:239–256.

Stadtman, V. A. 1980. *Academic adaptations.* San Francisco: Jossey-Bass.

Stevens, J. 1996. *Applied multivariate statistics for the social sciences.* 3d ed. Mahwah, N.J.: Lawrence Erlbaum Associates, Publishers.

Strauss, A. L., & J. Corbin. 1990. *Basics of qualitative research: Grounded theory procedures and techniques.* Newbury Park, Calif.: Sage.

Strong, E. K., Jr. 1943. *Vocational interests of men and women.* Stanford, Calif.: Stanford University Press.

Stroup, H. H. 1966. *Bureaucracy in higher education.* New York: Free Press.

Stryker, S. 1977. Development in 'two social psychologies': Toward an appreciation of mutual relevance. *Sociometry* 40:145–160.

Super, D. E. 1957. *The psychology of careers.* New York: Harpers.

Super, D. E., & J. O. Crites. 1962. *Appraising vocational fitness.* New York: Harper & Row.

Tallmadge, G. K. 1982. An empirical assessment of norm-referenced evaluation methodology. *Journal of Educational Measurement* 19:97–112.

Tallmadge, G. K., C. T. Wood, & N. N. Gamel. 1981. *User's guide: ESEA Title I evaluation and reporting system.* Mountain View, Calif.: RMC Research Corporation.

Thompson, M. D., & J. C. Smart. 1999. Student competencies emphasized by faculty in disparate academic environments. *Journal of College Student Development* 40:365–376.

Tinto, V. 1975. Dropout from higher education: A theoretical synthesis of recent research. *Review of Educational Research* 45:89–125.

———. 1987. *Leaving college: Rethinking the causes and cures of student attrition.* Chicago: University of Chicago Press.

———. 1993. *Leaving college: Rethinking the causes and cures of student attrition.* 2d ed. Chicago: University of Chicago Press.

Tranberg, M., S. Slane, & E. Ekeberg. 1993. The relation between interest congruence and satisfaction: A metaanalysis. *Journal of Vocational Behavior* 42:253–264.

Trow, M. 1988. American higher education: Past, present, and future. *Educational Researcher* 17:13–23.

U.S. Department of Labor. 1977. *Dictionary of occupational titles.* 4th ed.. Washington, D.C.: U.S. Government Printing Office.

Vreeland, R., & C. E. Bidwell. 1966. Classifying university departments: An approach to the analysis of their effects upon undergraduates' values and attitudes. *Sociology of Education* 39:237–254.

Walsh, W. B. 1973. *Theories of person-environment interaction: Implications for the college student.* Iowa City: American College Testing Program.

Walsh, W. B., & J. L. Holland. 1992. A theory of personality types and work environments. In *Person-environment psychology: Models and perspectives,* ed. W. B. Walsh, K. H. Craik, and R. H. Price, 35–69. Hillsdale, N.J.: Lawrence Erlbaum Associates.

Walsh, W. B., & D. W. Lacey. 1969. Perceived change and Holland's theory. *Journal of Counseling Psychology* 16:348–352.

———. 1970. Further exploration of perceived change and Holland's theory. *Journal of Counseling Psychology* 17:189–190.

Walsh, W. B., & R. O. Lewis. 1972. Consistent, inconsistent, and undecided career preferences and personality. *Journal of Vocational Behavior* 2:309–316.

Walsh, W. B., & J. H. Russell. 1969. College major choice and personal adjustment. *Personnel and Guidance Journal* 47:685–688.

Walsh, W. B., A. R. Spokane, & E. Mitchell. 1976. Consistent occupational preferences and academic adjustment. *Research in Higher Education* 4:123–129.

Walsh, W. B., D. M. Vaudrin, & R. A. Hummel. 1972. The accentuation effect and Holland's theory. *Journal of Vocational Behavior* 2:77–85.

Watkins, C. E., B. D. Bradford, D. E. Lew, & C. D. Himmell. 1986. Major contributors and major contributions to the vocational behavior literature. *Journal of Vocational Behavior* 28:42–47.

Weber, M. 1947. *The theory of social and economic organizations.* New York: Free Press.

Weidman, J. 1989. Undergraduate socialization: A conceptual approach. In *Higher education: Handbook of theory and research,* ed. J. C. Smart, vol. 5, 289–322. New York: Agathon Press.

Wiener, Y., & R. Vaitenas. 1977. Personality correlates of voluntary midcareer change in enterprising occupations. *Journal of Applied Psychology* 62:706–712.

Wiggins, J. D. 1976. The relation of job satisfaction to vocational preferences among teachers of the educable mentally retarded. *Journal of Vocational Behavior* 8:13–18.

Wiggins, J. D., D. A. Lederer, A. Salkowe, & G. S. Rys. 1983. Job satisfaction related to tested congruence and differentiation. *Journal of Vocational Behavior* 23:112–121.

Zuckerman, H., & R. K. Merton. 1971. Patterns of communication in science: Institutionalization, structure and functions of the referee system. *Minerva* 9:66–100.

INDEX

John C. Smart is professor of higher education at the
University of Memphis.

Kenneth A. Feldman is professor of sociology at the State
University of New York at Stony Brook.

Corinna A. Ethington is professor of educational research at
the University of Memphis.